# Investment Valuation and Asset Pricing

James W. Kolari · Seppo Pynnönen

# Investment Valuation and Asset Pricing

## Models and Methods

palgrave
macmillan

James W. Kolari
Mays Business School
Texas A&M University
College Station, TX, USA

Seppo Pynnönen
Departent of Mathematics and Statistics
University of Vaasa
Vaasa, Finland

ISBN 978-3-031-16783-6 ISBN 978-3-031-16784-3 (eBook)
https://doi.org/10.1007/978-3-031-16784-3



This Palgrave Macmillan imprint is published by the registered company Springer Nature Switzerland AG
The registered company address is: Gewerbestrasse 11, 6330 Cham, Switzerland

*For my wife Karie and family Wes and Mary.*

*—James W. Kolari*

*For my wife Marja Leena and family Lauri, Erno, and Laura and Nicklas and grandchildren*

*Sebastian, Benjamin, and Vanessa.*

*—Seppo Pynnönen*

*with admiration and love.*

# Preface

A major change in the field of finance was marked by the advent of the Capital Asset Pricing Model (CAPM). Numerous authors are credited with this famous model of how asset prices are determined, including Treynor (1961, 1962), Sharpe (1964), Lintner (1965), Mossin (1966), and Black (1972). According to Black (1981) and recounted by French (2003), Jack Treynor is now recognized to have developed the first version of the CAPM as early as 1958 during a summer vacation to Colorado. As a former graduate of Harvard University, he shared his writings with John Lintner at Harvard in 1960. Never formally publishing his work, in the early 1960s he presented the CAPM as a graduate student at the Massachusetts Institute of Technology (MIT) to finance faculty, including Robert Merton.[1] A close friend and colleague was Fischer Black, with whom numerous discussions of the model likely led to Black's later work on the related zero-beta CAPM. Additionally, Jan Mossin was from Norway but attended Ph.D. studies at Carnegie Mellon University in the United States. Together, these students and professors worked contemporaeously on the fundamental relation between risk and return (or prices) of assets.

An important foundation underlying the CAPM is the mean-variance analyses of Markowitz (1952, 1959) and Tobin (1958). Harry Markowitz received his Ph.D. in Economics from the University of Chicago on portfolio theory. His work led to the fundamental concept of diversification in portfolio investments. By combining assets in a portfolio with returns that are less than perfectly correlated, investors can reduce risk as measured by the variance of returns. In theory, by varying expected returns, an infinite number of portfolios comprised of assets can be constructed that have minumum risk at different return levels. These portfolios trace out an *efficient frontier* in expected return/variance space. Relevant to the CAPM, total risk (or variance of returns) can be divided into diversifiable and nondiversifiable risks. It is the nondiversifiable portion of risk, known as *systematic risk*, that is the focus of the CAPM. Markowitz worked for some time at the Cowles Foundation of Yale University, where he met James Tobin, a Harvard trained economist and Yale professor. Tobin's insightful *separation principle* posited that risk-averse

[1] See Chapter 2 of Korajczyk (1999) for a reproduction of Treynor (1962).

investors seek: (1) efficient portfolios and (2) some optimum fraction of an efficient portfolio and a riskless asset as determined by their risk aversion. Importantly, these two investment decisions are separate from one another.

It is interesting that the lives of these early pioneers in asset pricing crossed paths with one another during the development of the CAPM. Their interaction was instrumental in the evolution of breakthroughs that transformed our thinking about risk and return in finance. Of course, it helps to be smart too! In this regard, Nobel Prizes in Economics were awarded to Tobin (1981), Markowitz (1990), and Sharpe (1990). Other contributors did not receive this honor due to death or nonpublication but are no less appreciated for their intellectual achievements. Certainly all of these notable scholars played important roles in shaping our understanding of modern finance. This book pays tribute to their accomplishments by retracing their steps in financial history.

*Investments Valuation and Asset Pricing: Models and Methods* is intended to fill a gap in undergraduate finance curriculums by providing an asset pricing text that is accessible to undergraduate students. The course is most suitable for senior finance students in the last year of their undergraduate studies. Also, it can be used in a graduate finance class, including Executive M.B.A. and Executive Business Education. The book has three unique features that set it apart from other finance textbooks.

1. Original published studies by researchers on the foundations of asset pricing are reviewed in chronological order over time. Retracing their steps in financial history, each chapter stays close to their authentic works, including quotations, examples, graphical exhibits, and empirical results. We want undergraduate students to gain a firm grasp of their achievements in the theory and practice of finance.
2. Important statistical concepts and methods relevant to the field of finance are covered. These statistical materials are crucial to learning asset pricing, which often employs statistical tests to evaluate different asset pricing models. Also, statistical skills are important tools for any finance professional.
3. Practical examples, questions, and problems are included in the text to help students check their learning and better understand the fundamentals of asset pricing.

The roadmap for our journey through the emergence and development of asset pricing is as follows.

- Chapter 1 reviews the diversification principles of Markowitz (1952, 1959).
- Chapter 2 introduces the basic assumptions of investor behavior and financial markets that are foundational to asset pricing models.
- Chapter 3 builds upon these principles by following Sharpe's (1964) derivation of the CAPM under equilibrium market conditions.
- Chapter 4 covers the CAPM market model that is used for empirical estimation using real world return data.

- Chapter 5 reviews the first extension of the CAPM known as the *zero-beta CAPM* by Black (1972).
- Chapter 6 overviews a number of other forms of the CAPM developed by researchers, including the intertemporal CAPM, international asset pricing model (IAPM), consumption CAPM (CCAPM), production CAPM (PCAPM), and conditional CAPM.
- Chapter 7 reviews the famous arbitrage pricing model (APT) by Ross (1976).
- Chapter 8 introduces the innovative Fama and French (1993) three-factor model.
- Chapter 9 expands the discussion to other multifactor models that have become increasingly popular over the past few decades.
- Chapter 10 reviews theory and evidence with respect to a recently proposed special case of the zero-beta CAPM dubbed the *ZCAPM* by Kolari, Liu, and Huang (2021).
- Chapter 11 applies asset pricing models to event studies that investigate the effects of market news announcements on stock returns.

College Station, USA — James W. Kolari
Vaasa, Finland — Seppo Pynnönen

**Acknowledgements** The authors would like to express their sincere gratitude to our Editor Tula Weis as well as Production Manager Redhu Ruthroyoni at Springer. This book would not have been possible without the support of Editor Weis, who worked with us in developing the proposal and shaping the title and content of our book. A number of anonymous referees of our proposal provided valuable comments that were useful in writing the book. Of course, the entire team at Springer is very much appreciated for all their work in making this dream possible.

## References

Black, F. 1972. Capital market equilibrium with restricted borrowing. *Journal of Business* 45: 444–454.

Black, F. 1981. An open letter to Jack Treynor. *Financial Analysts Journal* July/August. Letters to the Editor, p. 14.

Fama, E.F., and K.R. French. 1993. The cross-section of expected returns. *Journal of Financial Economics* 33: 3–56.

French, C. W. 2003. The Treynor capital asset pricing model. *Journal of Investment Management* 1: 60–72.

Kolari, J.W., W. Liu, and J.Z. Huang. 2021. *A New Model of Capital Asset Prices: Theory and Evidence*. Cham, Switzerland: Palgrave Macmillan.

Korajczyk, R.A. 1999. *Asset Pricing and Portfolio Performance*, 15–22. London, UK: Risk Books.

Lintner, J. 1965. The valuation of risk assets and the selection of risky investments in stock portfolios and capital budgets. *Review of Economics and Statistics* 47: 13–37.

Markowitz, H.M. 1952. Portfolio selection. *Journal of Finance* 7: 77–91.

Markowitz, H. M. 1959. *Portfolio Selection: Efficient Diversification of Investments*. New York, NY: John Wiley & Sons.

Mossin, J. 1966. Equilibrium in a capital asset market. *Econometrica* 34: 768–783.

Ross, S. A. 1976. The arbitrage theory of capital asset pricing. *Journal of Economic Theory* 13: 341–360.

Sharpe, W. F. 1964. Capital asset prices: A theory of market equilibrium under conditions of risk. *Journal of Finance* 19: 425–442.

Tobin, J. 1958. Liquidity preference as behavior toward risk. *Review of Economic Studies* 4: 65–86.

Treynor, J. L. 1961. *Market value, time, and risk*. Unpublished manuscript.

Treynor, J. L. 1962. *Toward a theory of market value of risky assets*. Unpublished manuscript.

# Contents

# List of Figures

# List of Tables

# 1 Portfolio Theory and Practice

This chapter overviews the portfolio selection process developed by Nobel Laureate Harry Markowitz (1952, 1959). Basic concepts are introduced that are important in the field of asset pricing. These concepts are fundamental to understanding the relation between return and risk, which is the central theme of finance. Markowitz showed how to reduce risk by diversification in assets with less than perfect correlation. Many experts agree that diversification is the only "free lunch" available to investors in the market for real and financial assets. Diversification leads to the mean-variance parabola that describes the lowest risk portfolios for any given return. These major advances in modern portfolio theory have laid the foundation for general equilibrium asset pricing models in forthcoming chapters. Moreover, they have revolutionized investment management practices around the world.

## 1.1 Ex Ante Valuation

Markowitz viewed portfolio selection as a two-step process. First, investors assess the potential future performance of securities. Because it is expected or anticipated in the future, we refer to this analysis as *ex ante*. Second, they use this information to choose a portfolio of securities. Focusing on the second step, what rule should an investor use to guide their portfolio choices? A simple rule is to maximize the discounted value of future investment returns using the present value formula.

---

**Supplementary Information** The online version contains supplementary material available at https://doi.org/10.1007/978-3-031-16784-3_1.

 
J. W. Kolari and S. Pynnönen, *Investment Valuation and Asset Pricing*,
https://doi.org/10.1007/978-3-031-16784-3_1

As an example, assuming a three-year investment, the present value for a risky security can be written as:

$$V = \frac{\$10}{(1 + 0.10)} + \frac{\$12}{(1 + 0.10)^2} + \frac{\$8}{(1 + 0.10)^3} \approx \$25, \tag{1.1}$$

where risky cash flows in each future year are shown in the numerator, and the discount rate is 10%. The discount rate is the required rate of return of investors. We can re-write the formula in general terms as:

$$V = \frac{E(CF_1)}{[1 + E(R)]} + \frac{E(CF_2)}{[1 + E(R)]^2} + \frac{E(CF_3)}{[1 + E(R)]^3}, \tag{1.2}$$

where $E(CF_t)$ = the expected cash flow at time $t$, and $E(R)$ = the expected rate of return or discount rate in the three-year investment period. The expected value operator is used here to make clear that future cash flows are not known with certainty and therefore are risky. Given expected cash flows, discount rate $E(R)$ sets their present value equal to the current price of the investment. Investors form expectations about uncertain cash flows based on available information gathered about the firm, industry, and general economy.

The discount rate takes into account the risk of uncertain cash flows. Assuming that investors are risk averse (or do not like risk), higher risk implies a higher discount rate and, in turn, lower present value or asset price. That is, investors demand a higher expected return as compensation for the risk that they bear. If there is no risk of future cash flows, the discount rate is the riskless rate of interest. U.S. government bond rates are often used to proxy the riskless rate. Hence, the expected risky discount rate has two components:

$$E(R) = R_f + RP, \tag{1.3}$$

where $R_f$ is the riskless rate, and *RP* is the risk premium. The latter risk premium increases as: (1) the risk of the security increases, and (2) investors become more risk averse.

Let's take a closer look at how investors could evaluate expected rates of return. Since the future is uncertain, we do not know exactly what the cash flows will be over time. However, investors can estimate probabilities of different possible outcomes or states. In Table 1.1 we provide an example of how to compute the expected return for security *j*. Assume that there are three possible future states: (1) pessimistic, (2) average, and (3) optimistic. The states $s = 1, 2, 3$ are assigned probabilities $p_s = 0.25, 0.50, 0.25$ and possible returns $R_{sj} = 5\%, 10\%, 15\%$, respectively. Let's assume that we hold the security for one year. The expected annual return is computed as:

$$E(R_j) = \sum_{s=1}^{S} p_s R_{sj}, \tag{1.4}$$

**Table 1.1** Expected rate of return calculation (in percent terms)

| State | $p_s$ = probability | $R_{sj}$ | $p_s R_{sj}$ | $R_{sj} - E(R_{sj})$ | $[R_{sj} - E(R_{sj})]^2$ | $p_s[R_{sj} - E(R_{sj})]^2$ |
|---|---|---|---|---|---|---|
| 1 | 0.25 | 5 | 1.25 | −5 | 25 | 6.25 |
| 2 | 0.50 | 10 | 5.00 | 0 | 0 | 0.00 |
| 3 | 0.25 | 15 | 3.75 | 5 | 25 | 6.25 |
| | 1.00 | | $E(R_j) = 10$ | | | $\sigma^2(R_j) =$ 12.50 |
| | | | | | | $\sigma(R_j) =$ 3.5355 |

which equals 10% in Table 1.1.

Should investors seek securities that *maximize expected returns*? On its surface, the answer to this simple question would seem to be "yes." However, Markowitz (1952, p. 77) argued that, "The hypothesis (or maxim) that the investor does (or should) maximize discounted return must be rejected." In his words, any rule of investment behavior that ignored "... the superiority of diversification must be rejected." A better rule is to *maximize expected returns per unit of risk*. Risk can be conveniently measured as the variance of returns.

Returning to Table 1.1, the variance of returns across states for security $j$ is equal to 12.50. Variance is a measure of the dispersion, volatility, or variability of returns across the states. The formula for the variance of returns is:

$$\sigma^2(R_j) = \sum_{s=1}^{S} p_s[R_{sj} - E(R_j)]^2. \tag{1.5}$$

The variance of returns is not in percentage terms like expected returns. However, the standard deviation of returns is an equivalent measure of total risk that has units of measurement in percentage terms like expected returns. We can easily compute the standard deviation of returns as:

$$\sigma(R_j) = \sqrt{\sigma^2(R_j)}. \tag{1.6}$$

Using the data in Table 1.1, we get approximately $\sigma(R_j) = \sqrt{12.50} \approx 3.54\%$. Given a one standard deviation change in returns due to volatility, returns can vary around the expected return from a low of 6.46% (= 10% − 3.54%) to a high of 13.54% (= 10% + 3.54%). A two-standard deviation change implies a range from 2.92% to 17.08%. From statistics, it is known that two-standard deviations encompass all possible future return outcomes with a 95% probability. This wide range of values suggests that security $j$ is fairly risky, which explains the relatively high expected return of 10%.

Based on these return and risk concepts, Markowitz established straightforward methods for evaluating portfolio effects. The expected return of a portfolio is defined as:

$$E(R_P) = w_1 E(R_1) + w_2 E(R_2), \tag{1.7}$$

where $w_1$ is the proportion invested in security 1, and $w_2$ is the proportion invested in security 2. Note that the sum $w_1 + w_2 = 1$, i.e., $w_2 = (1 - w_1)$. What is the variance of portfolio returns? Here is where Markowitz made an important contribution to our thinking about risk. The variance formula from basic statistical methods is:

$$\sigma^2(R_P) = w_1^2\sigma^2(R_1) + 2w_1 w_2 Cov(R_1, R_2) + w_2^2\sigma^2(R_2), \tag{1.8}$$

where $Cov(R_1, R_2)$ = the covariance of returns between security 1 and security 2 over time. Covariance can be expressed in terms of deviations from expected returns for each security:

$$Cov(R_1, R_2) = E\{[R_1 - E(R_1)][R_2 - E(R_2)]\}. \tag{1.9}$$

A useful statistical definition of return covariance is:

$$Cov(R_1, R_2) = \rho_{12}\sigma(R_1)\sigma(R_2), \tag{1.10}$$

where $\rho_{12}$ = the correlation of returns between security 1 and security 2 over time. For two securities, denoting the covariance term $Cov(R_j, R_k)$ in the simpler notation $\sigma_{jk}$, we can re-write Eq. (1.8) in matrix form as:

$$\sigma_P^2 = (w_1, w_2)\begin{pmatrix}\sigma_{11} & \sigma_{12}\\ \sigma_{21} & \sigma_{22}\end{pmatrix}\begin{pmatrix}w_1\\ w_2\end{pmatrix} = w_1^2\sigma_1^2 + w_1 w_2(\sigma_{12} + \sigma_{21}) + w_2^2\sigma_2^2, \tag{1.11}$$

where $w_1 + w_2 = 1$, $\sigma^2(R_1) = \sigma_{11} = \sigma_1^2$, and $\sigma^2(R_2) = \sigma_{22} = \sigma_2^2$. Notice that the covariance terms $\sigma_{12}$ and $\sigma_{21}$ are equal to one another and, therefore, their sum equals $2\sigma_{12}$ such that:

$$\sigma_P^2 = w_1^2\sigma_1^2 + 2w_1 w_2\sigma_{12} + w_2^2\sigma_2^2, \tag{1.12}$$

which is the same as Eq. (1.8).

## 1.2 Ex Post Returns and Risk

Instead of assessing future expected returns, which requires dealing with uncertainty about the future, let's consider how to measure expected returns and risk from *ex post* or historical data. We can measure past returns and risk over time. Suppose securities 1 and 2 have actual or realized returns in previous years 1 to 5

**Table 1.2** Actual or realized (ex post) return and risk over time (in percent terms)

| Years | $R_1$ | $R_2$ | $R_1 - E(R_1)$ | $[R_1 - E(R_1)]^2$ | $R_2 - E(R_2)$ | $[R_2 - E(R_2)]^2$ |
|---|---|---|---|---|---|---|
| 1 | 7 | 7 | −5.2 | 27.04 | 0.4 | 0.16 |
| 2 | 13 | 8 | 0.8 | 0.64 | 1.4 | 1.96 |
| 3 | 8 | 5 | −4.2 | 17.64 | −1.6 | 2.56 |
| 4 | 16 | 3 | 3.8 | 14.44 | −3.6 | 12.96 |
| 5 | 17 | 10 | 4.8 | 23.04 | 3.4 | 11.56 |
| | $\bar{R}_1 = 12.2$ | $\bar{R}_2 = 6.6$ | | $\sigma^2(R_1) =$ 82.8/4 = 20.70 | | $\sigma^2(R_2) =$ 29.20/4 = 7.30 |
| | | | | $\sigma(R_1) = 4.55$ | | $\sigma(R_2) = 2.70$ |

after investment as shown in Table 1.2. To compute the sample mean or average return for security $j$ over $t = 1, \ldots, T$ periods, we can use the following formula:

$$\bar{R}_j = \frac{\sum_{t=1}^{T} R_{jt}}{T}. \tag{1.13}$$

The sample variance of returns over time $t$ related to risk is:

$$\sigma^2(R_j) = \frac{\sum_{t=1}^{T} (R_{jt} - \bar{R}_j)^2}{T - 1}. \tag{1.14}$$

As shown in Table 1.2, the returns for securities 1 and 2 over the past five years are known. From this data we can compute their average returns over the five years—namely, $\bar{R}_1 = 12.2\%$ and $\bar{R}_2 = 6.6\%$, respectively. The variance of their returns can be computed, which yields $\sigma^2(R_1) = 20.70$ with $\sigma(R_1) = 4.55\%$ and $\sigma^2(R_2) = 7.30$ with $\sigma(R_2) = 2.70\%$.

This information can be utilized to see how the average portfolio return $\bar{R}_P$ and variance of portfolio returns $\sigma^2(R_P)$ changes as the proportion investment weights $w_1$ and $w_2$ are changed. Table 1.3 shows the portfolio results. A naive investor that sought to maximize average portfolio returns would choose weights $w_1 = 1$ and $w_1 = 0$ to earn an average return $(\bar{R}_P)$ equal to 12.20%; hence, such investor would put all their funds in security 1.

However, according to Markowitz, we need to evaluate how the security weights affect *both* $\bar{R}_P$ and $\sigma(R_P)$. Table 1.3 shows that, as $w_1$ increases from 0.1 to 0.9 and $w_2$ decreases from 0.9 to 0.1, the portfolio variance increases. If we take the ratio of average returns/standard deviation of returns, we see that this ratio reaches a maximum at 8.28/2.25 = 3.68 using weights $w_1 = 0.3$ and $w_2 = 0.7$. Investing only in security 1, such that $w_1 = 1.0$ and $w_2 = 0.0$, this ratio equals 12.20/4.55 = 2.68, which is not as high as 3.68 for the two-security portfolio with $w_1 = 0.30$ and $w_2 = 0.70$. It is clear that, per unit standard deviation of returns (or risk), the investor is better off holding a portfolio containing both securities 1 and 2 with weights 0.30 and 0.70, respectively. This example demonstrates that investment returns should only be evaluated in the context of portfolio returns per unit risk.

**Table 1.3** Portfolio return and risk effects (in percent terms)

| $w_1$ | $w_2$ | $\bar{R}_1$ | $\bar{R}_2$ | $\bar{R}_P$ | $\sigma(R_1)$ | $\sigma(R_2)$ | $\rho_{12}$ | $Cov(R_1, R_2)$ | $\sigma^2(R_P)$ | $\sigma(R_P)$ | $\bar{R}_P/\sigma(R_P)$ |
|---|---|---|---|---|---|---|---|---|---|---|---|
| 0.0 | 1.0 | 12.2 | 6.6 | 6.60 | 4.55 | 2.70 | 0.1708 | 0.0000 | 7.29 | 2.70 | 2.44 |
| 0.1 | 0.9 | 12.2 | 6.6 | 7.16 | 4.55 | 2.70 | 0.1708 | 2.0983 | 4.40 | 2.10 | 3.41 |
| 0.3 | 0.7 | 12.2 | 6.6 | 8.28 | 4.55 | 2.70 | 0.1708 | 2.0983 | 5.05 | 2.25 | 3.68 |
| 0.5 | 0.5 | 12.2 | 6.6 | 9.40 | 4.55 | 2.70 | 0.1708 | 2.0983 | 7.40 | 2.72 | 3.46 |
| 0.7 | 0.3 | 12.2 | 6.6 | 10.52 | 4.55 | 2.70 | 0.1708 | 2.0983 | 11.45 | 3.38 | 3.11 |
| 0.9 | 0.1 | 12.2 | 6.6 | 11.64 | 4.55 | 2.70 | 0.1708 | 2.0983 | 17.19 | 4.15 | 2.80 |
| 1.0 | 0.0 | 12.2 | 6.6 | 12.20 | 4.55 | 2.70 | 0.4549 | 0.0000 | 20.70 | 4.55 | 2.68 |

Investors should seek to maximize portfolio returns per unit risk as measured by the standard deviation or variance of returns.

In the above portfolio analyses, portfolio risk can be dramatically affected by the correlation between security 1 returns and security 2 returns, which can be measured by the correlation coefficient $\rho_{12}$. If $\rho_{12} < 1$, Markowitz argued that the total risk of the portfolio as measured by $\sigma^2(R_P)$ can be reduced. This reduction in risk is due to a diversification benefit arising from less than perfect positive correlation at $\rho_{12} = 1$. The old adage that to diversify you should not "... put all your eggs in one basket" needed amendment. According to Markowitz's insight, to successfully diversify, you need to "... put your money in multiple securities that are not perfectly correlated with one another."

Using the simpler notation in Eq. (1.12), if securities 1 and 2 are perfectly positively correlated such that $\rho_{12} = 1$, then $\sigma_P^2 = w_1^2\sigma_1^2 + 2w_1w_2\sigma_1\sigma_2 + w_2^2\sigma_2^2$ (i.e., $\sigma_{12} = 1\sigma_1\sigma_2$). If they are uncorrelated with $\rho_{12} = 0$ so that $\sigma_{12} = 0$, then $\sigma_P^2 = w_1^2\sigma_1^2 + w_2^2\sigma_2^2$, as the term $2w_1w_2\sigma_{12} = 0$. Clearly, dropping this covariance term reduces the variance of portfolio returns. Surprisingly, if securities 1 and 2 have perfectly negatively correlated returns with $\rho_{12} = -1$, such that $\sigma_P^2 = w_1^2\sigma_1^2 - 2w_1w_2\sigma_1\sigma_2 + w_2^2\sigma_2^2$ (i.e., $\sigma_{12} = -1\sigma_1\sigma_2$), portfolio variance can be substantially reduced. Remarkably, assuming that the investment proportions $w_1$ and $w_2$ are chosen optimally, perfect negative correlation of two securities can drive total risk down to zero! Appendix A shows how to compute the optimal weights for two securities.

Figure 1.1 provides graphical depictions of how the correlation between the returns of securities 1 and 2 over time affects portfolio returns. The top panel shows that, if the securities' returns are perfectly positively correlated with $\rho_{12} = 1$, the combined portfolio exhibits an identical pattern of returns over time. If $\rho_{12} = -1$, portfolio returns could be flat line indicating zero total risk or volatility. In the more likely case that $0 < \rho_{12} < 1$, the portfolio return is less volatile than either security due to diversification that results in risk reduction.

In the real world, it is most likely that $0 < \rho_{12} < 1$. Indeed, it can be difficult to find securities that have negative correlations with other securities over time. Given $\rho_{12}$, the investor should seek to minimize the variance of portfolio returns by optimally choosing the investment proportions or weights $w_1$ and $w_2$ to achieve

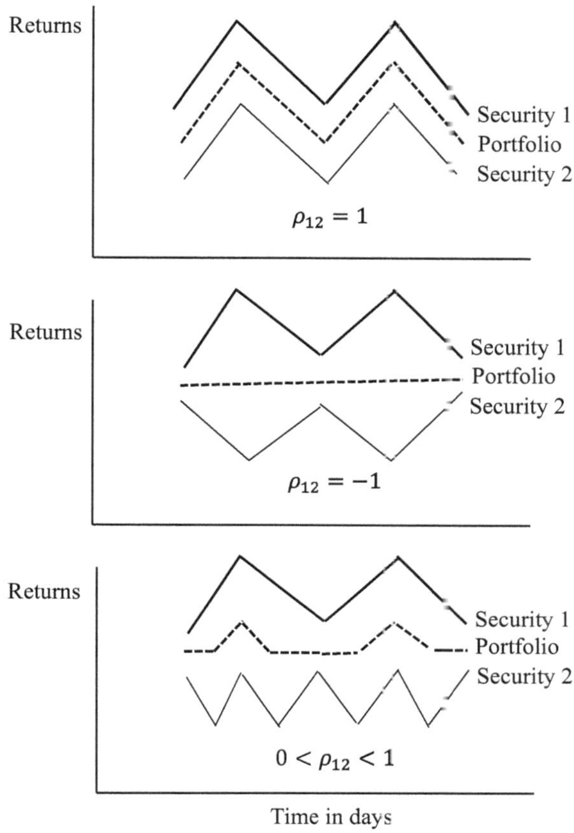


**Fig. 1.1** Correlation of security returns and effects on portfolio returns

this goal. These optimal weights can be solved to generate the average return and variance of a minimum variance portfolio, or $\bar{R}_P$ and $\sigma_P^2$. In this regard, at each level of $\bar{R}_P$, a different minimum variance portfolio is possible.

Figure 1.2 illustrates the basic principles of Markowitz diversification. We assume that only two securities are considered. Securities 1 and 2 have correlation somewhere in the reasonable range $0 < \rho_{12} < 1$. Average returns are on the Y-axis, and standard deviations of returns are on the X-axis. The locations of securities 1 and 2 are shown in return/standard deviation space. The set of portfolios that would exist if these securities were perfectly positively correlated ($\rho_{12} = 1$) is shown by the dashed line. Two other dashed lines coincide with different combinations of these securities if they were perfectly negatively correlated. Portfolio $X$ is the zero variance combination of these portfolios at some optimal weights. Here we interchangeably use the words variance and standard deviation of returns, which measure total risk.

The curved bold line in Fig. 1.2 shows the infinite number of optimal combinations of securities 1 and 2 with minimum variance based on varying the average

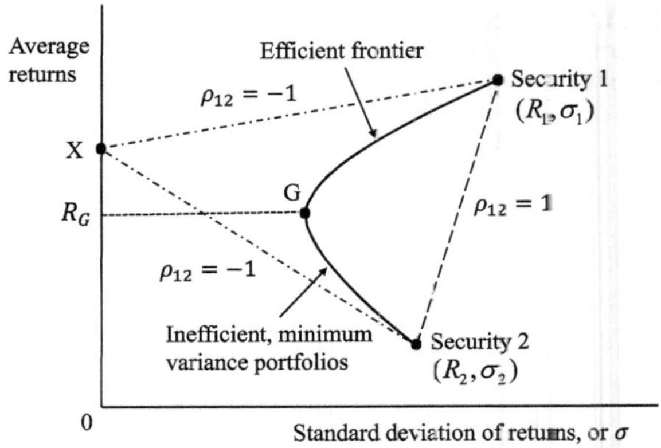


**Fig. 1.2** Combinations of two securities to form a portfolio

return of the portfolio. Markowitz referred to this curve as the *mean-variance parabola*. The range of average portfolio returns runs from all security 1 (i.e., $w_1 = 1$ so the $\bar{R}_P = R_1$) to all security 2 (i.e., $w_2 = 1$ so the $\bar{R}_P = R_2$). Portfolio $G$ is the global minimum variance portfolio that has the smallest variance of returns for all possible combinations of these two securities. Portfolio $G$ has average return $R_G$. Importantly, Markowitz named the set of minimum variance portfolios on the upward sloping boundary of the bold curve the *efficient frontier*. These portfolios are efficient in the sense that they have: (1) the lowest variance for any given average portfolio return, and (2) the highest average portfolio return for any given variance of returns. He argued that rational, risk-averse investors would only be interested in these efficient portfolios. Other portfolios on the downward sloping boundary of the bold curve are inefficient minimum variance portfolios.

Figure 1.3 shows the efficient frontier based on security 1 and security 2 data for average portfolio returns and standard deviations of portfolio returns in Table 1.3. Recalling this table, we varied the security weights $w_1$ and $w_2$ from 0 to 1 for each security. The returns of securities 1 and 2 equal to 8.40% and 9.60% respectively, are represented by the endpoints of the bold frontier. Since their correlation

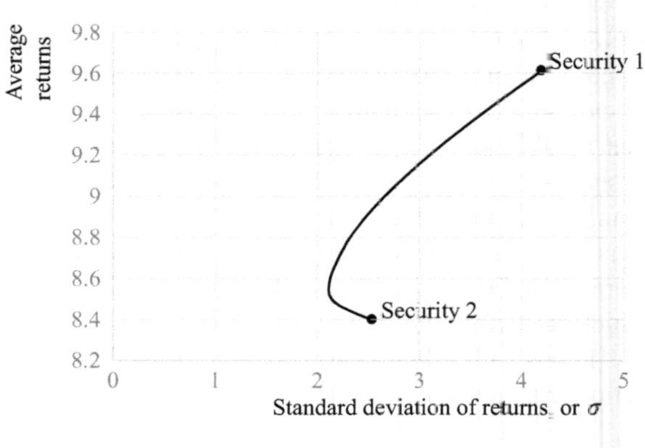


**Fig. 1.3** The minimum variance boundary of portfolios based on data for securities 1 and 2 in Table 1.3

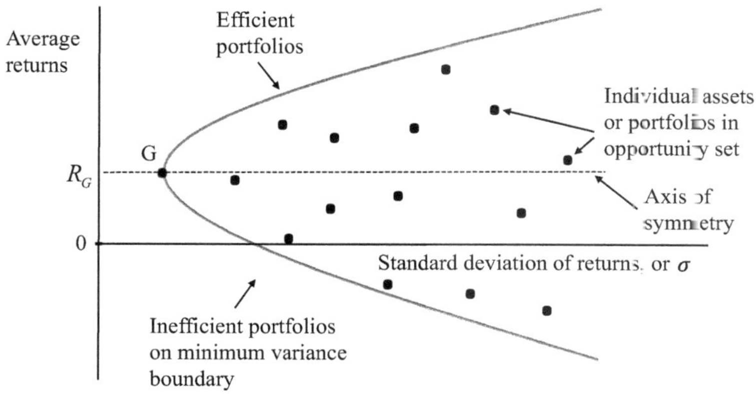


**Fig. 1.4** The minimum variance boundary of portfolios and opportunity set of all assets

coefficient $\rho_{12} = 0.3544 < 1$, different combinations of securities 1 and 2 generate a Markowitzian efficient frontier. Referring to the data in Table 1.3, the global minimum variance portfolio $G$ has weights of approximately $w_1 \approx 0.1$ and $w_2 \approx 0.90$. Portfolios on the minimum variance boundary from $G$ to security 1 comprise the efficient frontier. Investors would choose different minimum variance portfolios based on their risk preferences. The most risk averse investors would logically choose $G$. As risk aversion decreases, investors would choose portfolios with higher average returns on the efficient frontier.

Lastly, consider the more realistic and general case of many assets, not just securities but all assets. The population of assets includes both financial and non-financial (real) assets such as stocks, bonds, real estate, commodities, etc. As the number of assets under consideration increases, the efficient frontier will gradually move left due to increasing diversification benefits. Figure 1.4 illustrates the efficient frontier for all assets in the opportunity set at a single point in time.

It is interesting to consider what happens to the shape of the parabola over time. Some assets may experience higher returns and others lower returns than in previous periods (e.g., days). Over time the vertical width of the parabola could increase or decrease on a daily basis in response to changes in the cross-sectional return dispersion among assets (i.e., the variability of returns across all assets at any given time).

Assuming a large number $N$ of assets that is not infinite in number, in theory a return/standard deviation hyperbola exists (or a return/variance parabola).[1] A dashed line is shown at $E(R_G)$ that divides the hyperbola into equal and symmetric halves. This line is known as the *axis of symmetry*.

[1] Kolari et al. (2021) observed that the efficient frontier could collapse to the Y-axis in the unrealistic case of infinite number of assets. In the real world, the total number of assets is large but far from this infinite limit condition.

For a large number of $N$ securities, the average portfolio return can be written more generally as follows:

$$\mu_P = \sum_{j=1}^{N} w_j E(R_j), \tag{1.15}$$

where $\mu$ denotes the population mean return, $w_j$ is the weight for the $j$th security, $\sum_{j=1}^{N} w_j = 1$, and other notation is as before. The variance of portfolio returns for $N$ securities is:

$$\sigma_P^2 = \sum_{j=1}^{N} w_j^2 \sigma_j^2 + \sum_{j=1}^{N} \sum_{k \neq j}^{N} w_j w_k \rho_{jk} \sigma_j \sigma_k, \tag{1.16}$$

where $Cov(R_j, R_k) = \sigma_{jk} = \rho_{jk}\sigma_j\sigma_k$. In terms of the covariances of security returns, the same formula can be alternatively written as:

$$\sigma_P^2 = \sum_{j=1}^{N} \sum_{k=1}^{N} w_j w_k Cov(R_j, R_k) = \sum_{j=1}^{N} \sum_{k=1}^{N} w_j w_k \sigma_{jk}. \tag{1.17}$$

In this realistic case of many securities or assets, the computation of the optimal weights to minimize variance at different feasible expected return levels is considerably more complicated than the two-asset case discussed above. Appendix B reviews Markowitz's solution to this optimization problem. In the real world, some problems can arise in this solution. For example, some assets will get very low weights that do not allow their inclusion in the portfolio (e.g., the cost of the investment is less than determined by the weight). Another challenge is that the portfolio weights need to be adjusted over time to maintain efficient portfolios. To do this, rebalancing transactions costs must be incurred by buying and selling assets. These costs can offset potential diversification benefits. Yet another issue is that some researchers have documented that the out-of-sample performance of Markowitz portfolios is not very good. In this regard, Michaud (1989) found that even simple equal-weighted portfolio returns have outperformed optimally weighted mean-variance efficient portfolios.

What could explain this poor performance? It is well known that estimation errors can be serious in terms of accurately measuring input values such as expected returns that are proxied by average historical sample returns. Also, portfolio performance can be diminished due to other issues, including liquidity requirements, management policy guidelines, and benchmarks to use for performance evaluation.

## 1.3 Summary

According to Markowitz (1952, 1959), investors follow a two-step portfolio section process. First, they assess the potential future (ex ante) performance of securities. Second, they choose a portfolio of securities based on maximizing the discounted values of future returns by using the present value formula. In this formula, expected cash flows are in the numerator, and the expected rate of return or discount rate is in the denominator. The discount rate contains the riskless rate plus a risk premium related to the risk of the security and the risk aversion of investors. The expected return and variance of returns (or risk) can be computed from the probabilities of returns in different states of the world.

In a portfolio, the expected return and variance of returns (risk) are affected by the proportionate weights used for the securities, their individual expected returns and variances of returns, and the correlation of their returns. The latter correlation results in a covariance term. If two assets have less than perfect correlation, the covariance term will be reduced, which decreases the variance of returns. Hence, diversification reduces the risk of the portfolio but not its expected return.

Investors can use ex post return information to compute average returns and the variance of returns over time for any security. By weighting security holdings, an investor can evaluate the optimal weights that maximize average returns per unit standard deviation of returns (or variance of returns). Mathematical methods exist to compute the optimal weights of different securities in a portfolio. Minimum variance portfolios define the mean-variance investment parabola of Markowitz. The smallest variance portfolio is the minimum variance global portfolio *G*. The efficient frontier is the upper boundary of the parabola to the right of *G*. Minimum variance portfolios on the lower boundary of the parabola are inefficient. In the real world, some challenges exist in implementing minimum variance portfolios on the efficient frontier. Extremely small weights for assets, trading costs, and estimation of expected returns from average historical returns have led to poor out-of-sample portfolio performance of optimally weighted portfolios. Further work is needed to realize the dream of highly diversified, efficient portfolios in professional investment management.

## Questions

1. What is the two-step investment process proposed by Markowitz?
2. Write the general present value formula used to maximize the discounted value of future investment returns. What are the two components of the discount rate?
3. Assume that there are *s* states of nature. Write the formulas for the expected return of security *j* and the variance of security *j* returns. Next assume that there are two securities 1 and 2 in a portfolio. Write the formulas for the expected return and variance of portfolio returns.
4. What is the difference between *ex ante* and *ex post* returns?

5. Write the formulas for ex post computation of mean or average returns for security $j$ for time $t = 1, \ldots, T$ periods and the sample variance of returns.
6. According to Markowitz, what is wrong with maximizing returns of a portfolio as an investment goal? How can investors use ex post data to evaluate an investment?
7. How does the correlation between different assets in a portfolio affect the risk of the portfolio?
8. Figure 1.2 in the text plots the mean-variance parabola of Markowitz. Why is the parabola curved in shape? What is the minimum variance portfolio? What is the efficient frontier? Are some portfolios on the parabola inefficient?
9. In the real world, there are millions of assets. Why have investors had difficulty implementing Markowitz's optimization methods to find the optimal weights of assets to hold and therefore hold portfolios on the mean-variance parabola?

## Problems

1. Table 1.1 contains some computations of the expected rate of return and variance of returns for an asset. Assume that the probability $p_s$ are changed to 0.30, 0.40, and 0.30 in states 1, 2, and 3, respectively. Recompute the results to create a new Table 1.1.
2. Table 1.2 computes the average return and variance of returns for two securities. For security 1, change the returns for years 1 through 5 to the return series 5, 10, 6, 12, and 15. For security 2, change the return series to 8, 9, 8, 5, and 12. Recompute the results to create a new Table 1.2.
3. Table 1.3 computes the portfolio return and risk (in percent) using the data in Table 1.2. Use the data in your new Table 1.2 from problem 2 to create a new Table 1.3.

## Appendix A: Optimal Weights for Two Securities

Here we assume two securities with returns that have correlation $-1 < \rho < 1$. We want to find the optimal weights to minimize the portfolio variance. We invest proportion $w$ in security 1 and proportion $(1 - w)$ in security 2 that add to one. Using previous formulas, the variance of portfolio returns is defined as:

$$\sigma_P^2 = w^2\sigma_1^2 + 2w(1 - w)\rho_{12}\sigma_1\sigma_2 + (1 - w)^2\sigma_2^2. \tag{A1.1}$$

Expanding terms, we have:

$$\sigma_P^2 = w^2\sigma_1^2 + 2w\rho_{12}\sigma_1\sigma_2 - 2w^2\rho_{12}\sigma_1\sigma_2 + (1 - w)^2\sigma_2^2. \tag{A1.2}$$

Taking the partial derivative, we get:

$$\frac{\partial \sigma_P^2}{\partial w} = 2w\sigma_1^2 + 2(1-2w)\rho_{12}\sigma_1\sigma_2 - 2(1-w)\sigma_2^2. \quad \text{(A1.3)}$$

Setting the above expression to 0 (where variance is no longer reduced for a small increase in $w$), the optimal weight for security 1 is:

$$w^* = \frac{\sigma_2^2 - \rho_{12}\sigma_1\sigma_2}{\sigma_1^2 - 2\rho_{12}\sigma_1\sigma_2 + \sigma_2^2}, \quad \text{(A1.4)}$$

and the optimal weight for security 2 equals $(1 - w^*)$. Note that, if $\rho = 0$ is assumed, such that the covariance is zero, then $w^* = \frac{\sigma_2^2}{\sigma_1^2+\sigma_2^2}$ and $(1-w^*) = \frac{\sigma_1^2}{\sigma_1^2+\sigma_2^2}$. When covariance is nonzero, it will affect the optimal weights.

## Appendix B: Optimal Weights for Many Assets

This appendix reviews the standard mean-variance portfolio problem. Given the expected returns and matrix of covariances of returns for $N$ assets, we seek to find the minimum variance parabola based on the set of optimal asset weights that minimizes the return variance for each feasible portfolio $P$ expected return. Following Markowitz (1959), a Lagrangian function is used to find the minimum variance portfolio $I$ subject to the constraints that its expected return equals $E(R_I)$ and constituent asset weights sum to one (i.e., associated with Lagrangian multipliers $\eta$ and $\kappa$):

$$\underset{\omega,\eta,\kappa}{\text{Min}}\, L = \frac{1}{2}\omega'\Sigma\omega + \eta[E(R_I) - \omega' E(R_P)] + \kappa(1 - \omega' e), \quad \text{(B1.1)}$$

where $\omega$ is the vector of weights (with dimension $N \times 1$), $e$ is a vector of ones (with dimension $N \times 1$), $E(R_P) = [E(R_1), E(R_2), \ldots, E(R_N)]'$ is the expected one-period return vector for $N$ assets (with dimension $N \times 1$), and $\Sigma$ is the covariance matrix for $N$ assets (with dimension $N \times N$).

To optimize function $L$, we take the following first derivatives for each asset weight in the vector $\omega$ to obtain $N + 2$ first-order conditions:

$$\frac{\partial L}{\partial \omega} = \Sigma\omega - \eta E(R_P) - \kappa e = 0 \quad \text{(B1.2)}$$

$$\frac{\partial L}{\partial \eta} = E(R_P) - \omega' E(R_P) = 0 \quad \text{(B1.3)}$$

$$\frac{\partial L}{\partial \kappa} = e - \omega' e = 0. \quad \text{(B1.4)}$$

From Eq. (B1.2),

$$\begin{aligned}\omega &= \Sigma^{-1}(\eta E(R_P) + \kappa e)\\ &= \eta \Sigma^{-1} E(R_P) + \kappa \Sigma^{-1} e.\end{aligned} \tag{B1.5}$$

Multiplying Eq. (B1.5) by $E(R_P)'$:

$$E(R_P)'\omega = \eta E(R_P)'\Sigma^{-1}E(R_P) + \kappa E(R_P)'\Sigma^{-1}e = E(R_I). \tag{B1.6}$$

Multiplying Eq. (B1.5) by $e'$:

$$e'\omega = \eta e'\Sigma^{-1}E(R_P) + \kappa e'\Sigma^{-1}e = 1. \tag{B1.7}$$

Setting

$$\begin{aligned}A &\equiv E(R_P)'\Sigma^{-1}e\\ B &\equiv E(R_P)'\Sigma^{-1}E(R_P)\\ C &\equiv e'\Sigma^{-1}e,\end{aligned} \tag{B1.8}$$

and solving for $\eta$ and $\kappa$, we obtain the known scalars:

$$\eta = \frac{CE(R_I) - A}{D} \tag{B1.9}$$

$$\kappa = \frac{B - AE(R_I)}{D}, \tag{B1.10}$$

where $D = BC - A^2$.

Solving for the optimal weights $\omega^*$, we get

$$\begin{aligned}\omega^* &= \frac{B - AE(R_I)}{BC - A^2}\Sigma^{-1}e + \frac{CE(R_I) - A}{BC - A^2}\Sigma^{-1}E(R_P)\\ &\equiv \phi + \psi E(R_I),\end{aligned} \tag{B1.11}$$

where

$$\begin{aligned}\phi &\equiv \frac{B\Sigma^{-1}e - A\Sigma^{-1}E(R_P)}{BC - A^2}\\ \psi &\equiv \frac{C\Sigma^{-1}E(R_P) - A\Sigma^{-1}e}{BC - A^2}\end{aligned} \tag{B1.12}$$

are known $N \times 1$ vectors. From these equations, the familiar definition of the variance of efficient portfolio $I$ is

$$\sigma_I^2 = \frac{1}{C} + \frac{C\left[E(R_I) - \frac{A}{C}\right]^2}{BC - A^2}. \tag{B1.13}$$

A wide variety of computer programs have been developed to estimate the above equations. Quadratic programs are known to provide exact optimal solutions, and other programs estimate approximate solutions. There is an extensive literature on computer algorithms used to estimate mean-variance optimal portfolios. Programs are readily available for purchase on the internet.

## References

Kolari, J.W., W. Liu, and J. Huang. 2021. *A New Capital Asset Pricing Model: Theory and Evidence.* New York, NY: Palgrave Macmillan.

Markowitz, H.M. 1952. Portfolio selection. *Journal of Finance* 7: 77–91.

Markowitz, H.M. 1959. *Portfolio Selection: Efficient Diversification of Investments.* New York, NY: Wiley.

Michaud, R.O. 1989. The Markowitz optimization enigma: Is "optimized" optimal? *Financial Analysts Journal* 45: 31–42.

# Capital Market Conditions

# 2

This chapter covers different aspects of capital markets that are essential to understanding asset pricing. In the previous chapter, we learned that market participants make investment choices based on the expected returns and risks of assets. Total risk is measured by the variance or standard deviation of returns. According to Markowitz, investors should diversify to minimize risk and, in turn, seek to maximize their returns per unit risk. We begin this chapter by considering the following market conditions that facilitate asset pricing by investors: perfect capital markets, efficient markets, risk aversion, and normally distributed returns. While these market conditions do not always hold in the real world, they may be sufficiently justified by regulatory and legal practices in countries that promote the development of modern capital markets.

Next, we discuss the concept of efficient markets in which asset prices reflect all available market information. The Random Walk Hypothesis (RWH) posits that asset prices move randomly over time; consequently, it is not possible to profit from trading on past patterns of prices. Contrary to the RWH, anomalous price patterns such as momentum in asset prices have supported behavioralist views that trends in prices can occur due to psychological factors.

Another important construct in financial markets is investor risk aversion. Utility theory is used to define risk aversion and measure the risk premium demanded by investors on risky assets. An indifference curve shows how risk-averse investors trade-off expected returns and variance of returns. Assuming quadratic utility, increasing mean returns increases investor utility, whereas increasing variance of returns decreases utility.

---

**Supplementary Information** The online version contains supplementary material available at https://doi.org/10.1007/978-3-031-16784-3_2.



J. W. Kolari and S. Pynnönen, *Investment Valuation and Asset Pricing*,
https://doi.org/10.1007/978-3-031-16784-3_2

Lastly, an important market condition is normally distributed returns. Different returns need to be defined, including simple returns, log returns, gross returns, arithmetic mean returns, geometric mean returns, and portfolio returns. Assuming normally distributed returns, the mean and variance of simple returns can be defined. Additionally, return distributions are characterized by the skewness and kurtosis of returns. We demonstrate return distribution concepts using real-world stock return data.

## 2.1 Perfect Capital Markets

A perfect capital market is an ideal standard. Some characteristics of this utopic market are:

- rational behavior;
- all information is freely available;
- no taxes or transactions costs;
- all investors are price takers;
- perfect certainty.

**Rational Behavior**. In financial markets investors rationally prefer more to less wealth. This behavior is consistent with the nonsatiation principle of economics, which says that people always prefer more to less goods, money, stocks, bonds, etc. People are indifferent to these different forms of wealth. They simply want to increase their wealth. Consistent with Markowitz as discussed in the previous chapter, rational investors seek to maximize their wealth per unit risk.

In the real world, however, investors may not always act rationally. For example, suppose that you have a choice between increasing your wealth and compromising a friendship or family relation. It is possible that you would not seek to maximize your personal wealth in this situation. For personal reasons, you may choose to sacrifice potential wealth gains in favor of your ethical values. From a broader perspective, financial markets can behave in irrational ways at times. History is replete with price crashes in financial markets. Asset prices begin to fall in the market due to some bad news. As prices fall, panic can break out among investors, which causes large numbers of investors to sell en masse with severe downward pressure on prices. Conversely, at times market optimism or irrational exuberance[1] can push asset prices up to excessively high levels known as a *bubble*. Normally, bubbles are precursors of crashes as they later burst with devastating consequences to asset prices.

[1] See Shiller (2000), who titled his book "Irrational Exuberance" after a warning by Federal Reserve Chairman Alan Greenspan of a possible market bubble in 1996.

So-called *behavioralists* argue that human psychology plays an important role in financial markets. Investors can over- or underreact to market news and conditions in response to emotions, biases, social preferences, environmental factors, etc. Do you fear losses more than you enjoy gains from investments? Do you weight more recent events more heavily than all events? Do you feel pressure to conform or follow your peers? Do you follow fixed rules without fully evaluating all available information? Is a dollar earned by working at a job valued differently by you from a dollar received as a gift? Is bad news something that you tend to avoid thinking about? These questions suggest that human psychology can influence our investment decisions.

Like so many things, rational behavior can be considered as a continuum from totally rational to totally irrational. Rationality in asset pricing lies somewhere along this continuum, with a tendency toward rationality. If irrationality was fairly common, then rational investors would take advantage of irrational agents. Rational investors would earn abnormal returns by buying and selling assets from irrational investors, which creates *arbitrage profits*. Assuming there are many rational investors, these arbitrage profits would gradually diminish and eventually disappear as prices are pushed up or down by arbiteurs and all such profits are exhausted. Hence, no-arbitrage profits should exist as long as a sufficient number of investors are rational. This condition is necessary to achieve equilibrium asset prices. If arbitrage is unrestricted, arbiteurs will buy and sell to reach some equilibrium market price.[2]

**All Information Is Freely Available**. In order for arbitrage to occur, information needs to be available to investors. If information is freely available equilibrium prices can be rapidly attained. Today, due to the internet, most investors have access to large amounts of free information.[3] Even so, search costs still remain for investors seeking information about firms which can be significant, especially for large, complex firms.

**No Taxes and Transactions Costs**. A strong assumption in a perfect capital market is that no taxes and transactions costs exist. Clearly, taxes can affect the relative attractiveness of different investment choices beyond their return and risk characteristics. Investors with different tax rates on income and capital gains would not evaluate prices on a before-tax but rather after-tax return basis. Hence, an asset could have different after-tax returns and risks across investors with different tax exposures. Likewise, transactions costs can vary across investors and change

---

[2] It is possible that *limits to arbitrage* can occur due to constraints on traders arising from institutional or structural restrictions in the financial market. For example, an investor that borrowed money to buy an asset could face a margin call to cover losses on the asset that are short run in nature due to a temporary market panic. These sudden losses could prevent arbitrage gains from being realized such that equilibrium prices cannot be achieved.

[3] As discussed shortly in the context of strong-form efficiency, private or inside information of managers of companies exists, but managers cannot legally trade on this information. Also, securities firms cannot pay firms for inside information that is not publicly available.

the returns and risks of assets. Accounting practices, regulatory constraints, institutional trading, and other market imperfections can alter transactions costs and impede the formation of equilibrium prices. The question is: Are arbitrage profits consistently available due to market imperfections such as tax and transactions costs?

In answer to this question, operational efficiency in financial markets is steadily increasing due to technological advances in computers, software, and communications. These trends reduce transactions costs and make markets more perfect than otherwise. Also, at least among big institutional investors, which dominate a large proportion of investment activities in the markets nowadays, tax exposures are similar. Although tax and transaction imperfections exist, their magnitudes are likely insufficient to prevent the formation of equilibrium prices in capital markets.

**All Investors Are Price Takers**. No investor should be able to move prices by buying and selling assets, thereby becoming a price maker. Instead, all investors should be price takers. Investors have equal and costless access to information needed to price assets. If an investor did have an ability to set prices, they could unfairly achieve arbitrage profits. Again, arbitrage profits do not exist in a perfect capital market.

**Perfect Certainty**. Lastly, all investors agree about the future expected returns and risks of assets. This certainty implies homogeneous beliefs among investors concerning the mean-variance investment parabola proposed by Markowitz. Without this assumption, no equilibrium prices are available to construct the investment parabola. In this regard, it should be noted that, even in uncertain markets, homogeneous expectations are essential to equilibrium asset prices.

Are capital markets perfect in the real world? Of course, this possibility is far from reality. Nonetheless, this assumption is a useful simplification in theoretical derivations of asset pricing models, which we cover in forthcoming chapters. No model is completely valid due to the violation of perfect markets. Instead, the validity of models is determined by their empirical success in helping to explain realized returns and risks in the financial marketplace. If they do a good job based on actual price data, we can infer that violations of the perfect capital markets assumption are not so large as to prevent us from measuring returns and risks with a fair degree of accuracy.

## 2.2 Efficient Markets

Efficient markets depend on the existence of a perfect capital market with no-arbitrage profits. Prices are efficient if they reflect all available information at any point in time. It is worthwhile to note that a perfect capital market is a sufficient but not necessary condition for an efficient market. That is, absolutely perfect capital market conditions are not needed for the market to operate efficiently, only some reasonable level of such conditions. How can we determine if sufficient conditions have been met? According to the efficient market hypothesis (EMH) proposed by Eugene Fama (1970), who won the Nobel Prize in Economics in 2013, the following empirical tests of market efficiency can provide insights into the answer to this question:

- *weak-form efficiency* in which future prices cannot be predicted from current or past historical prices;
- *semi-strong-form efficiency* in which prices reflect publicly available information; and
- *strong-form efficiency* in which prices reflect private information.

Weak-form efficiency implies that an investor cannot make profits from trading on past price movements. Some investors use "technical analysis" that takes into account past patterns of prices and then seek to trade on these patterns. In general, most experts would agree that so-called *technicians* are unable to earn abnormal trading profits. One reason is that prices tend to randomly change over time. The Random Walk Hypothesis (RWH) of Burton Malkiel (2003) says that prices move around in a random manner much like a random particle in physics. Indeed, tests of prices using physics models have confirmed this description of price behavior. Prices over time appear to be independent of past prices.[4]

A major challenge to RWH is the well-known anomaly of *momentum* in asset prices. In a seminal paper in this large field of academic study and professional practice, Jegadeesh and Titman (1993) showed that abnormal trading profits can be earned on simple strategies that buy (sell) recent winners (losers). Because momentum relies upon choosing asset investments based on recent trends in prices over the past 3-to-12 months, it violates the EMH. How can such profits be possible?

As mentioned earlier, behavioralists argue that investors are affected by overconfidence, herding, and other psychological factors that can lead to overreactions or underreactions to information that cause trends in prices. Alternatively, momentum profits may arise from risks associated with such investment portfolios. Here is where Fama's EMH plays an important role. If prices are efficiently priced with respect to all risks, no abnormal profit should exist. By implication, in order to test the EMH, a joint hypothesis is required: (1) the asset pricing model used to measure risk is correct; and (2) prices reflect all available information related to risk. This joint hypothesis creates difficulties for asset pricing models. If the empirical evidence does not support a particular model, we do not know if the model failed or if market efficiency failed. Conversely, if evidence did support a model, this finding would corroborate both the model and market efficiency.

Many tests of publicly available news about companies have shown that semi-strong efficiency holds in financial markets. Fama showed that prices react rapidly to news of a stock split by a company. Many *event studies* of news announcements about new products, patent approvals, changes in profits, etc., have confirmed that

---

[4] According to Fama and Miller (1972, p. 339, footnote 19), further RWH assumptions are that prices are identically distributed and that expected price changes can be nonzero due to drift.

prices are fairly efficient in response to most public information. However, there are numerous studies that find persistent abnormal price movements lasting over a year or more in response to major corporate actions, including mergers and acquisitions, new issues of stocks, stock repurchases, dividend initiations, etc. Again, behavioralists attribute these long-run abnormal prices (and returns) to psychological factors. Others believe that changing risk explains these long-run anomalies. If an asset pricing model correctly adjusts for risk, no long-run abnormal returns or profits are possible. In Chapter 11, we provide further discussion of event studies, which employ asset pricing models in their analyses.

Strong-form market efficiency implies that investors cannot profit from private, inside (or monopolistic) information. In this regard, it is illegal for managers as insiders to trade on information about the company. If they knew that a merger with another company was imminent, they cannot legally trade in the company's stock until this information is publicly disclosed. Hence, the market is strong-form inefficient in a regulated financial world.

In sum, sufficient conditions appear to be present for the existence of efficient markets in modern financial systems. If market prices are efficient, we can infer that expected returns reflect all available information. As such, expected returns are conditional on information about both future cash flows and risks. As discussed in the previous chapter, Markowitz established the two-parameter, mean-variance paradigm to measure expected returns and associated risks. How do individuals make decisions about investment choices when faced with risk? We turn next to understanding investor preferences for risk.

## 2.3 Risk Aversion

Early writers von Neumann and Morgenstern (1944) as well as Friedman and Savage (1948) considered the problem of an individual that must choose among investment alternatives with different risks. To solve this problem, individuals must quantify their preference for one investment over another using a construct called *utility* (U). If the expected return of investment A has more utility than B, and B over C, then we know that they can be ranked in terms of expected utility as $U(A) > U(B) > U(C)$. This rank takes into account the probability distributions of returns that embody the riskiness of assets.

Another characteristic of utility is that, for risk-averse investors, it is concave in shape. As expected utility increases, each incremental increase is worth less to the individual. In terms of mathematics, the first derivative of utility is positive (i.e., individuals want more to less utility) but the second derivative is negative (i.e., each additional unit of utility has less value to the investor than the previous unit). Risk loving investors would actually have a positive second derivative, as they enjoy each unit of utility more than the previous unit. Risk neutral investors have a zero second derivative, such that each increment of utility is the same as the previous increment. In the real world, most investor behavior conforms to risk aversion with diminishing marginal utility.

As an example of risk, Friedman and Savage proposed the following alternative choice problem. Investment $A$ offers the portfolio combination of investment return $I_1$ with probability $\alpha$ $(0 < \alpha < 1)$ and investment return $I_2$ with probability $(1 - \alpha)$. Investment $B$ is a riskless return paying certain return $I_0$. Using these probabilities, the expected utility of investment $A$ is:

$$\bar{U}(A) = \alpha U(I_1) + (1 - \alpha)U(I_2). \tag{2.1}$$

If $\bar{U}(A)$ is greater than $U(I_0)$, the investor will choose $A$ over $B$. Also, if $\bar{U}(A)$ is less than or equal to $U(I_0)$, then the investors will prefer $B$ or be indifferent between $A$ and $B$, respectively. Now let's define the actuarial value of $A$ in dollars as:

$$\bar{I}(A) = \alpha I_1 + (1 - \alpha)I_2. \tag{2.2}$$

Assuming that $\bar{I}(A) = I_0$, what if the investor prefers $A$ to $B$? This preference for risk means that $\bar{U}(A) > U(I_0)$, such that $\bar{U}(A) - U(I_0)$ equals the utility gained by the investor in taking the risk associated with choice $A$. An investor that does not like risk will choose a certain investment $B$ with $\bar{U}(A) < U(I_0)$. And, an investor that is indifferent to risky investment $A$ and certain investment $B$ has $\bar{U}(A) = U(I_0)$.

This framework enables an analysis of investment choice under risk. To see this, suppose that there is some certain return $I^*$ with the same utility as $A$, i.e., $\bar{U}(A) = U(I^*)$. If this *certainty equivalent* return $I^*$ is less than the actuarial value of $A$, then the investor is risk averse and is willing to pay up to $\bar{I}(A) - I^*$ as insurance against the risk of $A$. However, what if the investor likes risk? In this case, the investor prefers to gamble and is willing to pay up to $I^* - \bar{I}(A)$ to do so.

Based on graphs in Friedman and Savage (1948), Fig. 2.1 depicts the above utility analysis of alternative investments under risk. The actuarial value of investment A in assets $I_1$ and $I_2$ is shown along the straight line at $\bar{I}(A)$ Investment A has utility equal to the certainty equivalent return $I^*$, or $\bar{U}(A) = U(I^*)$. Recall also that investment B has certain return $I_0$. The left (right) graph illustrates risk averse (risk preference) behavior by an investor. To simplify matters, we adopt the reasonable assumption that certain return $I_0$ from investment B is less than risky return $\bar{I}(A)$ from investment A.[5]

In the risk averse graph on the left, with diminishing marginal utility, if $I_0$ is greater than certainty equivalent return $I^*$, the investor will prefer certain investment B with higher utility. Furthermore, in the likely case that $I_0 < \bar{I}(A)$, the investor would be willing to pay $\bar{I}(A) - I_0$ for this certainty, which is the same as "buying insurance" to obtain the certain outcome. This payment for risky investment A is referred to as the *risk premium*, which is required by the investor for taking risk. However, if $I_0 < \bar{I}(A)$ and also $I_0 < I^*$, investment A is preferred with higher utility. This framework describes risk-averse behavior among investors.

[5] See Friedman and Savage for the case in which $I_0 > \bar{I}(A)$.

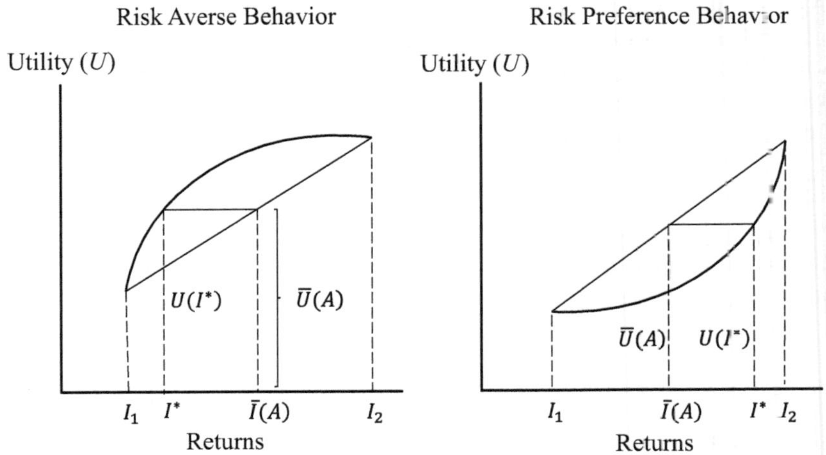


**Fig. 2.1** Utility analysis of choices involving risk

The graph on the right shows how investors who prefer risk behave. As discussed above, risk loving behavior is reflected in the utility curve increasing at an increasing rate and $I^* > \bar{I}(A)$. In the likely case that $I_0 < \bar{I}(A)$, higher utility is gained from risky investment A compared to certain investment B. But unlike risk-averse behavior, the investor would be willing to pay $\bar{I}(A) - I_0$ for risky investment A, i.e., this situation can also be interpreted as "selling insurance."

The previous utility analysis of risk focused on a simple choice between investments A and B. In the real world, investors are confronted with many investment choices. For example, Fig. 2.2 provides data for different investments with alternative payoff gains and losses. Based on probabilities of gains ($\alpha$) and losses $(1 - \alpha)$ for each investment, expected returns and expected utilities can be computed. The graph illustrates the diminishing marginal utility of returns as returns increase for a risk-averse investor.

When evaluating multiple investments, as proposed by Markowitz, risk-averse investors take into account not only the expected return but the variance of returns also. The variance (or standard deviation) measures the dispersion of returns around the expected return (or mean return). High (low) dispersion implies more (less) negative and positive deviations from the mean and is associated with higher (lower) risk. Higher expected returns can be obtained by taking higher risks. Hence, according to Tobin (1958), investors are indifferent between the utility of various combinations of expected returns on investments and their variances

Figure 2.3 shows a graph of Tobin's mean-variance indifference curves The investor is indifferent between all mean-variance points that lie on the indifference curve. As variance (or risk) increases, risk-averse investors demand increasingly

| Gain | Loss | Probability of Gain | Utility of Gain | Utility of Loss | Expected Return | Expected Utility |
|---|---|---|---|---|---|---|
| 100 | -100 | 0.60 | 5.0 | -6.0 | 20.0 | 0.60 |
| 150 | -100 | 0.55 | 7.8 | -6.0 | 37.5 | 1.59 |
| 210 | -100 | 0.50 | 10.1 | -6.0 | 55.0 | 2.05 |
| 290 | -100 | 0.45 | 12.8 | -6.0 | 75.5 | 2.46 |
| 380 | -100 | 0.40 | 15.7 | -6.0 | 92.0 | 2.68 |
| 520 | -100 | 0.35 | 19.3 | -6.0 | 117.0 | 2.86 |
| 600 | -100 | 0.30 | 23.4 | -6.0 | 110.0 | 2.82 |

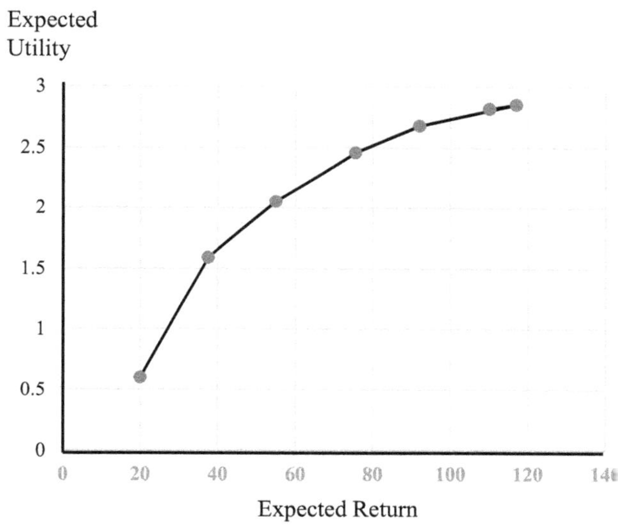


**Fig. 2.2** Expected returns and utility for multiple risky investment choices

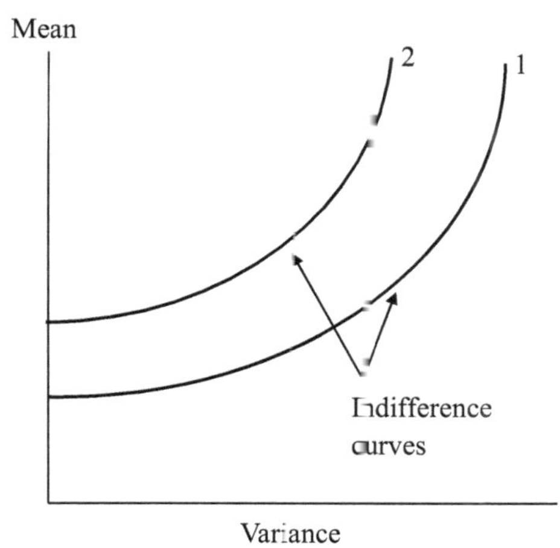


**Fig. 2.3** Mean-variance indifference curve of a risk-averse investor

higher mean returns per unit risk, which gives the curve its concave upward shape.[6] Investors will prefer the indifference curve 2 to 1 due to the fact that, for a fixed variance (risk), a higher mean return can be obtained from investments along curve 2 compared to curve 1. Also, for a fixed mean return, risk-averse investors prefer the lower variance (or risk) of curve 2 compared to curve 1.

Tobin further proposed that the mean-variance paradigm can be justified by assuming a quadratic utility function. Given mean returns $R$ and variance of returns $R^2$, the utility function of the investor takes the form:

$$U(R) = (1 + b)R + bR^2, \tag{2.3}$$

where $-1 < b < 0$ for a risk-averse investor.[7] The first term $(1 + b)R$ implies that utility increases as mean returns increase. The second term $bR^2$ indicates that utility decreases as variance (or risk) increases (as the $b$ coefficient has a negative sign). Here it must be assumed that marginal utility is always positive with respect to increasing returns.[8]

Quadratic utility is an important assumption in the Markowitz two-parameter, mean-variance framework. Also, as we will see in the next chapter, quadratic utility is foundational to the Capital Asset Pricing Model (CAPM) of Treynor (1961, 1962), Sharpe (1964), Lintner (1965), and Mossin (1966), which assumes that investors obtain equilibrium prices by taking into account the mean and variance of returns.

## 2.4 Normally Distributed Returns

Let's take a closer look at the effects of mean and variance on the distribution of returns. Before doing so, we briefly discuss some useful definitions of stock returns. The major reason for analyzing returns rather than prices is that, while prices are highly persistent and therefore predictable, returns bear no predictability in efficient markets. Therefore, returns are the major ingredients when investigating the behavior of financial markets.

Asset returns are based on price changes between adjacent time periods $t - 1$ to $t$. Using stocks as the asset, *simple returns* are defined as

$$R_t = (P_t + D_t - P_{t-1})/P_{t-1}, \tag{2.4}$$

where $P_t$ is the stock price at time $t$, $D_t$ is the dividend paid on the stock during the period from $t - 1$ to $t$, and $P_{t-1}$ is the stock price at previous time $t - 1$. Assuming an infinite number of subperiods within period $t$, *continuously compounded*

---

[6] Risk lovers would have a concave downward-shaped indifference curve.

[7] For a risk lover, we have $0 < b < 1$.

[8] As shown by Tobin (1958, p. 76), this assumption limits the range of mean returns $R$.

*returns* can be computed using *log returns* as

$$r_t = \log(P_t + D_t) - \log(P_{t-1}), \tag{2.5}$$

where log is the natural logarithm. Simple and log returns are related to one another as follows:

$$r_t = \log(1 + R_t), \tag{2.6}$$

where $1 + R_t$ is the *gross return*, and $1 + r_t$ is the *gross log return*.

It is important to note that returns are scale free but not unitless, which means that they are always defined with respect to some time interval, e.g. one month. The typical jargon is (for example) "5 percent per month" for $R_t = 0.05$ measured over a one-month period of time.

Assuming no dividends, and using the definition of the gross return $1 + R_t = P_t/P_{t-1}$, we can compute the $k$-period gross return as a product of the single-period returns from $t - k + 1$ to $t$ as follows:

$$\begin{aligned} 1 + R_t(k) &= (1 + R_{t-k+1}) \times (1 + R_{t-k+2}) \times \cdots \times (1 + R_t) \\ &= \frac{P_{t-k+1}}{P_{t-k}} \times \frac{P_{t-k+2}}{P_{t-k+1}} \times \cdots \times \frac{P_t}{P_{t-1}} = \frac{P_t}{P_{t-k}}. \end{aligned} \tag{2.7}$$

This relation only holds if dividends are ignored. If dividends are paid at some point within the period, then the single-period returns in the equation can be adjusted to compute the $k$-period return. In this case, the equation implicitly assumes that dividends are reinvested in the stock over time. In the same fashion, other adjustments such as stock splits or new issues can be taken into account at the time they occur.

Computing a mean return over some time period $k$ is more complicated. The arithmetic mean over the whole sample period of $t = 1, \ldots, T$ is defined as

$$\bar{R} = \frac{1}{T} \sum_{t=1}^{T} R_t. \tag{2.8}$$

The arithmetic mean of $k$ period returns from $t - k + 1$ to $t$ is mathematically defined as:

$$\bar{R}_t(k) = \frac{1}{k} \sum_{j=1}^{k} R_{t-j+1}. \tag{2.9}$$

However, this mean return is always biased upward and therefore is too high. The main problem is that returns on investment develop in a compounded manner, not additive. A simple example illustrates the bias. If you start with \$200 and lose 20% in the first period, you have $(1 - 0.20) \times \$200 = \$160$ to invest in the second period. If the gain in this second period is 30%, the end value becomes $(1 + 0.30) \times \$160 = \$208$, such that the 2-period return of your investment is $(208 - 200)/200 = 4\%$, i.e., $(1 - 0.20) \times (1 + 0.30) - 1$. The additive return of 10% $(= -0.20 + 0.30)$ in the arithmetic mean formula is clearly too high and therefore yields an upward-biased mean return equal to 5% $(= 10\%/2)$.

The correct mean return in a multiperiod context is the *geometric mean* computed as:

$$\bar{R}_g = \left[\prod_{t=1}^{T}(1 + R_t)\right]^{1/T} - 1 \tag{2.10}$$

for the whole sample period, and for a subperiod of $k$ returns from $t - j + 1, \ldots, t$ the geometric mean becomes:

$$\bar{R}_{g,t}(k) = \left[\prod_{j=1}^{k}(1 + R_{t-j+1})\right]^{1/k} - 1. \tag{2.11}$$

Note that the whole sample notations are simplifications of the subperiod notations. That is, for the whole sample $k = T$ and therefore for example $\bar{R}_{g,t}(k) = \bar{R}_{g,T}(T) = \bar{R}_g$.

The geometric mean is more complex in mathematical terms but simplifies matters in the sense that, given the geometric mean, the $k$-period gross return becomes $1+R_t(k) = [1+\bar{R}_{g,t}(k)]^k$. Thus, in the simple example above, the correct mean return is $[(1 - 0.2) \times (1 + 0.3)]^{1/2} - 1 = 1.98\%$ (rather than the arithmetic mean of $(-0.2+0.3)/2 = 5\%$). The 2-period return is then $(1+0.0198)^2-1 = 4\%$ which matches the correct 2-period return computed above.

Using log returns, again called continuously compounded returns, the logarithm of $1 + R_t(k)$ transforms the product of the gross returns of securities to a sum as follows:

$$r_t(k) = \log[1 + R_t(k)] = \sum_{j=1}^{k}\log(1 + R_{t-j+1}) = \sum_{j=1}^{k} r_{t-j+1} \tag{2.12}$$

with $r_{t-j+1} = \log(1 + R_{t-j+1})$. Therefore the arithmetic mean

$$\bar{r}_t(k) = \frac{1}{k}\sum_{j=1}^{k} r_{t-j+1} \tag{2.13}$$

correctly measures the average multiperiod log return also. Moreover, it is useful to observe that $\bar{R}_{g,t}(k) = e^{\bar{r}_t(k)} - 1$ and $1 + R_t(k) = (1 + \bar{R}_{g,t}(k))^k = e^{k\bar{r}_t(k)}$, where $e \approx 2.718$ is the Neper's or Napierian number after the Scottish mathematician John Napier ($e$ is also known as Euler's number after the Swiss mathematician Leonard Euler).

As noted earlier, while returns are scale free, they are not unit free. That is, they depend on the time unit. Therefore, when discussing returns, it is important to indicate the unit, whether it is daily, weekly, monthly, yearly, etc. In particular, when making comparisons, it is important to transform returns to the same time unit. It is not useful to annualize single daily returns. A simple example demonstrates the problem. Assume a 1% return on some day. If annualized by assuming 365 days, one gets $(1 + 0.01)^{365} - 1 \approx 36.78$ or 3,678%, implying that the transformation explodes the numbers. However, average daily returns can be annualized as averaging smooths single day variation. The $k$-period geometric mean in Eq. (2.11) can be used for the annualization. Also, even though it is biased, sometimes the $k$-period arithmetic mean in Eq. (2.9) is used.

Regarding simple versus log returns, in high frequency data based on daily or weekly returns, the numerical value differences between simple returns and log returns are usually negligible as demonstrated shortly. However, there are fundamental differences between these return concepts. One difference is that the simple return is bounded below by $-1$ when the stock price falls to zero. In this case, log returns approach minus infinity. Therefore, while simple returns can take values from minus one upward, log returns can be all real values.

A more important difference between these returns is the way they aggregate with multiple assets in a portfolio. We previously observed that, unlike log returns, summing simple returns over time does not aggregate correctly to total returns. The opposite is true when summing cross-sectionally stocks into portfolios at a point in time. Portfolio returns can be obtained as weighted sums of the simple returns, while log returns of a portfolio cannot be obtained as a weighted sum of log returns of multiple stocks. For this reason, it is common to use simple returns when the cross-section of assets is studied in some period of time and log returns when the temporal behavior of returns over time is under study.

In discussing statistical properties, it is convenient to start with the log return because of its summation property shown in Eq. (2.12). We can think of each one-period return, $r_t$, as the sum of subperiods between times $t - 1$ and $t$—for example, days can be divided into hours or even minutes. Thus, dividing the time interval from $t - 1$ to $t$ into $n$ (nonoverlapping equal length) subperiods, or $t-1 = t_0 < t_1, \ldots, < t_n = t$, and defining log returns as $r_{t_i} = \log(P_{t_i})-\log(P_{t_{i-1}})$, we have

$$r_t = \sum_{i=1}^{n} r_{t_i}. \tag{2.14}$$

If markets are efficient, intra-period returns should be approximately independent. Under some fairly general conditions, the Central Limit Theorem (CLT) implies that, as $n$ grows (i.e., we take finer and finer subperiods), the distribution of the sum approaches that of a normal distribution. That is, if the assumptions hold, the CLT predicts that $r_t$ is normally distributed. Furthermore, the properties of normally distributed random variables imply that, if we take an exponential transformation (anti-log transformation) of a normally distributed random variable, the transformed random variable follows the lognormal distribution. Therefore, because the gross return $1 + R_t = e^{r_t}$, the theory predicts that $1 + R_t$ follows a lognormal distribution.

Unfortunately, due to complexities in the real world, the normal distribution has proven often to be a fairly poor approximation of returns, particularly for the distribution of high frequency returns (intra-day and daily returns). Stock returns appear to have the feature that, while they are serially virtually uncorrelated over time, squared returns and absolute values of returns are highly serially correlated from period to period. This breaks the independence assumption of the CLT and disallows the normality implication of the theorem. This issue is a concrete example of the fact that zero correlation and statistical independence are not the same It is an important fact that stock return distributions have far fatter tails than those of the normal distribution.

In spite of these drawbacks, the means and variances of returns that characterize the (multivariate) normal distribution are the key parameters in asset pricing. Let's assume for the moment that the log return, or $r_{it}$, for stock $i$ is normally distributed, which can be denoted as

$$r_{it} \sim N(\mu_i, \sigma_i^2), \tag{2.15}$$

where $\mu_i = E(r_{it})$ and $\sigma_i^2 = Var[r_{it}]$ are, respectively, the mean and variance of returns. Then the relation between the normal distribution and the lognormal distribution implies that the mean and the variance of the simple return $R_{it}$ are

$$E(R_{it}) = e^{\mu_i + \frac{1}{2}\sigma_i^2} - 1 \tag{2.16}$$

and

$$Var(R_{it}) = e^{2\mu_i + \sigma_i^2}\left(e^{\sigma_i^2} - 1\right). \tag{2.17}$$

Obviously, the corresponding lognormal formulas would be much more complicated. However, for high frequency daily returns, the Taylor expansion:[9]

$$R_{it} = e^{r_{it}} - 1 = r_{it} + \frac{1}{2}r_{it}^2 + \text{higher order terms}, \tag{2.18}$$

shows that

$$R_{it} \approx r_{it}.$$

[9] See Wikipedia on the internet for an excellent review of the Taylor series. This mathematical method enables the evaluation of a general function with incremental accuracy by a polynomial of finite order. Often even the first-order approximation provides a sufficiently accurate approximation for practical purposes.

Therefore, for daily returns, the two return concepts do not differ materially. A rule of thumb is that the above approximation is precise up to a 10% return. Using Eq. (2.18), for a 10% return the error is only about $\frac{1}{2}(.01)^2 \approx .005$, or about half of a percentage point.

In addition to the mean and variance, two additional popular measures utilized in summarizing return distributions are *skewness* and *kurtosis* defined, respectively, as

$$\mu_3 = E\left(\frac{r_t - \mu}{\sigma}\right)^3 \tag{2.19}$$

and

$$\mu_4 = E\left(\frac{r_t - \mu}{\sigma}\right)^4. \tag{2.20}$$

Skewness measures the asymmetry of the distribution, whereas kurtosis measures the peakedness of the distribution or fatness of the tails. Because the normal distribution is symmetric, its skewness is zero, i.e., $\mu_3 = 0$. The kurtosis of the normal distribution is 3. Therefore, it is a common practice to use *excess kurtosis* defined as the difference $\mu_4 - 3$, rather than the original kurtosis.

Given $T$ return observations, the sample counterparts for these population measures are the sample skewness

$$\text{sk} = \frac{1}{T-1}\sum_{t=1}^{T}\left(\frac{r_t - \bar{r}}{s}\right)^3 \tag{2.21}$$

and sample kurtosis

$$\text{ku} = \frac{1}{T-1}\sum_{t=1}^{T}\left(\frac{r_t - \bar{r}}{s}\right)^4, \tag{2.22}$$

where

$$\bar{r} = \frac{1}{T}\sum_{t=1}^{T} r_t \tag{2.23}$$

is the sample mean of the returns, and $s$ is the return standard deviation, which is the square root of the sample variance

$$s^2 = \frac{1}{T-1}\sum_{t=1}^{T}(r_t - \bar{r})^2. \tag{2.24}$$

**Table 2.1** Sample statistics for S &P 500 index, DAX index, and Microsoft Corporation: daily, weekly, and monthly returns (in percent)

| | Daily | | | Weekly | | | Monthly | | |
|---|---|---|---|---|---|---|---|---|---|
| | MS | S &P 500 | DAX | MS | S &P 500 | DAX | MS | S &P 500 | DAX |
| Mean | 0.09 | 0.05 | 0.04 | 0.44 | 0.22 | 0.19 | 1.89 | 1.01 | 0.77 |
| Median | 0.07 | 0.07 | 0.08 | 0.52 | 0.31 | 0.42 | 2.23 | 1.50 | 0.71 |
| Volatility | 25.39 | 17.50 | 20.55 | 22.69 | 13.90 | 20.84 | 21.33 | 14.07 | 17.76 |
| Skewness | 0.04 | −0.58 | −0.38 | −0.25 | −0.49 | −0.82 | 0.03 | −0.31 | −0.50 |
| Kurtosis | 9.91 | 15.13 | 7.21 | 2.89 | 1.84 | 5.69 | 0.34 | 0.93 | 1.65 |
| Min | −14.74 | −11.98 | −12.24 | −14.37 | −7.19 | −20.01 | −15.52 | −12.51 | −19.19 |
| Max | 14.22 | 9.38 | 10.98 | 15.02 | 7.39 | 10.91 | 19.63 | 12.68 | 15.01 |
| N | 2,768 | 2,768 | 2,785 | 574 | 526 | 574 | 132 | 132 | 132 |

*Notes* Mean and median are percentage returns per indicated period, and volatility is annualized. Kurtosis is the excess kurtosis, or ku − 3, with ku defined in Eq. (2.22).

If the returns are normally distributed, the skewness and kurtosis are normally distributed in large samples with respective means 0 and 3 and variances $6/T$ and $24/T$. Consequently, these features can be utilized in testing for the normality of a return distribution. Empirically speaking, it has been observed that the skewness of daily returns of individual stocks is close to zero and slightly negative for stock indices based on a portfolio of stocks (e.g., the S &P 500 index).

The excess kurtosis, or ku−3, tends to be positive for both individual stocks and stock indices, which indicates fatter tails with a more peaked mean than the normal distribution. Therefore, various alternatives, such as *stable distributions*, have been proposed. However, the popularity of these alternatives has diminished today due to some counterintuitive properties (e.g., increasing variance with the sample size). On the other hand, some fatter tailed distributions, like the *t*-distribution and generalized error distributions of which the normal distribution is a special case, have gained popularity over time. In spite of these issues, normal and lognormal distributions continue to play a central role in theoretical financial economics. Hence, the empirical challenge is to assess how critical the normality assumption is for the predictions of theory.

The following empirical example illustrates the concepts and issues discussed above. We use daily, weekly, and monthly price data downloadable from Yahoo Finance[10] for Microsoft and two stock market indices, including the S &P 500 Index for the U.S. markets and the DAX Index for German markets. Our sample time period is from January 1, 2010 until December 31, 2020.

Table 2.1 supports the general observation of slight negative skewness of stock indices (S &P 500 and DAX), which indicates that the left-hand-side tail is

[10] https://finance.yahoo.com.

longer than the right-hand-side tail. Using the large-sample test statistic defined as $z = \text{sk} \cdot \sqrt{T/6}$ for testing symmetry (i.e., whether the population symmetry is zero), in unreported results, both index skewness measures appear highly statistically significant for different return frequencies. For individual stocks (Microsoft), skewness can vary for different sampling frequencies, with both positive and negative skewness shown in the table. In this regard, the weekly returns are significantly negatively skewed. These features are observable from the means and medians in Table 2.1. A positively skewed distribution has a mean greater than the median, and vice versa for negatively skewed distributions. Volatilities are annualized in percentage terms. Index volatilities are generally lower than those of individual stocks due to the diversification effect discussed in Chapter 1. It is interesting to note that, while the mean return of the S &P 500 is greater than that of the DAX, volatility (risk) is lower for the S &P 500, which means that the reward-to-risk ratio is higher for the S &P 500 over the period 2010 to 2020.

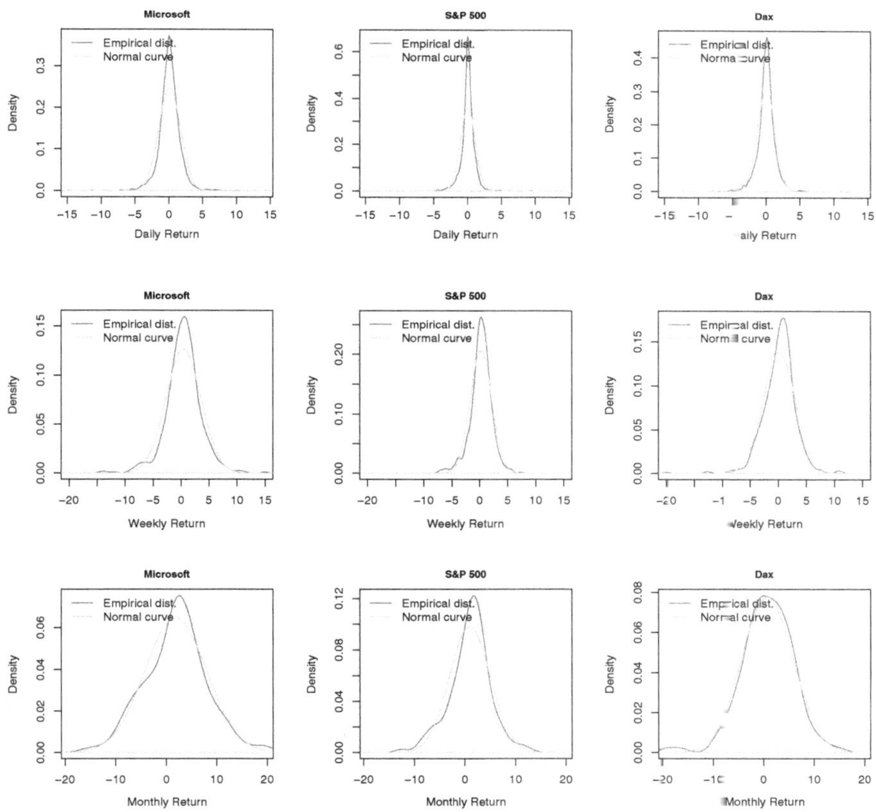


**Fig. 2.4** Empirical return distributions for Microsoft, U.S. S &P 500 index, and German Dax index using daily, weekly, and monthly returns

Figure 2.4 shows the return frequency distributions (in blue) for Microsoft as well as U.S. S &P 500 and German DAX stock price indexes. Distributions are shown using daily, weekly, and monthly return frequencies. These empirical distributions are compared to the imposed normal curves (in red) calibrated by respective sample means and sample variances. The peakedness of the empirical distributions illustrates graphically the kurtosis feature, which is characteristic of both individual stocks and indexes (portfolios). Fat tails, even though not that obvious from the graphs, are well-recognized features associated with stock returns due to high kurtosis. The mild skewness of the return distributions is not obvious from the graphs. Scanning down the rows of graphs reveals that, as return frequency decreases from daily to monthly returns, the normal approximation improves.

Finally, we should note that the above sample statistics and graphs are produced using simple returns (in percentages). We have left as an exercise for the student to reproduce these results using log returns and compare if there are material differences.

## 2.5 Summary

A number of capital market conditions are foundational to asset pricing. Perfect capital markets assume rational investor behavior, all information is freely available, no taxes and transactions costs, all investors are price takers, and perfect certainty. The efficient market hypothesis (EMH) by Nobel Laureate Eugene Fama (1970) posits that prices reflect all available information. Weak-form, semi-strong form, and strong-form efficiency describe different types of market efficiency. In an efficient market, the random walk hypothesis (RWH) of Malkiel (2003) argues that prices move randomly over time and therefore are independent of past prices. Behavioralists counter that price trends can occur due to investor psychology which can cause over- or underreactions to information in the market.

Investors are assumed to be risk averse in capital markets. Research by von Neumann and Morgenstern (1944) and Friedman and Savage (1948) employed utility theory to study risky investment choices. If the expected utility of a risky investment exceeds the utility of a certain return, assuming their actuarial values is the same, a risk-averse investor will purchase the risky investment. In the more likely case that the actuarial value of the risky investment is greater than that of the certain return, a risk premium is paid by the investor. In a graph of utility (Y-axis) and returns (X-axis), the utility curve increases at a decreasing rate for risk-averse investors, who obtain less utility per unit of return as returns increase. For risk loving behavior, the utility curve increases at an increasing rate as utility per unit risk increases for each incremental return. In a portfolio context with multiple investments, Tobin (1958) defined an indifference curve with trade-offs between mean returns and the variance of returns. Assuming quadratic utility, investors' utility is increasing in mean returns and decreasing in the variance of returns.

Stock returns can be defined in a variety of ways. Simple returns take into account dividends and capital gains on a stock for a discrete time period. Log returns provide a continuously compounded return. The log of one plus the simple return (or gross simple return) equals the log return. An arithmetic mean takes the average of simple returns over a number of time periods. Because the arithmetic mean return has an upward bias, the geometric mean is used to compute an average multiperiod return. Alternatively, the simple arithmetic mean of log returns over a number of time periods can be used to measure the average multiperiod return. For high frequency data, such as daily or weekly returns, simple returns, and log returns are similar to one another, at least up to about a 10% return. When aggregating returns in a portfolio, simple returns should be used in cross-sectional analyses of assets at a point in time, and log returns should be used in time-series analyses of returns over multiple periods. Using log returns defined as the sum of many subperiod log returns, the Central Limit Theorem (CLT) says that returns are normally distributed. However, in the real world, stock returns are not normally distributed; instead, they tend to have some degree of asymmetry (i.e., skewness) and fatter tails (i.e., kurtosis). Mean, variance, skewness, and kurtosis measures are used to characterize return distributions. Individual stocks normally have higher variances of returns than portfolios due to the diversification benefit in portfolios. As the return frequency decreases from daily to monthly returns, the distribution of stock returns becomes closer to a normal curve.

## Questions

1. In a perfect capital market, rational behavior dictates that investors prefer more to less wealth. Give some examples of irrational market behavior. Why might investors act irrationally?
2. Give three characteristics of a perfect capital market and briefly discuss them.
3. Under the efficient markets hypothesis (EMH), what are the three types of market efficiency? Briefly describe them.
4. What is the Random Walk Hypothesis (RWH)? Is there any evidence against this hypothesis?
5. What is a certainty equivalent return of a risky investment?
6. What is a risk premium on an investment?
7. Figure 2.2 gives an example of a utility curve for a risky investment. For this risky investment, expected utility is on the Y-axis, and expected returns are on the X-axis. What is the main concept conveyed by this graph?
8. When risk-averse investors evaluate multiple investments in a portfolio context, what do investors use to evaluate investments? Also, what is an indifference curve in this respect? Is this curve related to investor utility? If so, write a utility function that is relevant to the indifference curve.
9. Write the simple return for a stock. Also, write the continuously compounded rate of return. How are these two returns related to one another?

10. Are simple returns and log returns similar to one another? In a portfolio, which type of return should be used to compute the cross-sectional average return at a point in time? Which one should be used to compute returns over time in a time-series analysis?
11. How can the Central Limit Theorem (CLT) be applied to explain why log returns approach a normal distribution?
12. Suppose that the simple returns of stocks are normally distributed. What can you say about the distribution of the return of a portfolio of these stocks?

## Problems

1. Assume that investment $A$ offers the portfolio combination of investment return $I_1$ with probability $\alpha$ $(0 < \alpha < 1)$ and investment return $I_2$ with probability $(1 - \alpha)$. What is the expected utility of investment $A$, or $\bar{U}(A)$? What is the actuarial value of A in dollars, or $\bar{I}(A)$?
2. Suppose that there is some certain return $I^*$ with the same utility as $A$, i.e., $\bar{U}(A) = U(I^*)$. Also, assume that this *certainty equivalent* return $I^*$ is less than the actuarial value of $A$. What does this tell you about the investor? How much is the investor willing to pay as insurance against the risk of $A$?
3. Draw a graph of the utility curve showing risk-averse investor behavior with respect to the risky investment opportunity in problem 1 above. How would this graph change for risk loving investors?
4. How would you compute the $k$-period gross return $1 + R_t(k)$ for an investment from $t - k + 1$ to $t$? Assume no dividends are paid. Write the general formulas using gross return $1 + R_t = P_t/P_{t-1}$. Also, compute $1 + R_t(k)$ assuming that $(1 + R_1) = 100/90$, $(1 + R_2) = 105/100$, and $(1 + R_3) = 110/105$ (note $t = k = 3$ here).
5. How can we compute the mean return for an investment over some time period $k$? Show the formulas for the arithmetic mean and geometric mean. Utilizing the gross returns in problem 4, i.e, $(1 + R_1) = 1.1111$, $(1 + R_2) = 1.0500$, and $(1 + R_3) = 1.0476$, compute the arithmetic and geometric mean returns. Which mean return should you use and why?
6. How would we compute the gross return $1 + R_t(k)$ over some time period $k$ using log returns? In this case, what is the simple arithmetic mean of these gross returns? Is the average of this multiperiod correct (unbiased)? Assuming that $(1 + R_1) = 1.1111$, $(1 + R_2) = 1.0500$, and $(1 + R_3) = 1.0476$, compute these returns. What is the formula for the geometric mean return?
7. Consider the monthly returns of a stock. Assume that the returns are normally distributed with mean $\mu = 1\%$ and standard deviation $\sigma = 9\%$ (per month). How often would you expect to see a monthly return that exceeds 10%? How about 20%.
8. Download Microsoft stock prices in addition to S &P 500 and German DAX index values for the sample period from January 1, 2010 until December 31,

2020 and reproduce the sample statistics in Table 2.1 using log returns. Are there material differences?

## References


Fama, E.F. 1970. Efficient capital markets: A review of theory and empirical work. *Journal of Finance* 35: 383–417.

Fama, E.F., and M.H. Miller. 1972. *The Theory of Finance*. Hinsdale, IL: Dryden Press.

Friedman, M., and L. Savage. 1948. The utility analyses of choices involving risk. *Journal of Political Economy* 56: 279–304.

Jegadeesh, N., and S. Titman. 1993. Returns to buying winners and selling losers: Implications for stock market efficiency. *Journal of Finance* 48: 65–91.

Lintner, J. 1965. The valuation of risk assets and the selection of risky investments in stock portfolios and capital budgets. *Review of Economics and Statistics* 47: 13–37.

Malkiel, B.G. 2003. *A Random Walk Down Wall Street: The Time-Tested Strategy for Successful Investing*. New York, NY: W.W. Norton.

Markowitz, H.M. 1952. Portfolio selection. *Journal of Finance* 7: 77–91.

Markowitz, H.M. 1959. *Portfolio Selection: Efficient Diversification of Investments*. New York, NY: Wiley.

Mossin, J. 1966. Equilibrium in a capital asset market. *Econometrica* 34: 768–783.

Sharpe, W.F. 1964. Capital asset prices: A theory of market equilibrium under conditions of risk. *Journal of Finance* 19: 425–442.

Shiller, R.J. 2000. *Irrational Exuberance*. Princeton, NJ: Princeton University Press.

Tobin, J. 1958. Liquidity preference as a behavior toward risk. *Review of Economic Studies* 25: 65–86.

Treynor, J.L. 1961. Market value, time, and risk. Unpublished manuscript.

Treynor, J.L. 1962. Toward a theory of market value of risky assets. Unpublished manuscript.

von Neumann, J., and O. Morgenstern. 1944. *Theory of Games and Economic Behavior*. Princeton, NJ: Princeton University Press.

# 3 Capital Asset Pricing Model (CAPM)

This chapter covers the now famous Capital Asset Pricing Model (CAPM) as proposed by William Sharpe (1964), for which he was awarded the Nobel Prize in Economics in 1990. Other authors credited with contributions to the CAPM are Jack Treynor (1961, 1962), John Lintner (1965), and Jan Mossin (1966). The CAPM builds upon the mean-variance paradigm of Harry Markowitz (1952, 1959) and risk-aversion concepts of Tobin (1958). Interestingly, Sharpe was a Ph.D. student working closely with Markowitz at University of California at Los Angeles (UCLA), who shared the Nobel Prize with him along with Merton Miller.

The CAPM represents a landmark that established the study of *asset pricing*. Up until that time, finance as an academic and professional discipline was grounded primarily in accounting principles, present value of cash flow mathematics, and descriptive risk measures. The CAPM changed everything. Combining portfolio theory in Chapter 1 with capital market conditions in Chapter 2, including perfect capital markets, efficient markets, risk aversion, and mathematical return concepts, the CAPM provided the first equilibrium asset pricing model. It marked the beginning of a revolution that elevated the academic and professional field of finance around the world.

---

**Supplementary Information** The online version contains supplementary material available at https://doi.org/10.1007/978-3-031-16784-3_3.



J. W. Kolari and S. Pynnönen, *Investment Valuation and Asset Pricing*,
https://doi.org/10.1007/978-3-031-16784-3_3

## 3.1 The Present Value of Future Cash Flows

The present value formula is the workhorse of valuation. The current price of an asset $P$ at time 0 is determined as follows:

$$P_0 = \sum_{t=1}^{T} \frac{E(CF_t)}{(1 + E(R))^t}, \tag{3.1}$$

where $E(CF_t)$ are expected cash flows generated by the asset over time $t = 1, \ldots, T$, and $E(R)$ is the expected discount rate. Expected values of these variables are *ex ante* risky in the sense that they occur in the future and therefore are not known with certainty. Expected future cash flows in the numerator can be estimated from accounting, finance, and operating information about the firm. What were its past sales revenues, finance costs, and operating costs? Based on the firm's products and services, industry competition, and the general economy, what are the current projections for the cash flows or profits of the firm?

Nowadays many researchers express the present value formula in single-period $t$ as:

$$P_t = E_t(m_{t+1}x_{t+1}), \tag{3.2}$$

where $P_t$ is the beginning period price, $x_{t+1}$ represents cash flows or payoffs in the period from $t$ to $t+1$ equal to $1+R_{t+1}$, $E_t$ is the expectations operator conditional on market information at time $t$, and $m_{t+1}$ is the *stochastic discount factor*[1] (SDF) that discounts expected cash flows to present value prices. The SDF is defined as $m_{t+1} = 1/(1+R_{t+1})$. Assuming future cash flows are risky, the discount rate $R$ is random or stochastic. If future cash flows were certain, then $m_{t+1} = 1/(1+R_f)$ or the riskless discount factor. The above equation can be written in terms of returns by defining $R_{t+1} = x_{t+1}/P_t$ such that

$$E_t[m_{t+1}(1 + R_{t+1})] = 1. \tag{3.3}$$

This value equals 1 due to the *law of one price* for any asset. Accordingly, no possibility of arbitrage opportunities exists. As discussed in Chapter 2, arbitrage occurs when investors buy and sell the same asset at different prices to make trading profits. Of course, as they buy and sell, the trading profits are gradually eliminated to cause one price for the assets. This process assumes no frictions in the market that might prevent investor arbitrage (e.g., a brokerage firm that charges investors a fee for trading). Equations (3.2) and (3.3) are the most general forms of

[1] In different contexts, the variable $m$ is sometimes referred to as the *asset pricing kernel* or *marginal rate of substitution.*

asset pricing models. All models are special cases of these two equations, which fall under the general heading of "$m$-talk."[2]

The discount factor $m$ in the present value formula is central to asset pricing. To estimate the expected discount rate in $m$, it is necessary to understand the required rate of return of investors in the firm. This return on investment depends crucially on both the risks of the asset itself and investor aversion to risks. As discussed in Chapter 1, these two risk dimensions explain the *risk premium* equal to the difference between the risky expected rate of return for the $i$th asset and riskless rate, or $E(R_i) - R_f$.

To estimate discount rate $E(R_i)$ investors need to incorporate all potential risks affecting the price of the asset. For example, credit risk is related to the probability of bankruptcy of the firm. Liquidity risk takes into account the ability to buy and sell the asset with little change in price. Earnings risk considers the ability of the firm to generate profits in the future. Numerous other risks include (for example) management ability, legal issues, government regulation, technological change, and agency costs arising from differences in the objectives of management and shareholders. As the sum of these and other risks increases, the rate of return required by investors will increase. A number of questions naturally arise. How should we measure each of these many different risks? Is there a way to rank the risks from low to high? Can we combine these risks to estimate overall asset risk? To complicate matters further, expected future cash flows and expected discount rates change over time and cause the price of the asset to adjust or fluctuate in response to these changes.

Another way to estimate $E(R_t)$ is by observing historical prices. As defined in the previous chapter, the *ex post* rate of return in some period $t$ is:

$$R_t = \frac{P_t - P_{t-1}}{P_{t-1}}, \tag{3.4}$$

where no interest, dividends, or other payments to investors are assumed. The numerator gives the capital gain on the asset. A series of $R_t$ values can be computed over time to yield an estimate of the mean rate of return. The mean return could be used in the present value formula (3.1) as a proxy for $E(R_t)$.

This ex post rate is simple to estimate and provides an historical estimate of $E(R_t)$ but has a major drawback. Namely, it is backward looking and therefore does not consider future expected rates of return. Is the current price of the asset too high or low relative to the future rate of return? An investor could buy an asset that is overvalued with subsequent losses in its price over time. Likewise, an asset might be sold that is undervalued and then its price increases causing opportunity costs of lost gains. How can we determine if an asset is over- or undervalued at any point in time?

---

[2] See advanced textbooks by Cochrane (2005) and Ferson (2019) for excellent in-depth discussions and applications of m-talk in asset pricing models.

In forthcoming sections, we introduce the now famous Capital Asset Pricing Model (CAPM) of Treynor (1961, 1962), Sharpe (1964), Lintner (1965), and Mossin (1966). The CAPM proposes that, once the risk of an asset is estimated, ex ante rates of return can be determined. An overall measure of asset risk is derived relative to the market as a whole. In this sense, asset prices are relative to their market risks, which are jointly formed in equilibrium. To measure market risk, the CAPM relies upon the portfolio theory of Markowitz (1952, 1959), who defined the efficient frontier of all asset returns in the market. Let's see how Sharpe and other CAPM authors were able to use modern portfolio theory to solve the problem of estimating the expected rate of return and market risk of assets.

## 3.2 Market Equilibrium Assumptions

Sharpe (1964) observed that previous classroom discussions of capital asset prices lacked a theoretical foundation. Consequently, he sought to develop an equilibrium market framework for asset pricing. Some idealistic assumptions were needed to simplify matters. For market equilibrium to be reached, he assumed: (1) perfect competition exists in capital markets; (2) investors have homogeneous expectations concerning the probability distributions of returns on risky assets; (3) investors seek to maximize the expected utility of wealth; (4) risk-averse investors have quadratic utility functions; (5) investors can borrow and lend at the riskless rate; and (6) investors are not allowed to short sell assets in forming portfolios (i.e., only long asset positions are allowed).

As a starting point, he proposed the Capital Market Line (CML) as shown in Fig. 3.1. Equilibrium asset prices trade-off the expected rates of return of assets against their risks. The risk here is measured by the standard deviation of returns, or *total risk*. If there is zero risk, the investor earns the riskless rate $R_f$, which is based on the price of time or pure interest rate.[3] Given some expected rate of return per unit risk, under conditions of risk, the investor demands increasing risk premiums as risk increases.

Sharpe noted that Tobin (1958) used Markowitz's portfolio theory to propose a two-step investment process. First, the investor chooses a unique optimal combination of risk assets in a portfolio. Second, a separate choice is the allocation of funds to the risky portfolio and a riskless asset. This *Separation Theorem* set the stage for Sharpe's market equilibrium theory of asset prices under conditions of risk. While preparing his paper, Sharpe became aware of a similar equilibrium theory developed by Treynor[4] that no doubt influenced his work.

Combining Markowitz's efficient frontier (see Fig. 1.4 in Chapter 1) and Tobin's mean-variance indifference curves (see Fig. 2.3 in Chapter 2), Fig. 3.2 shows that

[3] For example, assuming no risk, if you indifferent between \$100 today or \$101 at the end of a year, your rate of time preference is 1%. This rate can be attributed to your utility preference of present consumption over future consumption.

[4] See Sharpe (1964, p. 427 footnote 7).

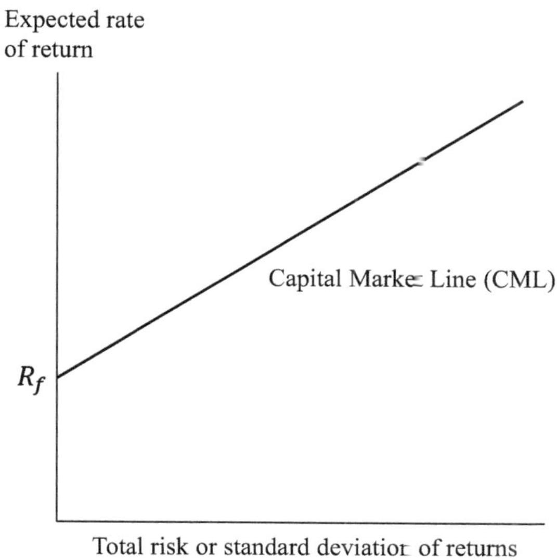


**Fig. 3.1** Equilibrium relationship between expected rates of return and risk

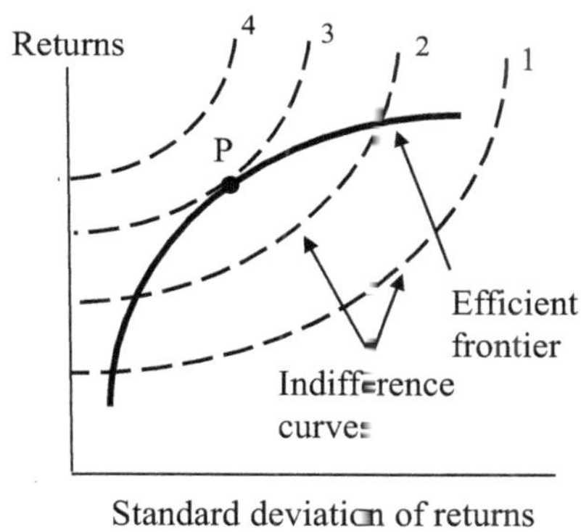


**Fig. 3.2** Combining the efficient frontier and indifference curves

the investor prefers optimal portfolio $P$. This portfolio lies at the tangency between indifference curve 3 and the efficient frontier. Any other portfolio will lower the expected utility of investors (e.g., portfolios intersecting indifference curves 1 and 2). The investor maximizes expected utility at $P$ in mean return and standard deviation return space. Assuming the investor commits their initial wealth ($W_i$) to portfolio $P$, Sharpe concluded that the investor would earn in one period $t$:

1. expected rate of return equal to $E(R_P) = (W_t - W_i)/W_i$; and
2. expected utility $E(U) = g[E(R_P), \sigma(R_P)]$, where $\sigma(R_P)$ denotes the standard deviation of portfolio $P$ returns.

Following Tobin's Separation theorem, the investor initially locates the efficient frontier and then selects one efficient portfolio with the highest expected utility.

## 3.3 Investment Choice with a Riskless Asset

Extending previous authors, Sharpe made a logical leap by introducing the existence of a riskless asset. Simplifying matters, he assumes a one-period model, such that we can drop the time subscript $t$ in the notation. Investors can allocate their wealth among both risky and riskless assets. Using risky efficient portfolio $P$ from Fig. 3.2, the expected return on this portfolio combination ($C$) is:

$$E(R_C) = aR_f + (1-a)E(R_P), \tag{3.5}$$

where $R_f$ is the constant riskless rate for asset $f$ held in wealth proportion $a$, and $E(R_P)$ is the expected return on portfolio $P$ held in wealth proportion $(1-a)$. The standard deviation of returns, or total risk, for this combination is:

$$\sigma(R_C) = [a^2\sigma^2(R_f) + (1-a)^2\sigma^2(R_P) + 2a(1-a)Cov(R_f, R_P)]^{1/2}, \tag{3.6}$$

where $Cov(R_f, R_P)$ denotes the covariance between asset $f$ and $P$ returns. Since the riskless rate $R_f$ is constant over time, we know that $\sigma^2(R_f) = 0$ and $\rho_{fP} = 0$ (i.e., the correlation of a constant with a random variable is zero). Consequently, the term $Cov(R_f, R_P) = \rho_{fP}\sigma(R_f)\sigma(R_P) = 0$, where $\rho_{fP}$ is the correlation coefficient between their returns. Conveniently, this result simplifies Eq. (3.6) to:

$$\sigma(R_C) = (1-a)^2\sigma^2(R_P). \tag{3.7}$$

The formulas for Eqs. (3.5) and (3.6) imply that combinations of the riskless rate and any efficient portfolio's risky return lie on a straight line. Figure 3.3 shows a variety of possible combinations of the riskless rate with different risky portfolios. It is obvious that the ray from riskless rate $R_f$ to the tangent point on the efficient frontier provides the highest expected return $E(R)$ per unit risk as measured by the standard deviation of returns $\sigma(R)$. Other combinations are less efficient than this optimal combination.

Sharpe referred to the optimal tangent point as the *market portfolio* denoted $M$. All points on the Capital Market Line (CML) from $R_f$ to $M$ represent different proportionate investments in the riskless asset $f$ and market portfolio $M$. All risk-averse investors buy market portfolio $M$, which is comprised of the value-weighted returns of all assets in the market with weights equal to the ratio of the market value of each asset to the aggregate market value of all assets. This theoretical result is remarkable! What about investors that buy other risky asset portfolios? According to Fig. 3.3, they would earn lower risk-adjusted returns than if they invested in $M$.

How do investors achieve expected return and total risk combinations along the CML? Points on the line from $R_f$ to $M$ require that the investor lend some

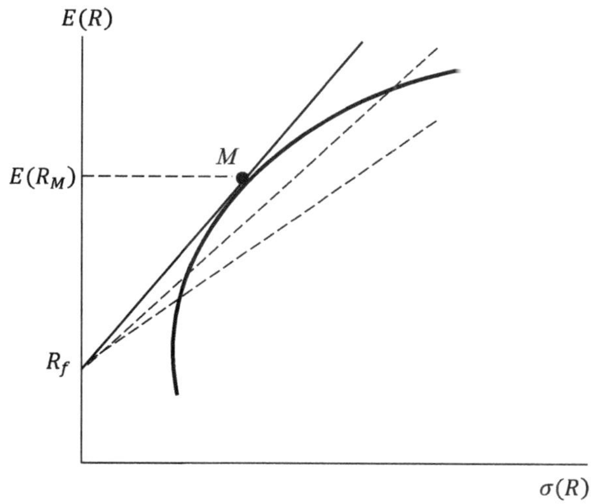


**Fig. 3.3** Locating market portfolio as a tangent point on the ray from riskless rate

proportion $a$ of their funds to earn the riskless rate $R_f$ (e.g., depositing funds in an insured bank deposit account or buying a riskless government bond) and invest the remainder in proportion $(1 - a)$ in market portfolio $M$. Where the investor lies on this section of the CML depends on their risk aversion as determined by the tangency point of their indifference curve with the CML. If the investor prefers points above $M$ on the CML, these points could be achieved by borrowing funds at the riskless rate $R_f$ and adding to their purchases of market portfolio $M$.

There is a long controversy about Sharpe's market portfolio results. Many professional investors argue that they can "beat the market" in the sense of actively managing investments to pick assets earning a higher rate of return per unit risk greater than market portfolio $M$. Opposing this claim, academics point to Sharpe's mean-variance theory. Historical evidence proves that over 90% of professional managers do not outperform common stock market indexes over reasonable investment horizons (e.g., the S &P 500 index over five years). This empirical fact led to the widespread adoption of index investing in well-diversified portfolios that contain all assets in the stock market. So-called *passive index funds* have very low transactions costs which help to further explain their relatively higher performance compared to *actively managed funds*. Professional managers in the latter funds seek to apply investment skills to choose portfolio assets and incur higher operating costs from this aggressive activity (e.g., transactions costs, management salaries, etc.).

## 3.4 The CAPM

The optimal CML tangent to the market portfolio defines a simple linear relationship between expected returns and their risk or standard deviation of returns. How does this general equilibrium relation affect individual assets? These assets are inefficient and lie within the investment opportunity set somewhere below the efficient frontier. Sharpe proved that individual assets are affected by their relationship to the market portfolio. Let's review his proof.[5]

Similar to forming combinations of the riskless asset and the market portfolio, investors can purchase combinations of an individual risky asset $i$ and market portfolio $M$. The expected rate of return on this combination is:

$$E(R_C) = aE(R_i) + (1 - a)E(R_M). \tag{3.8}$$

The standard deviation of returns for this portfolio is:

$$\sigma(R_C) = [a^2\sigma^2(R_i) + (1 - a)^2\sigma^2(R_M) + 2a(1 - a)Cov(R_i, R_M)]^{1/2} \tag{3.9}$$

where $Cov(R_i, R_M)$ denotes the covariance between asset $i$ and $M$ returns. Using Eq. (1.10) in Chapter 1, the covariance term for asset $i$ and market portfolio $M$ can be defined as $Cov(R_i, R_M) = \rho_{iM}\ \sigma(R_i)\ \sigma(R_M)$, where $\rho_{iM}$ is the correlation of returns between asset $i$ and $M$, and $\sigma(R_i)$ and $\sigma(R_M)$ are the standard deviations of returns (or total risks) of assets $i$ and $M$, respectively. Hence, covariance is related to correlation—positive (negative) correlation will result in positive (negative) covariance (as total risk is always positive). As we learned earlier, the covariance term plays an important role in the total risk of the combined portfolio $C$.

The slope of the efficient frontier can be derived as follows. From Eq. (3.8), we know that $dE(R_C)/da = E(R_i) - E(R_M)$. Also, from Eq. (3.9), we get $d\sigma(R_C)/da = [a\sigma^2(R_i) - \sigma^2(R_M) + a\sigma^2(R_M) + Cov(R_i, R_M) - 2a\,Cov(R_i, R_M)]/\sigma(R_C)$. Using these results, the change in portfolio $C$ returns per unit change in total risk, or slope of the CML, at the market portfolio where $a = 0$ is:

$$\frac{dE(R_C)}{d\sigma(R_C)} = \frac{[E(R_i) - E(R_M)]}{[-\sigma^2(R_M) + Cov(R_i, R_M)]/\sigma(R_M)}. \tag{3.10}$$

In Fig. 3.3 we know that the slope of the CML is $[E(R_M) - R_f]/\sigma(R_M)$.

Setting the slopes of the CML and efficient frontier (at the market portfolio $M$ with $a = 0$) equal to one another, we can write:

$$\frac{[E(R_M) - R_f]}{\sigma(R_M)} = \frac{[E(R_i) - E(R_M)]}{[-\sigma^2(R_M) + Cov(R_i, R_M)]/\sigma(R_M)}. \tag{3.11}$$

Rearranging terms yields:

$$E(R_i) = R_f + [E(R_M) - R_f]\frac{Cov(R_i, R_M)}{\sigma^2(R_M)}. \tag{3.12}$$

[5] See Sharpe (1964, p. 438, footnote 22).

The term $Cov(R_i, R_M)/\sigma^2(R_M)$ plays a pivotal role in this equation. It represents the slope of the line relating individual asset returns to market portfolio returns. To see this more clearly, we can substitute the parameter $\beta_i$ for the covariance term to get the more commonly used simplified form of the CAPM:

$$E(R_i) = R_f + \beta_i[E(R_M) - R_f], \tag{3.13}$$

where

$$\beta_i = \frac{Cov(R_i, R_M)}{\sigma^2(R_M)}. \tag{3.14}$$

The term $\beta_i$ is known as *beta*. It measures *systematic risk*, which is the risk of the asset relative to the market portfolio. If market portfolio $M$ is inserted for asset $i$ on the left-hand-side of the CAPM, its beta would equal 1. This benchmark value can be used to determine the relative risk of different assets. Assets with beta < 1 or beta > 1 have lower or higher risk, respectively, than the general market as represented by the market portfolio.

Beta risk assumes that the investor buys a diversified market portfolio $M$. As such, total risk as measured by $\sigma(R_i)$ for the $i$th assets can be broken down as follows:

$$\text{Total risk} = \text{systematic risk} + \text{unsystematic risk}, \tag{3.15}$$

where systematic risk is measured by beta, and unsystematic risk is an idiosyncratic component unrelated to systematic risk. Because the correlation of an asset with the market portfolio cannot be diversified away, beta risk is the only risk that is priced by investors. All other idiosyncratic risks can be eliminated by the diversifying behavior of investing in the market portfolio containing all assets. Notice that, while idiosyncratic risks do indeed exist, they do not affect the prices of capital assets as determined by diversified investors. This theoretical inference complements the earlier finding that all investors should purchase market portfolio $M$.

Figure 3.4 gives a graphical depiction of the CAPM. The linear relationship between the expected rate of return $E(R_i)$ and beta risk $\beta_i$ for individual assets is referred to as the *Security Market Line*. The market portfolio $M$ has expected rate of return $E(R_M)$ and systematic risk $\beta = 1$. Notice that the *market risk premium* or return in excess of the riskless rate equals $E(R_M) - R_f$. From Eq. (3.13), the risk premium for an individual asset, or $E(R_i) - R_f$, equals beta times the market risk premium, or $\beta_i[E(R_M) - R_f]$. These basic relationships describe the CAPM.

As an example, Fig. 3.5 illustrates how expected returns change with beta risk. We assume that the riskless rate $R_f = 4\%$ and expected market portfolio rate of return $E(R_M) = 9\%$, such that the market risk premium $E(R_M) - R_f = 5\%$. The table shows the expected rate of return for asset $i$, or $E(R_i)$, for different beta values, or $\beta_i$. Again, the beta of the market portfolio at one is a benchmark against which to evaluate the risk of different assets. Assets with betas less (more)

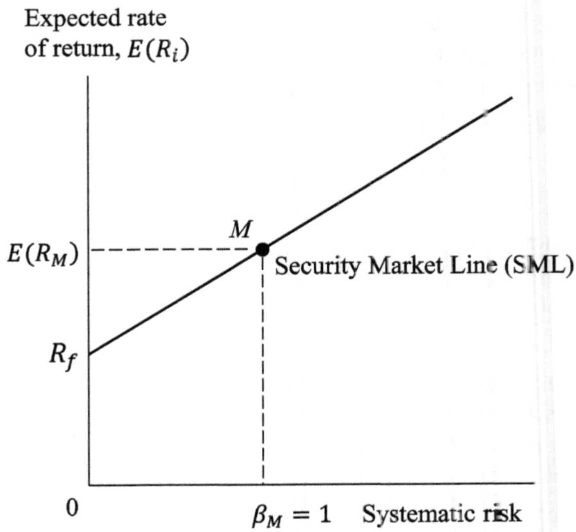


**Fig. 3.4** Pricing capital assets using systematic or beta risk

| Expected Rate of Return, $E(R_i)$ | Riskless Rate, $R_f$ | Beta, $\beta_i$ | Market Risk Premium, $E(R_M)-R_f$ |
|---|---|---|---|
| 4.00% | 4.00% | 0 | 5.00% |
| 5.25% | 4.00% | 0.25 | 5.00% |
| 6.50% | 4.00% | 0.50 | 5.00% |
| 9.00% | 4.00% | 1.00 | 5.00% |
| 10.25% | 4.00% | 1.25 | 5.00% |
| 11.50% | 4.00% | 1.50 | 5.00% |
| 14.00% | 4.00% | 2.00 | 5.00% |

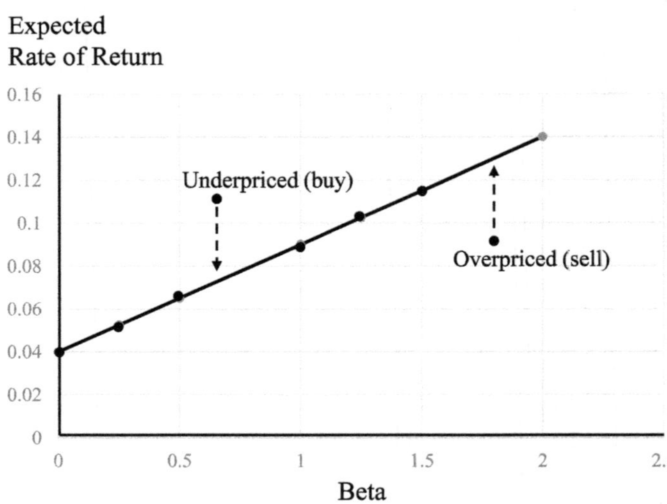


**Fig. 3.5** Expected rates of return and beta risk

than one, have less (more) risk than the market and commensurately lower (higher) expected returns. All $E(R_i)$ increase linearly with beta and lie on the SML. Assets in disequilibrium located above (below) the SML are underpriced (overpriced). Arbiteurs will buy (sell) these mispriced assets until they lie on the equilibrium SML.

We can write the CAPM in alternative forms that yield insights into the valuation of assets. We begin by defining the risky price of the $i$th asset at the end of a single-period as $P_{i1}$, where we now use a time subscript $t$. This risky price is a random variable. The asset's current price $P_{i0}$ is known and so is a constant. Referring back to Eq. (3.16) for the ex post return, we can similarly define the ex ante rate of return for the $i$th asset as:

$$E(R_i) = \frac{E(P_{i1}) - P_{i0}}{P_{i0}}, \tag{3.16}$$

where $E(P_{i1})$ is the expected future price of the asset at the end of the period at time 1, and $P_{i0}$ is the current equilibrium price of the asset at time 0. Here the time subscripts $t = 1$ and $t = 0$ only are used for prices, and no subscript is again used for single-period returns. Substituting this one-period return into the left-hand-side of CAPM relation (3.13), we have:

$$\frac{E(P_{i1}) - P_{i0}}{P_{i0}} = \frac{E(P_{i1})}{P_{i0}} - 1 = R_f + \beta_i[E(R_M) - R_f]. \tag{3.17}$$

Using some algebra, we can re-write this equation as:

$$P_{i0} = \frac{E(P_{i1})}{1 + R_f + \beta_i[E(R_M) - R_f]}. \tag{3.18}$$

Equation (3.18) is known as the *risk-adjusted rate of return valuation formula*.[6] The risky future price or cash flow $E(P_{i1})$ in the numerator is divided by the risky discount rate $1 + R_f + \beta_i[E(R_M) - R_f]$ in the denominator, where risk premium $\beta_i[E(R_M) - R_f]$ is added to the riskless one-period discount rate $1 + R_f$. If the asset has no risk, then this valuation equation reduces to $P_{i0} = E(P_{i1})/(1+R_f) = P_{i1}/(1 + R_f)$, as $E(P_{i1}) = P_{i1}$ when $P_{i1}$ is riskless.

Alternatively, if we define $\beta_i = Cov(R_i, R_M)/\sigma^2(R_M)$ as before, and substitute $[E(P_{i1}) - P_{i0}]/P_{i0}$ for $R_i$, beta can be re-written as:

$$\beta_i = \frac{1/P_{i0}Cov[(P_{i1} - P_{i0}), R_M]}{\sigma^2(R_M)}. \tag{3.19}$$

Because $P_{i1}$ is a random risky price, and $P_{i0}$ is the current price (a constant) with zero correlation with $R_M$, beta reduces to

$$\beta_i = \frac{1/P_{i0}Cov(P_{i1}, R_M)}{\sigma^2(R_M)} \tag{3.20}$$

[6] See Copeland and Weston (1980, p. 170).

or $\beta_i = Cov(P_{i1}, R_M)/P_{i0}\sigma^2(R_M)$. Next, we replace beta with this value in Eq. (3.18) to get

$$P_{i0} = \frac{E(P_{i1})}{1 + R_f + [Cov(P_{i1}, R_M)/P_0\sigma^2(R_M)][E(R_M) - R_f]}. \tag{3.21}$$

Again rearranging terms, we finally obtain the following *certainty equivalent valuation formula*:

$$P_{i0} = \frac{E(P_{i1}) - [Cov(P_{i1}, R_M)/\sigma^2(R_M)][E(R_M) - R_f]}{1 + R_f}. \tag{3.22}$$

Here the certainty equivalent cash flow in the numerator is discounted at the riskless rate to yield the equilibrium current price of the asset $P_{i0}$. Unlike the risk-adjusted rate of return valuation formula (3.18), wherein the risky discount rate in the denominator is adjusted upward by adding the risk premium to the riskless rate, cash flows in the numerator are adjusted for risk by subtracting the risk premium from the risky future price. In both of these alternative CAPM models, the value of an asset is determined by its expected future cash flow and beta risk as well as the market risk premium and riskless rate. Given homogeneous expectations among investors about these determinants, no individual risk preferences (as reflected by utility functions) affect asset value.

## 3.5 Implications of the CAPM

The CAPM is an elegantly simple theoretical model based on previously established portfolio theory and risk preference theories by Markowitz and Tobin. As mentioned earlier, Treynor, Lintner, and Mossin developed comparable versions of the CAPM. Unlike Sharpe, they allowed short sales of assets, which helps to make the model more general and applicable to the real world. Also, unlike Sharpe who allowed more than one risky portfolio to be efficient, the other authors found that tangent portfolio $M$ is the only efficient risky portfolio—that is, $M$ is located on the highest return/risk CML from the riskless rate that represents the efficient frontier in the presence of a riskless asset. In his paper, Sharpe argued that one asset might be in one efficient risky portfolio and a second asset could be in another efficient risky portfolio. Because all efficient risky portfolios are perfectly correlated, he inferred that the betas of all assets would be unchanged with respect to alternative efficient portfolios. However, Fama (1968) clarified this issue by observing that market portfolio $M$ must contain all assets. Since any assets not in $M$ would not be held by investors, this possibility is inconsistent with equilibrium in which markets are clear for all assets. In the CAPM, market portfolio $M$ contains all assets in proportion to their market values relative to total or aggregate market value.

Treynor (1961, 1962) never published his papers but over time received credit for being the first person to derive the CAPM.[7] He had given a copy of his first paper to Lintner at Harvard in 1960. As a matter of record, he publicly presented his work in 1962 to MIT university faculty in a research seminar. You can find his papers on the internet.[8]

Lintner (1965) considered different idealistic assumptions underlying the CAPM and concluded that the CAPM would hold under more complex real-world conditions. For example, he argued that the CAPM would hold even if borrowing rates exceeded lending rates. Securities firms typically charge clients a rate of interest greater than the riskless government interest rate on borrowed funds to invest in securities. However, this objection implies only that there is a kinked CML with a higher slope from $R_f$ to $M$ and a lower slope (due to borrowing rates being greater than lending rates) above $M$. And, some large investors may well be able to borrow at close to the riskless government rate (e.g., global banks, insurance, securities firms, etc.). Hence, Lintner inferred that the CAPM, while theoretically simplistic, was applicable to real-world decision-making, including capital budgeting and other financial problems.[9]

Mossin (1966) cited Sharpe's CML in his analysis. He employed the CML to define the "price of risk" for individual assets. This price was defined as the compensation for risk per unit of an individual asset's risk. In effect, similar to Sharpe's SML, he derived the asset pricing relation for individual assets from the general market equilibrium CML.

The significance of the CAPM rests in its implications to the theory and practice of finance. The following provides a short list of major implications.

1. All assets lie somewhere along the SML. Assets with prices above (below) the SML will be bought (sold) by arbiteurs until their prices change and fall back to the SML. Hence, the SML represents an equilibrium relationship between risk and return in the marketplace. It can be used to determine whether assets are over- or underpriced.
2. Market beta can be used to rank order stocks or portfolios by their risk. Returns for assets should be related to their beta risk levels. Investors can expect lower (higher) returns on assets with lower (higher) beta risk in portfolio selection decisions. For portfolios, assuming the investor has $x\%$ of their wealth in asset

[7] See Black (1981).

[8] See the following Social Science Network (SSRN) websites:
https://papers.ssrn.com/sol3/papers.cfm?abstract_id=2600356 and
https://papers.ssrn.com/sol3/papers.cfm?abstract_id=2600356.

[9] Linter also did not assume that all investors agree on the distribution of asset returns in the next period; instead, he argued that asset prices are based on the weighted average of investor expectations about asset returns.

X and $y\%$ in asset $Y$, the beta of the portfolio will be the simple weighted average of their betas, or $\beta_p = x\beta_X + y\beta_Y$.[10]

3. Investors do not need to spend countless hours identifying and measuring credit risk, liquidity risk, legal risk, management risk, etc., of individual stocks. All of these risks are incorporated in beta risk, which summarizes the relevant risk facing diversified investors holding the market portfolio.
4. Given beta for a stock, managers of firms can estimate the cost of equity and cost of capital (i.e., the cost of capital is the weighted costs of debt and equity capital). In turn, these costs can be used to select the highest net present value (NPV) projects in capital budgeting decisions.
5. Idiosyncratic risks unrelated to systematic risk will earn only the riskless rate of return. Only assets with positive systematic risk will have expected rates of return greater than the riskless rate.
6. Market imperfections, including perfect capital market frictions such as taxes, transactions costs, institutional structure, government regulation, etc., do not significantly affect the main results of the CAPM. However, real-world empirical tests are needed to confirm this implication.
7. Beta measures the sensitivity of an asset's rate of return to changes in the market rate of return. Since the market return is affected by general economic activity, asset returns are sensitive to fundamental economic forces also.
8. Investors are able to purchase a portfolio in the marketplace that is a close substitute or proxy for market portfolio $M$.
9. There are no other systematic risk factors than the market factor equal to the market risk premium. No mispricing exists after taking into account sensitivity to the market factor as measured by beta risk. Tests of other potential risk factors are needed to support this implication.

As we will see in forthcoming chapters, these implications motivated a tremendous amount of research in the years to come. Can such a simple model really be valid? Will it work in the real world? Does the CAPM lead to other theoretical discoveries? Are there competing models of asset pricing? As we will see, confirming the final remarks of Lintner at the end of his paper, the CAPM opened the doors to a flood of new theories and applied for empirical work.

## 3.6 Summary

The traditional approach to valuation employs the present value formula. This formula specifies asset prices as a function of expected future cash flows divided by expected discount rates. Fundamental accounting, finance, and operating information about the firm are used to estimate expected cash flows. A wide variety of

[10] Note that, to find Markowitz efficient portfolios, it is not necessary to use optimization methods such as quadratic programs. Conceptually at least, beta could be used to construct efficient portfolios with different levels of market risk.

risks are incorporated into the expected discount rate. Alternatively, historical rates of return on an asset can be used to approximate expected discount rates. However, historical rates have the drawback of being backward looking and, therefore, are not helpful in determining whether an asset is over- or undervalued relative to future returns.

The CAPM represents a breakthrough in terms of measuring the relevant risk to diversified investors. Based on idealistic assumptions of perfect competition, homogeneous expectations, utility maximization, risk aversion, and riskless borrowing and lending rates, Treynor, Sharpe, Lintner, and Mossin independently derived the price of risky assets in equilibrium. To do this, they assumed that Markowitz portfolio theory and the Tobin Separation Principle hold. Investors that practice Markowitz diversification will hold a single optimal portfolio on the efficient frontier. This efficient portfolio is obtained as the tangent point on a ray extending from the riskless rate to the efficient frontier. The resultant ray is the Capital Market Line (CML) relating expected rates of return to total risk as measured by the standard deviation of returns. All investors will purchase the tangent point known as the *market portfolio M*, which is a separate decision from their risk preferences. Depending on their risk preferences, investors will hold different combinations of the riskless rate and the market portfolio. Investors who want to take more risk than the market portfolio can borrow funds and increase their holdings of the market portfolio. These results are logical outcomes of Markowitz diversification and Tobin risk preference concepts.

The next step is to derive the price of an individual asset. By setting the slopes of the linear CML to the efficient frontier of risky assets, Sharpe showed that asset prices are determined by the riskless rate, expected rate of return on the market portfolio, and beta risk. Beta risk (denoted $\beta$) is a parameter relating the expected rate of return of asset $i$ to the market risk premium defined as the expected rate of return on the market portfolio return minus the riskless rate. The linear relationship between expected rates of return for assets and their beta risks is the *Security Market Line* (SML). The SML represents the equilibrium pricing relationship in which only beta measuring systematic risk is priced by investors. Hence, total risk as measured by the standard deviation of returns can be broken down into undiversifiable systematic risk (beta) and diversifiable unsystematic (idiosyncratic) risk. Assets that are underpriced (overpriced) lie above (below) the SML; arbiteurs will buy (sell) these assets until they lie on the SML. Thus, the SML is an equilibrium return/risk relation. Two alternative but equivalent forms of the CAPM are the risk-adjusted rate of return valuation formula and certainty equivalent valuation formula. Both of these formulas, like the CAPM itself, value assets without regard to the risk preferences of individuals that have homogeneous expectations. If investors have heterogeneous expectations, a single efficient market portfolio may not be identified by investors, which is critical to the CAPM. For this reason, empirical tests of the CAPM discussed in the next chapter jointly test the CAPM and the efficiency of the market portfolio.

The CAPM has many important implications. All investors buy the same market portfolio. All systematic risk is captured in beta risk related to the market portfolio. Besides identifying over- and underpriced assets, it can be used in portfolio management, capital budgeting, and other financial decisions. Its assumptions are idealistic but may well be relaxed in many cases, such as the allowance of risky borrowing rates and short sales. The simple elegance of the CAPM is both an advantage and disadvantage. If true, it allows investors to spend less time evaluating a myriad of different risks affecting assets (e.g., credit risk, liquidity risk, legal risks, regulation, etc.) and instead focus on beta risk. Contrary to the CAPM, many professional investment managers believe that they can outperform the market portfolio (e.g., a general market index) by means of skill in evaluating market information. As will see in forthcoming chapters, the CAPM opened the door to a large body of theoretical and applied research. Even today, researchers grapple with what we might call the *CAPM paradox*—are asset prices determined by the equilibrium mechanics of Treynor–Sharpe–Lintner–Mossin, or are they entangled in a more complex pricing mechanism?

## Questions

1. Write the present value formula for future cash flows. Re-write this present value formula using $m$-talk. Redefine the $m$-talk equation in terms of expected returns.
2. Draw the Capital Market Line (CML) of Sharpe (1964). What does this line show?
3. Assuming Markowitz's efficient frontier and Tobin's mean-variance indifference curves, what portfolio should the investor select? Illustrate this portfolio with a graph with mean returns on the Y-axis and standard deviation of returns on the X-axis.
4. Write the expected return of the portfolio combination of the riskless asset in proportion $a$ and risky efficient portfolio $P$ in proportion $(1 - a)$. What is the standard deviation of returns for this combination? Since the riskless rate $R_f$ is a constant over time, to what does this standard deviation reduce? What do these results imply to investors?
5. Given the results for question 4 above, which portfolio will an investor optimally select to maximize their expected returns per unit risk as measured by the standard deviation of returns $\sigma(R)$? Draw a picture of your Capital Market Line (CML) solution. How can investors locate themselves at different points along this CML?
6. Do you think that professional investors can buy a risky portfolio that "beats the market" in the sense of outperforming portfolio $M$?
7. Draw the Security Market Line (SML). Is this line an equilibrium relation between risk and return? Is systematic risk part of total risk?

8. A certainty equivalent form of the CAPM is as follows:

$$P_0 = \frac{E(P_1) - [Cov(P_1, R_M)/\sigma^2(R_M)][E(R_M) - R_f]}{1 + R_f}.$$

Why does the equation use the riskless rate to discount the cash flows in the numerator?

9. Give a definition of the market portfolio $M$. Are some assets in the market not contained in $M$?
10. The CAPM has a number of implications for the theory and practice of finance. Discuss five implications.

## Problems

1. Assume that investors hold a portfolio of an individual risky asset and riskless asset $f$. Starting with the expected return of this combination and its standard deviation, derive the slope of the efficient frontier and then set this slope equal to the slope of the efficient frontier at market portfolio $M$. Rearranging terms, write the equation for the CAPM in more general form as well its more common simplified form.
2. Using data in the following table, compute the expected returns for different assets using the CAPM.

| $E(R_i)$ | $R_f$ (%) | Beta, $\beta_i$ | $E(R_M) - R_f$ (%) |
|---|---|---|---|
| | 2.00 | -0.25 | 4.00 |
| | 2.00 | 0.00 | 4.00 |
| | 2.00 | 0.25 | 4.00 |
| | 2.00 | 0.75 | 4.00 |
| | 2.00 | 1.00 | 4.00 |
| | 2.00 | 1.50 | 4.00 |
| | 2.00 | 2.00 | 4.00 |

## References

Black, F. 1981. An open letter to Jack Treynor. *Financial Analysts Journal* 37: 14.

Cochrane, J. H. 2005. *Asset Pricing: Revised Edition.* NJ: Princeton University Press, Princeton.

Fama, E.F. 1968. Risk, return, and equilibrium: Some clarifying comments. *Journal of Finance* 23: 29–40.

Ferson, W. E. 2019. *Empirical Asset Pricing: Models and Methods.* MA: The MIT Press, Cambridge.

French, C.W. 2003. The Treynor Capital Asset Pricing Model. *Journal of Investment Management* 1: 60–72.

Lintner, J. 1965. The valuation of risk assets and the selection of risky investments in stock portfolios and capital budgets. *Review of Economics and Statistics* 47: 13–37.

Markowitz, H. 1952. Portfolio selection. *Journal of Finance* 7: 77–91.

Markowitz, H.M. 1959. *Portfolio Selection: Efficient Diversification of Investments*. New York, NY: John Wiley & Sons.

Mossin, J. 1966. Equilibrium in a capital asset market. *Econometrica* 34: 768–783.

Sharpe, W.F. 1964. Capital asset prices: A theory of market equilibrium under conditions of risk. *Journal of Finance* 19: 425–442.

Tobin, J. 1958. Liquidity preference as behavior toward risk. *Review of Economic Studies* 4: 65–86.

Treynor, J.L. 1961. Market value, time, and risk. Unpublished manuscript.

Treynor, J.L. 1962. Toward a theory of market value of risky assets. Unpublished manuscript.

Weston, T.E., and J.F. Weston. 1980. *Financial Theory and Corporate Policy*. Reading, MA: Addison-Wesley Publishing Company.

# The Market Model

# 4

The famed capital asset pricing model (CAPM) of Treynor (1961; 1962), Sharpe (1964), Lintner (1965), and Mossin (1966) is surprisingly elegant in design. It hypothesizes that only a single market factor is sufficient to measure systematic risk and price assets in financial markets. All investors will price assets using the market factor regardless of their individual risk preferences. To test this hypothesis, the market model was invented in the form of a simple regression equation. Using a proxy for the market portfolio and a riskless rate, this regression model enables the estimation of beta risk for assets.

The earliest applications of the market model focused on the U.S. stock market. As we will see, this early evidence did not entirely support the CAPM. High (low) beta stocks had lower (higher) returns than predicted by the CAPM. In effect, the slope of the Security Market Line (SML) was flatter than predicted by the theory. This flatter SML resulted in a higher than expected intercept term, which implies that other risks may well exist that are embedded in the intercept or $\alpha$ parameter in the market model. Given that $\alpha$ is fairly large in magnitude, as discussed in forthcoming chapters, researchers subsequently proposed various remedies that led to new forms of the CAPM as well as alternative models extending the CAPM to multiple factors.

In this chapter, we take a look at the market model and early CAPM evidence. Because the market model is a statistical model, we supplement the discussion with a primer on simple regression analysis, including the interpretation of regression coefficients, justification for ordinary least squares (OLS) estimation of regression coefficients, relation of the market model to the theoretical CAPM, and goodness-of-fit of regression models.

---

**Supplementary Information** The online version contains supplementary material available at https://doi.org/10.1007/978-3-031-16784-3_4.



J. W. Kolari and S. Pynnönen, *Investment Valuation and Asset Pricing*,
https://doi.org/10.1007/978-3-031-16784-3_4

## 4.1 Empirical Form of the CAPM

From Chapter 3, the theoretical CAPM specifies the expected rate of return on the $i$th asset in ex ante form as follows:

$$E(R_i) = R_f + \beta_i[E(R_M) - R_f]. \tag{4.1}$$

where $R_f$ is the riskless rate, $E(R_M)$ is the expected rate of return on the market portfolio, and $\beta_i$ measures systematic beta risk. How can we estimate this model in the real world?

To investigate the validity of the CAPM, an empirical model is needed. For this purpose, the variables in the CAPM need to be proxied with data available in financial markets. It is reasonable to proxy the riskless rate by using a high-quality government bond rate that has little or no default risk. The rate of return on the market portfolio $M$ is a more difficult variable to proxy. Since $M$ theoretically contains all assets by their market values, when applying the model to the stock market, researchers proposed using a general value-weighted market index. For example, the S &P 500 index contains the largest 500 stocks that comprise a large proportion of the total market capitalization of the U.S. stock market. A more comprehensive aggregate stock market portfolio is the CRSP index containing all U.S. stocks that are provided by the Center for Research and Security Prices at the University of Chicago.

Markowitz (1959) originally proposed an empirical model for the CAPM that Sharpe (1963) and Fama (1968) further developed. They proposed the following so-called *market model*:[1]

$$R_{it} - R_{ft} = \alpha_i + \beta_i(R_{mt} - R_{ft}), \tag{4.2}$$

where $R_{it} - R_{ft}$ is the excess realized rate of return on asset $i$ in time period $t$ (e.g., daily or monthly), and $R_{mt} - R_{ft}$ is the realized excess average rate of return on the stock market as a whole. Notice that an intercept term, or $\alpha$ parameter, is included to denote the excess realized rate of return assuming no beta risk (i.e., $\beta = 0$). According to CAPM theory, $\alpha$ should be zero. Also, we use the lower case notation $m$ for the stock market portfolio, which is a proxy for the theoretical (unobservable) market portfolio $M$.

The market model is a simple regression model of $y$ (excess asset returns) on $x$ (excess market returns). Typically, ordinary least squares (OLS) regression methods are used for estimation purposes. OLS is the most widely used type of regression analysis that is available in Excel and all statistical packages (e.g., Stata, Matlab, etc.). Free software on the internet is available for R and Python program codes to estimate OLS regression models. Forthcoming Sect. 4.4 provides a primer on regression analysis.

---

[1] See also Black et al. (1972).

Jensen (1968) recognized that $\alpha_i$ enables a test of the CAPM. So-called *Jensen's alpha* is a joint test of both the efficiency of the proxy for the market portfolio and the possibility of mispricing due to missing factors. If the empirical market portfolio $m$ is not a good proxy for the theoretical market portfolio $M$, then $\alpha$ would be nonzero. Roll (1977) argued that the CAPM cannot be tested without an efficient market proxy for $M$, which is known as the *Roll critique*. Moreover, if one or more other factors are important in pricing stocks beyond the market excess return factor, again $\alpha$ would not equal zero. Given the simplicity of the CAPM, the possibility of missing factors is certainly plausible.

In the real world, all stocks will not lie exactly on the Security Market Line (SML) relating asset returns to beta risks. Individual stocks' returns will randomly be located above or below the SML due to random movements in their stock prices (rather than over- or underpricing). Taking into account random stock prices, the market model can be modified as follows:

$$R_{it} - R_f = \alpha_i + \beta_i(R_{mt} - R_{ft}) + e_{it}, \tag{4.3}$$

where $e_{it}$ is a random error term (with mean zero and constant variance) that captures the scatter of assets' returns around the SML.

## 4.2 Early Tests of the Market Model

In this section we review some of the early evidence on the market model. Overall, stock market data suggested that the Security Market Line (SML) relating stock returns to beta risk was flatter than CAPM theory would predict. The slope of the SML was lower and the intercept was higher than hypothesized. This evidence caused considerable controversy about the CAPM. Were the data in the tests sufficient? Were the statistical tests appropriate? Was the CAPM too simplistic? These and other questions were addressed by researchers in the early studies.

### 4.2.1 Black, Jensen, and Scholes Study

Black, Jensen, and Scholes (BJS) (1972) proposed a direct test of the CAPM using the market model. According to the CAPM, the $\alpha$ intercept should be zero. Their data consisted of monthly returns for U.S. stocks trading on the New York Stock Exchange (NYSE) and U.S. government interest rates (i.e., 30-day Treasury rates) for the period 1926 to 1966.[2] The study included between 600 to 1,000 individual stocks in different years.

BJS is a landmark study that helped to establish the use of portfolios in asset pricing tests. They discovered that individual stocks should not be used in CAPM

[2] Treasury rates were only available from 1948 to 1966. From 1925 to 1947 they used the dealer commercial paper rate for the riskless rate proxy.

tests due to substantial measurement errors in estimating betas and, in turn, intercepts. These measurement errors tend to cancel one another out in portfolios. Consequently, their portfolio sorting method became the standard approach in later asset pricing tests.[3] One drawback of forming portfolios is that the range of beta values is decreased compared to their range among individual stocks. This more narrow range of betas makes it more difficult to detect a significant relation between stock returns and beta. In the extreme, if random portfolios were used, the portfolios would tend to have mean returns similar to that of the market portfolio proxy. In this case, all the alphas ($\alpha$s) would be zero with betas ($\beta$s) equal to approximately one. Of course, this test would be meaningless; no information on how beta affects returns would be gained. By sorting stocks into portfolios by their betas, BJS mitigated this potential pitfall but nonetheless constrained the full range of return/beta relations in the population of stocks.

They grouped stocks into 10 portfolios sorted on betas. In forming beta groups of stocks, they employed five years of monthly returns to estimate beta for all individual stocks. For example, the five-year period 1926 to 1930 was used to estimate individual stocks' betas. After forming 10 beta groups, their monthly returns in the next (out-of-sample) 12 months of 1931 were computed and their beta group was retained. They then rolled forward this process by one year, estimated betas for the five-year period 1927 to 1931, formed 10 beta groups, and computed the monthly returns in the next year 1932 for each beta group. This process was repeated to construct a 35-year time series of monthly returns from 1931 to 1965 (i.e., 420 observations). These time-series returns were used to estimate the market model Eq. (4.3) for each of the 10 beta portfolios. On average, the betas of the portfolios ranged from about 0.5 to 1.5 with some variation in this range from year-to-year in the sample period.

For the entire sample period, the results of BJS market model tests followed a definite pattern. Stock portfolios with betas greater (less) than one had negative (positive) intercepts. To evaluate the CAPM, a $t$-test of the intercept for each of the 10 portfolios was implemented as follows:

$$t = \frac{\hat{\alpha}_p - 0}{s_{\hat{\alpha}_p}}, \tag{4.4}$$

where $\hat{\alpha}_p$ is the OLS regression estimate for each portfolio $p$, $s_{\hat{\alpha}_p}$ is the OLS standard error of $\hat{\alpha}_p$, and 0 is the population value of $\alpha$ according to CAPM theory. Note that $\hat{\alpha}_p$ and $s_{\hat{\alpha}_p}$ are estimated for each portfolio using an OLS regression of the market model with monthly returns from 1931 to 1965. The $t$-test above assumes that the error terms of the market model are normally distributed.[4] The results of these $t$-tests for the 10 portfolios showed that 3-out-of-10 tests were significant at the 10% level. Stock portfolios with $\beta$s nearer to one had insignificant

[3] See Blume (1970) and Friend and Blume (1970).

[4] In forthcoming Sect. 4.4, we discuss the error term and other OLS assumptions in more detail.

$\alpha$s. But portfolios with very high or low $\beta$s had significant $\alpha$s. Again, CAPM theory hypothesizes that no significant $\alpha$s should occur; hence, some evidence was contrary to the CAPM. While a definite pattern in positive and negative $\alpha$s was obvious, they cautiously inferred that $t$-tests for the full sample of all stocks were not sufficient to make a clear interpretation of the results.

To more fully investigate their sample data and increase the number of tests, BJS divided their sample period into four subperiods with 105 months each. In the first period, the results flipped: stock portfolios with $\beta$s greater (less) than one had positive (negative) intercepts. In the other three subperiods, the results flipped back to agree with the total sample results: stock portfolios with betas greater (less) than one had negative (positive) intercepts. In the last two subperiods, the $t$-tests were stronger, with both higher negative and positive $t$-statistics associated with $\beta$ portfolios having high and low $\alpha$s, respectively. Related to the latter findings for the last two subperiods, average $\beta$ estimates for the 10 portfolios suggested that the slope of the SML was flatter than in the other subperiods. Thus, low $\beta$ stocks had higher returns than predicted, and high $\beta$ stocks had lower returns than predicted. No statistical tests of the $\beta$s were conducted using time-series monthly returns in the market model. To test the $\beta$s, they conducted cross-sectional regression tests that will be discussed shortly with respect to the Fama and MacBeth (1973) study.

It is noteworthy that the magnitudes of average $\alpha$s for portfolios were relatively high at between about $-0.50\%$ and $+0.35\%$ per month. In other words, on an annual basis, beta risk in the market model did not explain between $-6\%$ and $+4\%$ of stock returns in different beta portfolios. For comparison, the average market return on all NYSE stocks was 1.42% per month, or about 17% per year in their sample period. Hence, the magnitudes of average $\alpha$s suggested that something more than beta was needed to complete price stocks.

Based on their findings, BJS inferred the following:

1. the SML appears to be flatter (or less upward sloping) for the beta-sorted portfolios than predicted by CAPM theory;
2. portfolios with betas greater (less) than one tended to have negative (positive) $\alpha_p$ intercepts; and
3. there is some instability or nonstationarity of $\alpha$ and $\beta$ portfolio estimates that determines the shape of the SML over time.

Taken together, they concluded that the results rejected the CAPM. Due to this failure, in an effort to account for the large magnitudes of the $\alpha$ estimates discussed above, further tests were conducted by BJS on a second missing factor based on the theoretical CAPM model of Black (1972). In the next chapter, we cover Black's more general CAPM that contains a second factor uncorrelated with the market factor and discuss the BJS findings.

### 4.2.2 Fama and MacBeth Study

A number of studies confirmed the BJS finding that the SML was flatter than predicted by the CAPM, including Douglas (1969), Friend and Blume (1970), Miller and Scholes (1972), Fama and MacBeth (1973), Stambaugh (1982), Gibbons and Shanken (1983), and others. Here we take a closer look at the Fama and MacBeth (FM) study, which became famous in asset pricing tests due to its methodological advances.

FM gathered monthly returns for NYSE stocks in a longer sample period from January 1926 to June 1963. Like BJS, they used portfolios in their tests of the market model due to the potential *error-in-the-variables* problem that exists for individual stock estimates of beta. Since the market portfolio proxy $m$ is not the same as the latent (or unobserved) true market portfolio $M$, beta is estimated with error. If these errors in beta estimates are not perfectly positively correlated, they will tend to cancel out in portfolios, which provides a more accurate measurement of beta. Consequently, they formed 20 beta-sorted portfolios and constructed their equal-weighted average returns over time.

To test the CAPM, FM set up the following novel cross-sectional regression model:

$$R_{pt} = \alpha_0 + \lambda_m \beta_{pt-1} + \lambda_{nl} \beta_{pt-1}^2 + \lambda_s \bar{\sigma}(e)_{pt-1} + e_{pt}, \tag{4.5}$$

where $R_{pt}$ is the portfolio return in month $t$, $\alpha_0$ is the intercept term not explained by the other variables in the equation, $\beta_{pt-1}$ is the portfolio beta estimated using monthly returns in previous years (e.g., four or five years), $\beta_{pt-1}^2$ is used to test for a possible non-linear relation between returns and beta risk, $\bar{\sigma}(e)_{pt-1}$ is the average of the standard deviation of monthly residual errors for stocks in the portfolio in previous years, and $e_{pt}$ are independent and normally distributed error terms.[5] Independent variables on the right-hand-side of the regression model are measured prior to the portfolio returns on the left-hand-side. This out-of-sample approach to testing the CAPM is predictive. FM argued that *normative models*, such as Markowitz's (1959) portfolio theory that was intended to help investors make better decisions, are only valid to the extent that past information is related to future returns.

Importantly, the $\lambda$ terms in Eq. (4.5) are known as *market prices of risk* associated with the $\beta$ estimates (often called *loadings*). The cross-sectional regression coefficient $\lambda_m$ estimates the average market price of risk (or market risk premium) equal to $\bar{R}_{mt} - \bar{R}_{ft}$ in the sample period. We can compare this estimate to the actual average market risk premium in the sample period. Of course, if the CAPM holds, the estimated and actual market prices of beta risk should be approximately equal to one another. If non-linearity exists, then the market price of squared $\beta$, or

[5] The exact details of their data are somewhat complicated and beyond the scope of the present general discussion. See Fama and MacBeth (1973, pp. 616–617).

$\lambda_{nl}$, will be nonzero. And, if market price $\lambda_s$ is nonzero, some other non-beta risk must exist that is not captured by beta.

More generally, we can summarize the above two-step testing approach as follows:

1. In the first step, time-series regressions are estimated to obtain $\beta$ coefficients or other risk loadings in an estimation window (e.g., five years of monthly returns or one year of daily returns).
2. In the second step, cross-sectional regressions are estimated based on regressing step ahead returns (e.g., one-month-ahead) on $\beta$s from the first step, which provides coefficient estimates of the $\lambda$ risk premiums associated with $\beta$ and other loadings.

Most studies using this two-step approach roll forward one month at a time and repeat these steps over and over until the end of the sample period. A time series of $\lambda$ risk premium estimates (i.e., the coefficients in second step cross-sectional regressions) is generated for each $\beta$ or other risk parameter. Using these monthly risk premium estimates, the average $\lambda$ is computed and then a $t$-test of this average risk premium is performed. The $t$-test seeks to determine if the average $\lambda$ risk premium is significantly different from zero.[6]

Let's review FM's empirical results. They ran different versions of regression Eq. (4.5) that use all variables in the model as well as subsets of these variables (e.g., drop the squared $\beta$ variable). First, no evidence of non-linearity of $\beta$ was found, as the $t$-tests of $\lambda_{nl}$ were not significantly different from zero. They inferred that the relation between expected returns and beta risk is linear. Also, $t$-tests were insignificant for $\lambda_s$, which suggests that non-beta risks are not present. In their test period 1935 to 1968, the market price of beta risk, or $\lambda_m$, had a highly significant $t$-statistic. In subperiods, this $t$-statistic was smaller and not significant in a number of instances. Estimates of $\lambda_m$ were positive which is consistent with the CAPM relation between returns and beta risk. FM concluded that their findings supported the notion that beta risk is priced by investors in the capital market. As discussed earlier, this finding also implies that the market portfolio proxy $m$ is efficient.

Lastly, FM tested whether the market price of risk equaled the market portfolio proxy return minus the riskless government interest rate. Using their cross-sectional test, they compared the market price of beta risk, or $\lambda_m$, to actual $\bar{R}_{mt} - \bar{R}_{ft}$ in different periods. In some subperiods these two estimates were similar to one another, but in other subperiods they found that $\lambda_m < \bar{R}_{mt} - \bar{R}_{ft}$. The latter result means that a rate of return greater than the riskless rate should be used

[6] It is well known that this rolling FM procedure eliminates correlation between residuals, or $e_{pt}$, in cross-sectional regressions that can bias average risk premium $t$-tests. Some researchers conduct the cross-sectional regressions within the sample by regressing portfolio returns in each month in the sample period on average $\beta$ estimates for the entire period. In this case, it is necessary to make a correction to adjust the standard errors in the $t$-statistic. Excellent discussions of this correction can be found in Shanken (1992) and Cochrane (2005, Chapter 12).

in the market risk premium. In other words, the market risk premium should be defined as $E(R_{mt}) - E(R_{0t})$, where $E(R_{0t}) > R_{ft}$. Here the benchmark rate of return $E(R_{0t})$ contains some risk premium in excess of the riskless rate.

Further tests were conducted using time-series regressions of portfolio returns regressed on excess market returns, such that the intercept term should equal the riskless government rate. These tests confirmed that the intercept term was greater than the government rate. Importantly, FM's results help to explain the BJS findings discussed earlier. The slope of the SML is flatter and the intercept is higher than predicted by the CAPM due to this higher benchmark rate that should be used in estimating market risk premiums. Also, this result set the stage for the next innovation in the development of the CAPM. As presented in upcoming Chapter 5, Black (1972) proposed that $E(R_{0t})$ is the expected rate of return on a *zero-beta portfolio* that is greater than the riskless rate $R_{ft}$ and (like the riskless rate) uncorrelated with the expected market portfolio return $E(R_{Mt})$.

## 4.3 Estimating the Market Model

In this section we collect some real-world stock return data and estimate the market model. Monthly stock returns for Microsoft (ticker symbol MSFT) are analyzed. The market portfolio proxy is the Standard & Poor's (S &P) 500 index containing the largest 500 stocks in the U.S. stock market by market capitalization (i.e., number of shares outstanding times the current market price). This market index typically accounts for approximately 70–80% of the total market capitalization of all stocks trading in the U.S. market. We use adjusted closing prices that take into account dividends and stock splits. Monthly Treasury bill rates for one-month Tbills are downloaded from the FRED database of the Federal Reserve Bank of St. Louis available online.[7] We gather returns for the 36-month period from January 2018 to December 2020. Table 4.1 gives the return data series. Excess returns for MSFT and the S &P 500 index are computed by subtracting the Tbill rate from their monthly returns.

To implement the market model, we estimate the simple regression Eq. (4.3). Using our variables, we can re-write this equation as:

$$R_{MSFTt} - R_{ft} = \hat{\alpha}_{MSFT} + \hat{\beta}_{MSFT}(R_{S\&P500t} - R_{ft}) + e_{MSFTt}. \qquad (4.6)$$

In Excel, open the Data tab, then select Data Analysis. From the dropdown menu select Regression. Enter the Input Y Range (excess MSFT return) and Input X Range (excess S &P 500 return). You can do this by blocking off the data column values you want to enter into the regression analysis. As you block off the data column, you will see the Y or X Range values change. Finally, select the Output Options that you want, and click the OK button. Let's look at some of the output of the market model for MSFT.

---

[7] See https://fred.stlouisfed.org/series/DGS1MO.

**Table 4.1** Monthly returns for Microsoft (MSFT), S &P 500 index, and Treasury bills from January 2018 to December 2020

| Year/Month | MSFT | Tbill | S &P 500 | Excess MSFT | Excess S &P 500 |
|---|---|---|---|---|---|
| 18/1 | −1.31 | 0.11 | -3.89 | -1.41 | -4.00 |
| 18/2 | −2.67 | 0.12 | −2.69 | −2.78 | −2.80 |
| 18/3 | 2.47 | 0.14 | 0.27 | 2.33 | 0.14 |
| 18/4 | 5.69 | 0.14 | 2.16 | 5.55 | 2.02 |
| 18/5 | −0.23 | 0.14 | 0.48 | −0.37 | 0.34 |
| 18/6 | 7.58 | 0.15 | 3.60 | 7.42 | 3.45 |
| 18/7 | 5.89 | 0.16 | 3.03 | 5.73 | 2.87 |
| 18/8 | 1.82 | 0.16 | 0.43 | 1.65 | 0.27 |
| 18/9 | −6.61 | 0.17 | −6.94 | −6.78 | −7.11 |
| 18/10 | 3.82 | 0.18 | 1.79 | 3.64 | 1.60 |
| 18/11 | −8.40 | 0.19 | −9.18 | −8.59 | −9.36 |
| 18/12 | 2.82 | 0.20 | 7.87 | 2.62 | 7.67 |
| 19/1 | 7.28 | 0.20 | 2.97 | 7.08 | 2.77 |
| 19/2 | 5.28 | 0.20 | 1.79 | 5.07 | 1.59 |
| 19/3 | 10.73 | 0.20 | 3.93 | 10.53 | 3.73 |
| 19/4 | −5.30 | 0.20 | −6.58 | −5.50 | −6.78 |
| 19/5 | 8.31 | 0.20 | 6.89 | 8.11 | 6.69 |
| 19/6 | 1.72 | 0.19 | 1.31 | 1.54 | 1.13 |
| 19/7 | 1.17 | 0.18 | −1.81 | 0.99 | −1.99 |
| 19/8 | 0.85 | 0.17 | 1.72 | 0.68 | 1.55 |
| 19/9 | 3.12 | 0.17 | 2.04 | 2.96 | 1.88 |
| 19/10 | 5.59 | 0.14 | 3.40 | 5.44 | 3.26 |
| 19/11 | 4.17 | 0.13 | 2.86 | 4.04 | 2.73 |
| 19/12 | 7.95 | 0.13 | −0.16 | 7.82 | −0.29 |
| 20/1 | −4.83 | 0.13 | −8.41 | −4.96 | −8.54 |
| 20/2 | −2.65 | 0.13 | −12.51 | −2.79 | −12.64 |
| 20/3 | 13.63 | 0.03 | 12.68 | 13.60 | 12.65 |
| 20/4 | 2.25 | 0.01 | 4.53 | 2.25 | 4.52 |
| 20/5 | 11.06 | 0.01 | 1.84 | 11.05 | 1.83 |
| 20/6 | 0.74 | 0.01 | 5.51 | 0.73 | 5.50 |
| 20/7 | 10.01 | 0.01 | 7.01 | 10.00 | 7.00 |
| 20/8 | −6.74 | 0.01 | −3.92 | −6.75 | −3.93 |

(continued)

**Table 4.1** (continued)

| Year/Month | MSFT | Tbill | S &P 500 | Excess MSFT | Excess S &P 500 |
|---|---|---|---|---|---|
| 20/9 | −3.74 | 0.01 | −2.77 | −3.74 | −2.77 |
| 20/10 | 5.73 | 0.01 | 10.75 | 5.72 | 10.75 |
| 20/11 | 3.90 | 0.01 | 3.71 | 3.89 | 3.70 |
| 20/12 | −2.22 | 0.01 | 1.43 | −2.22 | 1.43 |

This table reports the monthly returns (in percent) for Microsoft (MSFT), the S &P 500 index, and Treasury bills from January 2018 to December 2020. Stock prices are downloaded from Yahoo Finance. Adjusted stock prices are used that take into account dividends and splits. Treasury bill rates are downloaded from the FRED database provided online by the Federal Reserve Bank of St. Louis (see https://fred.stlouisfed.org/series/DGS1MO)

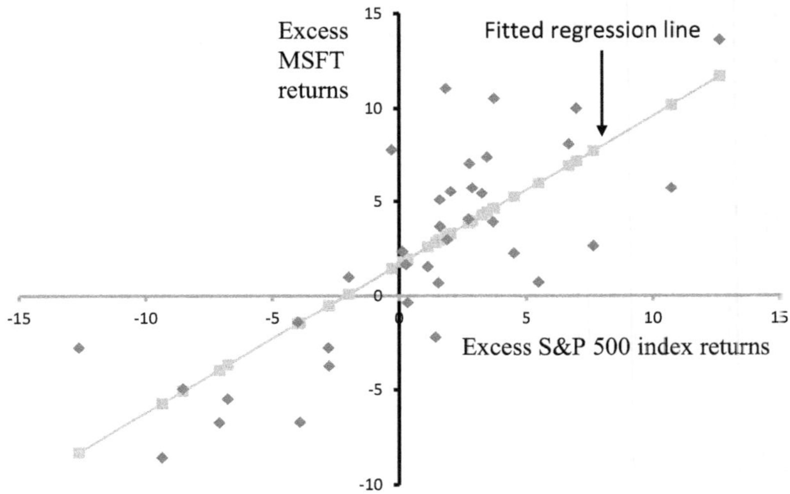


| | Coefficients | Standard error | *t*-statistic | *p*-value |
|---|---|---|---|---|
| Intercept | 1.67 | 0.58 | 2.88 | 0.01 |
| Excess S&P 500 returns | 0.79 | 0.11 | 7.35 | 0.00 |

**Fig. 4.1** The estimated market model for Microsoft (MSFT) stock returns with fitted regression line

Figure 4.1 plots the excess returns of MSFT (or Y variable) and the S &P 500 index (or X-variable) as well as the fitted regression line. The fitted line is comprised of the predicted values of the market model. The predicted MSFT return for each monthly S &P 500 return is computed as:

$$R_{MSFTt} - R_{ft} = \hat{\alpha}_{MSFT} + \hat{\beta}_{MSFT}(R_{S\&P500t} - R_{ft}), \tag{4.7}$$

where $\hat{\alpha}_{MSFT}$ is the estimated intercept parameter, and $\hat{\beta}_{MSFT}$ is the estimated slope measuring the beta risk of MSFT. We provide a screenshot of the Excel output below the diagram. The fitted line plots the predicted values of excess MSFT returns (see faded points on the straight line). The monthly returns for MSFT are represented by the scatter plot of points around the fitted line. The difference between each scatter plot point and the fitted line equals the residual $e_{MSFT,t}$ in Eq. (4.6). The larger the residuals, the lower the goodness-of-fit of the market model. In this regard, the Excel output reports the commonly used goodness-of-fit measure known as the *adjusted R-squared*. In the present case, MSFT had an estimated *R*-squared value of 61.4%, which means that the fit is fairly good.

The $\alpha$ estimate is greater than zero at $\hat{\alpha}_{MSFT} = 1.67$, and the $\beta$ estimate is less than one at $\hat{\beta}_{MSFT} = 0.79$. The *t*-statistics for these estimated parameters are 2.88 and 7.35, respectively, which have very low *p*-values below 0.01 suggesting at least a 1% level of significance. These results indicate that $\hat{\alpha}_{MSFT}$ and $\hat{\beta}_{MSFT}$ are highly significant in terms of their difference from zero. The positive and highly significant $\hat{\alpha}$ implies that other factors are needed to fully price MSFT. Also, the positive and even more highly significant $\hat{\beta}_{MSFT}$ can be interpreted to mean that the excess market factor proxied by S &P 500 index returns minus Tbill rates helps to explain movements in MSFT excess returns in our sample period. Because this estimate is less than one, we can infer that MSFT has less systematic risk than the market as a whole (or at least the largest 500 stocks).

The market model results for MSFT are consistent with the CAPM for the most part but not entirely. There appears to be a linear relation between its excess stock returns and excess market returns in line with the CAPM. However, according to the CAPM, the intercept or $\alpha$ parameter should be zero. Clearly, the large $\alpha$ term at 1.67% per month suggests that a large part of MSFT's excess returns are not explained by excess market returns. For comparison purposes, the average excess MSFT return and average excess market return in the sample period were 2.35% and 0.86% per month, respectively. Hence, 1.67% is quite large in terms of mispricing error captured by the $\alpha$ term. It appears that some additional factors are needed to more fully price MSFT and thereby reduce the magnitude of $\alpha$ mispricing.

## 4.4 A Primer on Regression Analysis

This section covers some fundamentals of regression models. Regression techniques are arguably the most commonly used empirical tools in economics and finance. The underlying idea is to empirically capture the relation between independent explanatory variables ($x$) and dependent variables ($y$). A simple regression with one explanatory variable is:

$$y_i = \alpha + \beta x_i + e_i, \tag{4.8}$$

where $i = 1, \ldots, n$ is the $i^{\text{th}}$ observation for a sample of size $n$ observations, $\alpha$ is the intercept term (or constant term), $\beta$ the slope coefficient, and $e$ is the unobserved error term. Note that $\alpha$ and $\beta$ are just generic notations for the regression coefficients and are not related to the CAPM discussed earlier. The task is to estimate the unknown regression parameters $\alpha$ and $\beta$ based on a sample of $n$ observed value pairs $(x_i, y_i)$, $i = 1, \ldots, n$.

The setup in Eq. (4.8) can be readily extended to multiple regression with $k$ explanatory variables, or $x_1, \ldots, x_k$,

$$y_i = \alpha + \beta_1 x_{i1} + \cdots + \beta_k x_{ik} + e_i, \tag{4.9}$$

where $\alpha$ is the intercept, $\beta_j$ are slope coefficients for $j = 1, \ldots, k$ independent variables, and $e$ is the unobserved error term. Now the estimation of the coefficients is based on $n$ observations on the variables $(x_1, \ldots, x_k, y)$ with the $i^{\text{th}}$ observation denoted as $(x_{i1}, x_{i2}, \ldots, x_{ik}, y_i)$. Hence, the sample of $n$ observations forms an $n \times k$ matrix similar to a data table in Excel with variable names occupying the first row of $p + 1$ columns and the $n$ rows containing the observed values of the $k$ $x$-variables and the dependent variable $y$ at each time $t$.

The above simple regression in (4.8) and multiple regression (4.9) are far more general than might be thought at first glance. For example, we can freely make transformations of the variables. For example, the logarithmic transformation is very popular in economics to transform absolute values into relative values. Importantly, fairly general non-linear relationships between the dependent variable and independent variable can be dealt with in the framework of the above linear setup. For example, polynomial extensions of individual variables are often utilized to capture possible non-linearities. Even so, the resulting equation can be represented by the above linear form. The second pass cross-sectional FM regression in Eq. (4.5) is a good example with $y_p = R_{pt}$, $x_{p,1} = \beta_{pt-1}$, $x_{p,2} = \beta^2_{pt-1}$, and $x_{p,3} = \bar{\sigma}(e)_{pt-1}$. Here the second explanatory variable, or $x_{p,2}$, is the square of the first variable—that is, $x_{p,2} = x^2_{p,1}$ in the regression equation.

### 4.4.1 On the Interpretation of Regression Coefficients

The properties of error term, or $e$, play a salient role in the statistical estimation of regression parameters. The expected value of the error terms is zero, i.e., $E(e) = 0$. This result can always be technically achieved in regression with an intercept term. A crucial assumption is that the error term is not correlated with the $x$ variables. In particular, it is assumed that $E(e|x) = 0$, which says that the conditional expectation of the error term given $x$ is zero. This property implies both zero correlation with $x$ variables as well as $E(e) = 0$. Given this assumption, $E(y|x) = \alpha + \beta x$ for the simple regression and $E(y|x_1, \ldots, x_k) = \alpha + \beta_1 x_1 + \cdots + \beta_k x_k$ in the multiple regression, so that we have straightforward interpretations of the regression coefficients. In the simple regression $\beta$ indicates the average change in $y$ when $x$

changes by one unit. For example, in the market model in Eq. (4.3), one percentage point change in the excess market return $R_{mt} - R_{ft}$ is expected to change the excess stock return $R_{it} - R_{ft}$ by $\beta_i$ percentage points.

The interpretation of multiple regression coefficients $\beta_j$ is similar. They indicate the (average) marginal effects of the $x_j$s on $y$. That is, $\beta_j$ indicates the expected change in $y$ when $x_j$ changes by one unit given that other $x$-variables remain unchanged. This interpretation assumes that $x_j$ is not functionally related to the other $x$ variables (i.e., the independent variables are uncorrelated with one another).

In mathematical terms, the slope coefficients capture marginal effects in that they are partial derivatives of the dependent variable with respect to the explanatory variable. In more complicated cases like the FM multiple regression in (4.5), the marginal effect of $\beta_{pt-1}$ is not constant $\lambda_m$ but $\lambda_m + 2\lambda_{nl}\beta_{pt-1}$. That is, the strength of the marginal effect of $\beta_{pt-1}$ depends on its level. If the slope coefficient $\lambda_{nl}$ were nonzero, it would indicate a non-linear relation, which contradicts the CAPM but reveals additional economic information about return-risk relationships. Positive $\lambda_{nl}$ would imply that investors demand an incremental premium for stocks with higher market risk. A negative $\lambda_{nl}$ implies the opposite. Hence, the interpretation of regression coefficients must be based on the functional form of the initial model.

In general, the intercept term is of lesser interest in most fields of study. It is used to improve the goodness-of-fit of the regression model and satisfy the OLS condition that $E(e) = 0$. In simple language, it captures the value of the dependent variable not explained by the independent variables. However, in asset pricing the intercept term has more than a statistical interpretation. It plays a central role in measuring mispricing by asset pricing models like the CAPM as discussed in the previous section. Indeed, Jensen's alpha is routinely reported alongside beta in many financial publications. From this perspective, mispricing alpha is an important metric for evaluating the validity of asset pricing models.

### 4.4.2 Justification for OLS

Statistical theory (related to the Gauss-Markov Theorem) shows that under certain assumptions OLS is the best linear unbiased estimator (BLUE) of the regression coefficients. This means that among linear estimators, the OLS estimator is unbiased and has smaller variance than any other linear unbiased estimator. Unbiasedness is a desirable property that guarantees the estimator does not systematically understate or overstate the population parameter. In this regard, the variance measures the precision of an estimator, wherein smaller is better. The underlying classical assumptions are itemized below.

i. Zero mean error terms: $E(e_i) = 0$ for all $i$.
ii. Homoskedasticity (constant variance of error terms): $Var(e_i) = \sigma_e^2$ for all $i$.
iii. Errors are uncorrelated: $Cov(e_i, e_j) = 0$ for all $i \neq j$.
iv. No perfect multicollinearity: $x$-variables are not linearly dependent.

v. $Cov\,(x_i, e_i) = 0$.

Under these assumptions with $n > k + 1$ sample observations, the solution to the minimum values of error terms in the regression equation or

$$(\hat{\alpha}, \hat{\beta}_1, \ldots, \hat{\beta}_k) = \text{argmin}_{\alpha, \beta_1, \ldots, \beta_k} \sum_{i=1}^{n} [y_i - (\alpha + \beta_1 x_{i1} + \cdots + \beta_k x_{ik})]^2 \quad (4.10)$$

gives the OLS estimators with the BLUE property.

In the case of the simple regression, the explicit solution is

$$\hat{\beta} = \frac{\sum_{i=1}^{n}(x_i - \bar{x})(y_i - \bar{y})}{\sum_{i=1}^{n}(x_i - \bar{x})^2} \quad (4.11)$$

and

$$\hat{\alpha} = \bar{y} - \hat{\beta}\bar{x}, \quad (4.12)$$

where $\bar{x}$ and $\bar{y}$ are the sample means of $x$ and $y$, respectively.

For the multiple regression, it is more convenient to use matrix notations and compile the $y$ observations to a column vector $\mathbf{y} = (y_1, \ldots, y_n)'$ and the $x$-observations to an $\mathbf{X}$ matrix of the form

$$\mathbf{X} = \begin{pmatrix} 1 & x_{11} & \cdots & x_{1k} \\ 1 & x_{21} & \cdots & x_{2k} \\ \vdots & \vdots & & \vdots \\ 1 & x_{n1} & \cdots & x_{nk} \end{pmatrix} \quad (4.13)$$

or $n \times (k+1)$ matrix. Using matrix notations, the multiple regression can be written compactly as

$$\mathbf{y} = \mathbf{X}\boldsymbol{\beta} + \mathbf{e}, \quad (4.14)$$

where $\boldsymbol{\beta} = (\alpha, \beta_1, \ldots, \beta_k)'$ is the $k + 1$-vector of regression coefficients, and $\mathbf{e} = (e_1, \ldots, e_n)'$ is the error term vector. Thus, the first column of constants equal to one in $\mathbf{X}$ has intercept $\alpha$ as the slope coefficient, which is often called the *coefficient of the constant term*. With these matrix notations, the OLS estimator of $\boldsymbol{\beta}$ becomes

$$\hat{\boldsymbol{\beta}} = (\mathbf{X}'\mathbf{X})^{-1}\mathbf{X}'\mathbf{y}. \quad (4.15)$$

The above classical assumptions guarantee desirable properties for OLS estimators. The properties even strengthen if we can assume that the errors are normally distributed, i.e., $e_i \sim N(0, \sigma_e^2)$. Then OLS also satisfies the properties of minimum variance unbiased estimators (MVUEs)—that is, OLS produces the best estimators among all unbiased estimators (not only among linear unbiased estimators).

Before continuing further, it is worthwhile to discuss the classical assumptions. Assumption (i) on the zero expected value of error terms is mechanical in nature as it holds whenever the intercept term $\alpha$ is freely estimated. Thus, intercept terms are routinely introduced in regression models. Reasonable justification is needed to exclude intercept terms from a model. By excluding an intercept, the slope coefficients may become biased.[8]

Assumption (ii) concerning homoskedasticity is technically desirable, as violation of this assumption causes OLS to lose the "best" in the BLUE qualities, i.e., best precision. The major problem is that the standard errors of the coefficient estimators become typically biased downward due to heteroskedasticity, thereby biasing inferences (e.g., over rejection of the null hypothesis in testing). However, under fairly general conditions, OLS is still consistent, meaning that as the sample size increases, the OLS estimator converges toward the corresponding population slope coefficient. By correcting the biases in standard errors with robust estimators, White (1980) heteroskedastic robust variance estimators (denoted HC) are nowadays routinely used as a solution to this potential problem.

Similarly, if the zero correlation of error terms assumption in (iii) is violated, robust alternatives are routinely used to help correct the problem. In time-series data, the solution is to use Newey and West (1987) heteroskedasticity and autocorrelation robust standard errors (denoted HAC). In cross-sectional observations, correlation of error terms can occur if observations form clusters (like industries) within which observations tend to be more alike than between clusters. In this situation, Cameron et al. (2011) have proposed clustering robust standard errors as a solution.

The fourth assumption (iv) is a technical problem that can lead to unstable regression parameter estimates. For example, a regression coefficient could flip from positive to negative in sign due to correlation of its independent variable with another independent variable in a multiple regression model. Unlike macroeconomics, multicollinearity is not a common problem in financial economics. Independent variables are normally not highly correlated with one another.

The last assumption (v) of zero correlation between the error terms and the explanatory variables is a serious and difficult problem that is more or less violated in virtually all empirical estimations. The simple reason is that the error term contains all the missing factors that affect the dependent variable. In economics, independent variables tend to be correlated. Therefore, missing factors absorbed

[8] In the estimation of the market model and other asset pricing models with multiple factors, the authors have found that the beta coefficients are changed little if any. Nonetheless, inclusion of an intercept is more appropriate to ensure that the regression coefficients are BLUE.

into the error term can be correlated with the explanatory variables. This complication is known as an endogeneity problem that biases the slope coefficient estimates. Economic variables that are typically positively correlated imply positive bias—that is, over-estimation of the coefficients. Various instrumental variable techniques have been developed to reduce the bias. However, finding appropriate instruments is a difficult practical issue. In some cases, panel data analysis can alleviate the problem. Unfortunately, there is no easy solution to this problem. Relevant to our focus on asset pricing models in finance, this problem is not generally serious.

## 4.5 OLS Estimation of the Market Model

We next apply the above discussion of OLS assumptions to show that the market model in Eq. (4.3) is indeed the empirical counterpart of the CAPM in Eq. (4.1). Under the CAPM, the classical Gauss–Markov assumptions are satisfied to justify OLS estimation of the market model using time series of stock returns. We begin by re-writing CAPM Eq. (4.1) with time index (assuming for simplicity that the riskless rate is a constant $R_f$) as:

$$E(R_{it}) - R_f = \beta_i\big[E(R_{Mt}) - R_f\big],$$

Next, adding and subtracting $R_{it}$ on the left-hand-side, and similarly adding and subtracting $\beta_i R_{Mt}$ on the right-hand-side, after rearranging terms in the equation, we get:

$$R_{it} - R_f + [E(R_{it}) - R_{it}] = \beta_i(R_{Mt} - R_f) - \beta_i[R_{Mt} - E(R_{Mt})].$$

Moving $[E(R_{it}) - R_{it}]$ to the right-hand-side and simplifying terms, we can write the market model:

$$R_{it} - R_f = \beta_i(R_{Mt} - R_f) + u_{it}, \tag{4.16}$$

where $u_{it} = [R_{it} - E(R_{it})] - \beta_i[R_{Mt} - E(R_{Mt})]$. Now if the CAPM holds, we can use this equation to estimate the unknown beta coefficient $\beta_i$ with OLS because all the classical assumptions hold. We leave the details for the student to check that: (i) $E(u_{it}) = 0$, (ii) $Var\,(u_{it}) = \sigma_i^2(1-\rho_{iM}^2) \equiv \sigma_{u_i}^2$ is constant, wherein $\rho_{iM} = \text{cor}\,(R_{it}, R_{Mt})$,[9] and (iii) $Cov\,(u_{it}, u_{is}) = 0$ for all $t \neq s$ due to being serially uncorrelated in an efficient market, which implies that $Cov\,(R_{it}, R_{is}) = 0$, $Cov\,(R_{Mt}, R_{Ms}) = 0$, and $Cov\,(R_{it}, R_{Ms}) = 0$ for all $t \neq s$. The condition (iv) can be satisfied directly by the researcher by choosing uncorrelated variables

[9] The term $Var\,(u_{it}) = \sigma_i^2 - 2\beta_i\sigma_{iM} + \beta_i^2\sigma_M^2$, where $\sigma_i^2 = Var\,(R_{it})$, $\sigma_M^2 = Var\,(R_{Mt})$, and $\sigma_{iM} = Cov\,(R_{it}, R_{Mt})$. In the CAPM, $\beta_i = \sigma_{iM}/\sigma_M^2 = \rho_{iM}(\sigma_i/\sigma_M)$, and using $\beta_i\sigma_M = \beta_i^2\sigma_M^2 = \sigma_i^2\rho_{iM}^2$ in $Var\,(u_{it})$ above, we get after adding up and rearranging terms $Var\,(u_{it}) = \sigma_i^2(1 - \rho_{iM}^2)$..

(i.e., no multicollinearity). Finally, condition (v) is satisfied due to properties of the covariance whereby $Cov(u_{it}, u_{is}) = Cov(R_{it}, R_{is}) - \beta_i Cov(R_{it}, R_{Ms}) + \beta_i^2 Cov(R_{it}, R_{Ms})$ in which all covariances are zero due to market efficiency whenever $t \neq s$. Consequently, we know that $Cov(u_{it}, u_{is}) = 0$ for all $t \neq s$. Due to satisfying these assumptions, the beta parameter can be efficiently estimated by the market model.

However, if the CAPM does not hold, and there are additional factors affecting stock returns, the situation changes. The missing factors will be absorbed into the error term $u_{it}$. If the factors are not correlated with the market return and only affect the mean return, such that $E(u_{it}) = \alpha_i \neq 0$, we can easily fix the problem by redefining the error term as $e_{it} = u_{it} - \alpha_i$ and balancing the subtraction by adding $\alpha_i$ into Eq. (4.16). The end result is Eq. (4.3), or

$$R_{it} - R_f = \alpha_i + \beta_i(R_{Mt} - R_f) + e_{it}.$$

Again all of the OLS assumptions are satisfied, and OLS can be used to produce efficient estimates (BLUE) for the parameters assuming the unknown factors are not (materially) correlated with the market factor. Is the beta estimate in the market model significant? Appendix A provides a discussion related to statistical inference from sampling theory, which enables tests of a beta estimate to see whether it is statistically significant or not.

### 4.5.1 Goodness-of-Fit

The most popular goodness-of-fit measure in regression analysis is $R$-squared (also known as the *coefficient of determination*) and its adjusted variant often denoted as $\bar{R}$-squared. These measures tell us how well the regression equation fits the data observations. The basic idea is that, if the regression equation yields predicted values that are close to the actual values of observations, it has strong goodness-of-fit, and vice versa if predicted and actual values are very different from one another. To compute goodness-of-fit, we need to decompose the total variation measure SST $= \sum_{i=1}^{n}(y_i - \bar{y})^2$ of the dependent variable. Letting $\hat{y}_i = \hat{\alpha} + \hat{\beta}_1 x_{i1} + \cdots + \hat{\beta}_k x_{ik}$ denote the fitted value, the decomposition becomes

$$\sum_{i=1}^{n}(y_i - \bar{y})^2 = \sum_{i=1}^{n}(\hat{y}_i - \bar{y})^2 + \sum_{i=1}^{n}(y_i - \hat{y}_i)^2, \tag{4.17}$$

or

$$\text{SST} = \text{SSE} + \text{SSR} \tag{4.18}$$

where SST $= \sum_{i=1}^{n}(y_i - \bar{y})^2$ is the total sum of squares, SSE $= \sum_{i=1}^{n}(\hat{y}_i - \bar{y})^2$ is the sum of squares explained by the regression which measures the share of variability around the mean $\bar{y}$ that is due to the independent variables in the regression model, and $\text{SSR} = \sum_{i=1}^{n}(y_i - \hat{y}_i)^2$ is the sum of squares due to residuals which is the variation not captured by the estimated regression model. The $R$-squared is the ratio of the total variation explained by the regression model,

$$R^2 = \frac{\text{SSE}}{\text{SST}} = 1 - \frac{\text{SSR}}{\text{SST}}. \tag{4.19}$$

The adjusted $R$-squared is based on the rightmost representation by adjusting the sums of squares using the respective degrees of freedom with $k$ independent variables such that

$$\bar{R}^2 = 1 - \frac{s_e^2}{s_y^2}, \tag{4.20}$$

where

$$s_e^2 = \frac{1}{n-k-1}\sum_{i=1}^{n}(y_i - \hat{y}_i)^2 \tag{4.21}$$

is the unbiased OLS variance estimator of the error variance $\sigma_e^2$, and $s_y^2$ is the usual unbiased estimator of the variance of $y$.

The major difference between $R^2$ and $\bar{R}^2$ is that the latter measure is penalized by the degrees of freedom. While adding a new variable can reduce $\bar{R}^2$ if the variable does not improve the explanatory power enough, the non-adjusted $R^2$ tends to increase or at least never decrease. By definition $0 \leq R^2 \leq 1$. Note that the adjusted R-squared can be negative if none of the explanatory variables helps to predict $y$. For these reasons, the adjusted R-squared is more popular to report, as a positive value indicates that the fitted model has some explanatory power.

## 4.6 Summary

The empirical form of the CAPM named the *market model* was proposed by Markowitz (1959) and developed by Sharpe (1963) and Fama (1968). Excess asset returns (dependent $y$ variable) are regressed on excess market portfolio proxy returns (independent $x$ variable) to yield an $\alpha$ intercept parameter and beta $\beta$ slope parameter. Jensen (1968) recognized that the $\alpha$ terms, so-called *Jensen's alpha*, can be used to jointly test whether the proxy for the market portfolio is efficient or mispricing exists due to missing factors. According to the CAPM, the $\alpha$ estimate should equal zero in the market model. In the real world, stocks and other assets do not lie exactly on the Security Market Line (SML), which results in a random error term in the market model.

Early tests of the CAPM employed the market model. Black, Jensen, and Scholes (BJS) (1972) found that the SML was flatter than predicted by the CAPM. They formed 10 portfolios of U.S. stocks sorted by beta. Contrary to the CAPM, 3-out-of-10 portfolios had significant $\alpha$ intercept terms. Also, stock portfolios with betas greater (less) than one tended to have negative (positive) intercepts. These results suggested that low (high) beta stocks had higher (lower) returns than predicted by the CAPM. Additionally, average $\alpha$s for their stock portfolios were significantly different from zero. This finding means that either the market portfolio proxy is inefficient or missing factors exist, which rejects the CAPM.

Another study by Fama and MacBeth (FM) (1973) conducted further market model tests using U.S. stock portfolio returns. They proposed a two-step estimation procedure: (1) a time-series regression model is used to estimate model parameters; and (2) a cross-sectional regression is used to estimate the market price of risk (or $\lambda$ coefficient) associated with the step (1) estimated model parameters (called *loadings*). Some key findings in their study were: (1) time-series regressions showed that non-linear beta and non-beta risks were not significant, only beta risk was significant; and (2) cross-sectional regression showed that $\lambda_m$ associated with beta risk was significant meaning that beta risk is priced in the cross-section of stock returns. Because the market price of beta risk tended to be less than the actual excess return of the market portfolio proxy, they inferred that the borrowing rate is greater than the riskless government bond rate.

Understanding the fundamentals of regression analyses is crucial to asset pricing. Simple regression with one independent variable and multiple regression with multiple independent variables are important tools in finance. Both regression models can be adapted to different transformations of the variables, including logarithms of variables, non-linear variables, etc. Regression $\beta$ coefficients measure the average change in $y$ when $x$ changes by one unit, given other independent variables are held constant in the model. The intercept $\alpha$ coefficient is used in regression models to improve the goodness-of-fit and ensure that the expected value of the error terms (denoted $e$) equals zero.

Under the Gauss–Markov Theorem, ordinary least squares (OLS) provide the best linear unbiased estimator (BLUE) of the regression coefficient. This theorem requires a number of statistical properties—(i) zero mean error terms: $E(e_i) = 0$ for all $i$; (ii) homoskedasticity (constant variance of error terms): $Var(e_i) = \sigma_e^2$ for all $i$; (iii) errors are uncorrelated: $Cov(e_i, e_j) = 0$ for all $i \neq j$; (iv) no perfect multicollinearity: $x$-variables are not linearly dependent; and (v) $Cov(x_i, e_i) = 0$. Assumption (i) is achieved by using an intercept term. If assumption (ii) is violated due to heteroskedaisticity (or nonconstant error variance), a White (1980) estimator (HC) can be used to adjust for this potential bias. If assumption (iii) is violated due to correlation of errors in a time-series regression, a Newey and West (1987) estimator (HAC) can be used. For cross-sectional regression, an adjustment by Cameron, Gelbach, and Miller (2011) can be implemented. The no multicollinearity assumption (iv) concerns the correlation between multiple independent variables, which normally is not a major problem in financial economics. Lastly, assumption (v) requires zero correlation between the error terms and independent variables. If nonzero, an endogeneity problem exists. This problem can be treated by introducing instrumental variables into the regression model but is not easily accomplished.

Interestingly, under the OLS assumptions, it can be proven that the market model represents an empirical counterpart of the theoretical CAPM. That is, due to satisfying these assumptions, the market model can efficiently estimate the beta parameter. To test whether beta is significantly different from zero, a $t$-ratio can be computed using the beta estimate and the standard error of this estimate. In the case that the CAPM does not hold, an intercept term is needed in the market model. This form of the market model is typically used in empirical studies. Finally, the goodness-of-fit of regression models is measured by $R$-squared measures. An adjusted $\bar{R}$-squared is normally used to adjust for the number of degrees of freedom that is affected by the number of regression parameters in the model. In words, this goodness-of-fit statistic measures the amount of variation around the mean value of the dependent variable explained by the independent variables in the regression model.

## Questions

1. Write the equation for the market model form of the CAPM. What is the intercept term in this model? Can the intercept be used to test the CAPM?
2. Why put a random error term in the market model? How would you estimate the market model with regression analysis?
3. Black, Jensen, and Scholes (BJS) (1972) tested the CAPM using the market model. Why did they use portfolios rather than individual stocks in their tests? How were the portfolios formed for their tests? Write the $t$-test that they performed to test whether the $\alpha_p$ for a portfolio was not equal to zero. What were the three main findings of their study? What did they conclude about the CAPM?
4. Fama and MacBeth (FM) (1973) tested the CAPM using cross-sectional regression analysis. What is the cross-sectional regression model that they tested?
5. What did Fama and MacBeth (1973) find in their cross-sectional tests of the CAPM?
6. Write a simple regression model with one explanatory variable. Also, write a multiple regression model with $k$ explanatory variables $x_1, \ldots, x_k$. How would you test for a non-linear relationship between an independent variable and the dependent variable?

7. What are the statistical properties of the error term, or $e$, in a regression model? How should the regression coefficient $\beta$ be interpreted? How should the intercept $\alpha$ be interpreted from both a statistical perspective and an asset pricing perspective?
8. List the underlying classical assumptions in OLS regression analysis. Why are these assumptions important to OLS estimation of regression coefficients?
9. What does homoskedasticity of error terms mean in regression analysis? Are error terms correlated with one another? What is multicollinearity and can it cause problems in a multiple regression model? Lastly, what is the problem if error terms in the regression model are correlated with an independent variable?
10. If the CAPM does not hold, how does this affect the market model?
11. You want to test whether an estimated $\beta_j$ coefficient in an OLS regression model is significant. What is the null hypothesis? What is the statistical test of this hypothesis? What values of the $t$-statistic are needed to reach 5% and 1% significance levels? (Hint: this question is based on Appendix A.)
12. What is goodness-of-fit mean in regression analysis? How would you estimate it? Show a formula and explain its terms. Can it be adjusted for the degrees of freedom in the estimation of the regression equation? Which measure of goodness-of-fit should be used?
13. You want to test whether the market risk of a stock is the same as the market portfolio in CAPM. What is the null hypothesis? What is the alternative hypothesis?

| x | y |
|---:|---:|
| 4.6 | 10.6 |
| 11.1 | 22.6 |
| 19.5 | 29.7 |
| 3.2 | 2.6 |
| 9.5 | 23.4 |
| 10.8 | 9.0 |
| 14.2 | 26.8 |
| 8.6 | 15.0 |
| 21.9 | 38.9 |
| 9.2 | 17.5 |

Compute the OLS estimates for the intercept and the slope coefficient for the simple regression $y = \alpha + \beta x + e$ using Eqns. (4.11) and (4.12).

## Problems

1. Update the data in Table 4.1 for Microsoft. Download monthly stock returns for MSFT and the S &P 500 index from Yahoo Finance. Download monthly Treasury bill rates from the Federal Reserve Bank of St. Louis (https://fred.stlouisfed.org/series/DGS1MO). Gather data for 36 months. What did you get for the intercept? Beta? Are these model parameters significant as determined by *t*-statistics? Also, draw a plot of the fitted regression line with excess MSFT returns on the Y-axis and excess S &P 500 index returns on the X-axis. Do the results support the CAPM?
2. In the text, it is proved that OLS estimation of the market model is the empirical counterpart of the CAPM under classical Gauss–Markov assumptions. Show that: (i) $E(u_{it}) = 0$, (ii) $Var\ (u_{it}) = \sigma_i^2(1 - \rho_{iM}^2) \equiv \sigma_{u_i}^2$ is constant, and (iii) $Cov\ (u_{it}, u_{is}) = 0$ for all $t \neq s$.
3. Consider the following observations for variables $x$ and $y$:

## Appendix A: Statistical Inference

Statistical inference gives us guidelines concerning what we can say about the population slope coefficients on the basis of the sample estimates. Confidence intervals and hypothesis testing are the major tools in this process. Statistical properties of the error term $e_{it}$ are critical. While the Gauss–Markov BLUE result needs only assumptions about the expected values, variances, and covariances, statistical inference needs more precise information about the whole distribution of the error terms.

The textbook assumption is that the error term is normally distributed, or $e_i \sim N(0, \sigma_e^2)$. While this assumption strengthens OLS estimator properties, as discussed in this chapter, it also determines the distribution (called the *sampling distribution*) of the estimator. An important property of the normal distribution is that any linear combinations of normal random variables are again normally distributed. Therefore, as an example considering $\hat{\beta}$ in Eq. (4.10), using fairly straightforward calculations, we can write

$$\hat{\beta} = \beta + \sum_{i=1}^{n} w_i e_i,$$

in which $w_i = (x_i - \bar{x}) / \sum_{i=1}^{n} (x_i - \bar{x})^2$, such that $\hat{\beta}_i$ indeed is a linear combination of $e_i$. Thus, given $x_i$, $\hat{\beta}$ is normally distributed with expected value $\beta$ and variance

$$\sigma_{\hat{\beta}}^2 = \frac{\sigma_e^2}{\sum_{i=1}^{n} (x_i - \bar{x})^2}.$$

In the same fashion, $\hat{\alpha}$ is normal with expected value $\alpha$ and variance

$$\sigma_{\hat{\alpha}}^2 = \sigma_e^2 \left( \frac{1}{n} + \frac{\bar{x}^2}{\sum_{i=1}^{n} (x_i - \bar{x})^2} \right).$$

In the general case of Eq. (4.15), the variances of respective OLS coefficients are obtained from the diagonal of the matrix

$$Var\,(\hat{\boldsymbol{\beta}}) = \sigma_e^2 (\mathbf{X}'\mathbf{X})^{-1}. \quad \text{(A4.1)}$$

If the error variance $\sigma_e^2$ were known, we could base our inferences directly on the normal distribution. In practice, however, variance $\sigma_e^2$ must be replaced by its regression estimate $s_e^2$ in Eq. (4.21) with the implication that inferences are based on the Student $t$-distribution. Thus, in a regression with $k$ independent variables, the $t$-ratio for testing the null hypothesis

$$H_0 : \beta_j = \beta_j^* \quad \text{(A4.2)}$$

becomes

$$t = \frac{\hat{\beta}_j - \beta_j^*}{s_{\hat{\beta}_j}}, \quad \text{(A4.3)}$$

where $\beta_j^*$ is the hypothesized value of the population coefficient (i.e., a fixed value defined by the researcher), $s_{\hat{\beta}_j}$ is the estimated standard error of $\hat{\beta}_j$ equaling the square root of the $j$th diagonal element of Eq. (A4.1) with $s_e^2$ substituted for $\sigma_e^2$, $j = 0, 1, 2, \ldots, k$, and $\beta_0$ the intercept term (equaling $\alpha$ in the text). Under the null hypothesis, the $t$-ratio in Eq. (A4.3) is $t$-distributed with $n - k - 1$ degrees of freedom. Regarding the null hypothesis in Eq. (A4.2), the most common case is that we are interested in whether variable $x_j$ has any impact on $y$. In this case, $\beta_j^* = 0$ in (A4.2) so that the null hypothesis becomes

$$H_0 : \beta_j = 0$$

and the $t$-statistic in (A4.3) reduces to

$$t = \frac{\hat{\beta}_j}{s_{\hat{\beta}_j}},$$

which is the $t$-ratio shown in standard computer outputs.

Confidence intervals are of the form $\hat{\beta} \pm t_p s_{\hat{\beta}}$ in which $t_p$ is an appropriate percentile from the $t$-distribution to match the desired confidence interval. Typical values are $p = .025$ for 95% and $p = .005$ for 99% interval. The $t_p$ value itself depends on the degrees of freedom. Typically in financial applications the number of observations is large. Therefore, as the $t$-distribution approaches the normal distribution when the degrees of freedom increases, $t_p \approx z_p$ such that for the 95% interval $t_{.025} = 1.96 \approx 2$ and for the 99% interval $t_{.005} = 2.58$. These $t$-statistics are interpreted as 5% and 1% significance levels, respectively. If $t$-statistics reach these levels or higher, they indicate that the estimated beta coefficient is statistically significant. Notably, even if the coefficient is statistically significant it may not be economically significant. The magnitude of the beta coefficient needs to be large enough to suggest that a change in the independent variable will result in a economically meaningful change in the dependent variable.

If the normality of the error term does not hold, the Central Limit Theorem (CLT) provides us with so-called large sample results under fairly mild assumptions. The CLT implies that the above normal distribution results can be reliably used when the sample size is reasonably large. There is no exact definition of how large the sample should be. In general, with as small as 50 observations, the approximation is fairly close for practical purposes.

As discussed earlier in the chapter, if the error terms are heteroskedastic and/or autocorrelated, the major implication is bias in the standard errors leading in most cases to overconfidence about the precision of the estimates. For cross-sectional data, the White (1980) heteroskedastic robust variance estimators (HC) are routinely used to correct the bias. In time-series regression, the Newey and West (1987) heteroskedastic autocorrelation robust measure (HAC) is used to correct standard errors. And, if data are clustered, Cameron, Gelbach, and Miller (2011) clustering robust standard errors can be used to take into account the correlation of error terms.

As an example, we apply HAC standard errors to our earlier example of Microsoft CAPM estimates in Sect. 4.3. For this purpose, we need more sophisticated regression software than provided by Excel. R (https://r-project.org) is a powerful open source software for general statistical analyses as well as a wide variety of regression estimation methods.

Below is R-code for the estimation in which we assume that the data is in an Excel file named `msft.xlsx` with the above headings on the first line.

```
### Preliminaries ('#' indicate comments and are ignored by the program)
## needed packages:
## 'readxl' to read Excel files,
## 'sandwich' to estimate HAC standard errors
## 'lmtest' to report HAC standard errors and related other statistics
  install.packages(c('readxl', 'sandwich', lmtest'),
                  repos = 'https://cloud.r-project.org') # if not installed
  library(readxl) # load the package, needed in every new session
  library(sandwich) # again, when starting a new session
  library(lmtest) # when starting a new session
###  Read data
  msdf <- read_xls('your excel folder/msft.xlsx') # read the excel file
  ## change column names for convenience
  colnames(msdf) <- c('date', 'msft', 'tbill', 'sp500', 'e_msft', 'e_sp500')

  head(msdf) # show a few first data points
        date  msft   rf sp500 e_msft e_sp500
1 2018-01-01 -1.31 0.11 -3.89  -1.42   -4.00
2 2018-02-01 -2.67 0.12 -2.69  -2.79   -2.81
3 2018-03-01  2.47 0.14  0.27   2.33    0.13
4 2018-04-01  5.69 0.14  2.16   5.55    2.02
5 2018-05-01 -0.23 0.14  0.48  -0.37    0.34
6 2018-06-01  7.58 0.15  3.60   7.43    3.45
##  Estimate the model
  fit <- lm(e_msft ~ e_sp500, data = msdf) # fit the market model
  summary(fit) # initial regression
## OLS results

lm(formula = e_msft ~ e_sp500, data = df)

Coefficients:
            Estimate Std. Error t value Pr(>|t|)
(Intercept)   1.6706     0.5797   2.882   0.0068 **
e_sp500       0.7921     0.1077   7.352 1.61e-08 ***
---
Signif. codes:  0 '***' 0.001 '**' 0.01 '*' 0.05 '.' 0.1 ' ' 1

Residual standard error: 3.434 on 34 degrees of freedom
Multiple R-squared:  0.6139,Adjusted R-squared:  0.6025
F-statistic: 54.06 on 1 and 34 DF,  p-value: 1.606e-08

### Results with HAC standard errors
```

```
coeftest(fit, vcovHAC(fit)) # regression with robust standard errors etc.
            Estimate Std. Error t value  Pr(>|t|)
(Intercept)  1.67059    0.61022  2.7377  0.009772 **
e_sp500      0.79209    0.13319  5.9470 1.009e-06 ***
---
Signif. codes:  0 '***' 0.001 '**' 0.01 '*' 0.05 '.' 0.1 ' ' 1
```

We observe that the HAC standard is just slightly larger than those of OLS, which indicates that there is no material heteroskedasticity and/or autocorrelation in the OLS residuals. Therefore, the OLS results are equally reliable as those produced by the HAC approach, and the conclusions of Sect. 4.3 pass this robustness check.

## References

Black, F. 1972. Capital market equilibrium with restricted borrowing. *Journal of Business* 45: 444–454.

Black, F., M.C. Jensen, and M. Scholes. 1972. The capital asset pricing model: Some empirical tests. In *Studies in the Theory of Capital Markets*, ed. M.C. Jensen. New York, NY: Praeger.

Blume, M. 1970. Portfolio theory: A step towards its practical application. *Journal of Business* 43: 152–174.

Cameron, A.C., J.B. Gelbach, and D.L. Miller. 2011. Robust inference with multiway clustering. *Journal of Business and Economic Statistics* 29: 238–249.

Cochrane, J.H. 2005. *Asset Pricing*. Revised. Princeton, NJ: Princeton University Press.

Douglas, G.W. 1969. Risk in the equity markets: An empirical appraisal of market efficiency. *Yale Economic Essays* 9: 3–45.

Fama, E.F. 1968. Risk, return, and equilibrium: Some clarifying comments. *Journal of Finance* 23: 29–40.

Fama, E.F., and J.D. MacBeth. 1973. Risk, return, and equilibrium: Empirical tests. *Journal of Political Economy* 81: 607–636.

Friend, I., and M. Blume. 1970. Measurement of portfolio performance under uncertainty. *American Economic Review* 60: 607–636.

Gibbons, M.R., and J. Shanken. 1983. A test of the Sharpe-Lintner CAPM. Working Paper, University of California, Berkeley, CA.

Jensen, M.C. 1968. The performance of mutual funds in the period 1945–1964. *Journal of Finance* 23: 389–416.

Lintner, J. 1965. The valuation of risk assets and the selection of risky investments in stock portfolios and capital budgets, *Review of Economics and Statistics* 47: 13–37.

Markowitz, H.M. 1959. *Portfolio Selection: Efficient Diversification of Investments*. New York, NY: Wiley.

Merton, R.C. 1972. An analytical derivation of the efficient portfolio frontier. *Journal of Financial and Quantitative Finance* 7: 1851–1872.

Miller, M., and M. Scholes. 1972. Rates of return in relation to risk: A re-examination of some recent findings. In *Studies in the Theory of Capital Markets*, ed. M.C. Jensen, 47–78. New York, NY: Praeger.

Mossin, J. 1966. Equilibrium in a capital asset market. *Econometrica* 34: 768–783.

Newey, W., and K. West. 1987. A simple, positive semi-definite, heteroskedasticity and autocorrelation consistent covariance matrix. *Econometrica* 55: 703–708.

Roll, R. 1977. A critique of the asset pricing theory's tests, part I: On past and potential future testability of the theory. *Journal of Financial Economics* 4: 129–176.

Roll, R. 1980. Orthogonal portfolios. *Journal of Financial and Quantitative Analysis* 15: 1005–1012.

Shanken, J. 1992. On the estimation of beta pricing models. *Review of Financial Studies* 5: 1–34.

Sharpe, W.F. 1963. A simplified model for portfolio analysis. *Management Science* 9: 277–293.

Sharpe, W.F. 1964. Capital asset prices: A theory of market equilibrium under conditions of risk. *Journal of Finance* 19: 425–442.

Stambaugh, R. F. 1982. On the exclusion of assets from tests of the the two-parameter model. *Journal of Financial Economics* 10: 237–268.

Treynor, J.L. 1961. Market value, time, and risk. Unpublished manuscript.

Treynor, J.L. 1962. Toward a theory of market value of risky assets. Unpublished manuscript.

White, H. 1980. A heteroskedasticity-consistent covariance matrix estimator and a direct test for heteroskedasticity. *Econometrica* 22: 193–218.

# 5 The Zero-Beta CAPM

In its early years, as discussed in the last chapter, the CAPM came under question. Empirical tests of the market model found that the relationship between CAPM beta and U.S. stock returns was weaker than expected. The estimated Security Market Line (SML) relating the excess returns of stock portfolios on the Y-axis and their estimated betas on the X-axis was flatter than predicted by the CAPM with a higher intercept (or $\alpha$ parameter). Black, Jensen, and Scholes (1972) found that low (high) beta stocks had higher (lower) returns than theorized by the CAPM. Consequently, they proposed that the borrowing rate in the real world is greater than the riskless rate used in the theoretical CAPM.

With this empirical evidence in hand, Black (1972) created the *zero-beta CAPM* by relaxing key assumptions in the CAPM: (1) investors can invest in both long and short positions in risky assets; and (2) investors can borrow in financial markets at interest rates greater than the riskless rate. Applying these assumptions, Black derived an alternative form of the CAPM. We next review of the zero-beta CAPM in addition to empirical tests of this model.

## 5.1 Zero-Beta CAPM

### 5.1.1 Assumptions

Black (1972) motivated his paper by overviewing the CAPM assumptions: (1) investors have homogeneous expectations or opinions about assets' distributions of returns; (2) asset returns follow a normal distribution; (3) risk-averse investors

**Supplementary Information** The online version contains supplementary material available at https://doi.org/10.1007/978-3-031-16784-3_5.

 
J. W. Kolari and S. Pynnönen, *Investment Valuation and Asset Pricing*,
https://doi.org/10.1007/978-3-031-16784-3_5

seek to maximize the end-of-period expected utility of wealth; and (4) investors can only hold long positions with unlimited borrowing and lending at the riskless asset. For interested readers, Fama (1968) provides an in-depth discussion of these assumptions. Contrary to the CAPM Black modified assumption (4) by allowing short sales of assets. Also, he believed that borrowing at the riskless rate was unrealistic. In support, he cited earlier evidence in Black et al. (1972) that showed the following model provides a better fit to U.S. stock returns than the CAPM market model:its zero-beta portfolio

$$R_{it} = a_i + \beta_i R_{mt} + (1 - \beta_i) R_{zt} + e_{it}, \tag{5.1}$$

where the return on market proxy portfolio $m$ (denoted $R_{mt}$) and the return on the zero-beta portfolioz (denoted $R_{zt}$) have zero correlation. Notice that the riskless rate $R_{ft}$ in the CAPM market model has been replaced with the risky rate $R_{zt} > R_{ft}$. Using this higher borrowing rate for investors helps to explain the higher intercept (or $\alpha$ parameter) in empirical tests of the CAPM as well as the lower slope of the SML. Upon relaxing short sale and borrowing rate restrictions, Black derived an alternative form of the CAPM dubbed the *zero-beta CAPM*.

### 5.1.2 Theoretical Model

Using the single-period framework of the CAPM, which enables us to drop the time $t$ subscript, Black's zero-beta CAPM is specified as follows:

$$E(R_i) = E(R_Z) + \beta_i [E(R_M) - E(R_Z)], \tag{5.2}$$

where $\beta_i$ is the beta risk of asset $i$ with respect to theoretical market portfolio $M$, $E(R_M)$ is the expected return on the market portfolio, and $E(R_Z)$ is the expected return on the zero-beta portfolio $Z$. This model differs from the CAPM with borrowing and lending at $R_f$ instead of $R_Z$. The excess return of the market portfolio is now $E(R_M) - E(R_Z)$ instead of $E(R_M) - R_f$. This excess return represents the return on the zero-investment portfolio with a long position in $M$ and a short position in $Z$. Assuming that $E(R_Z) > R_f$, the slope of this equilibrium relationship between expected excess returns and beta risk is lower than the SML of the CAPM. Given a lower SML slope, the intercept becomes higher than the theoretical CAPM. For interested readers, Appendix A contains a rigorous mathematical derivation of the zero-beta CAPM.

While Black assumed that investors cannot borrow at the riskless rate, it is possible for them to invest in this asset. Allowing investors to hold a portfolio consisting of market portfolio $M$, zero-beta portfolio $Z$, and riskless assets $f$, he re-wrote the zero-beta CAPM as follows:

$$E(R_i) - R_f = \beta_{i,M} [E(R_M) - R_f] + \beta_{i,Z} [E(R_Z) - R_f], \tag{5.3}$$

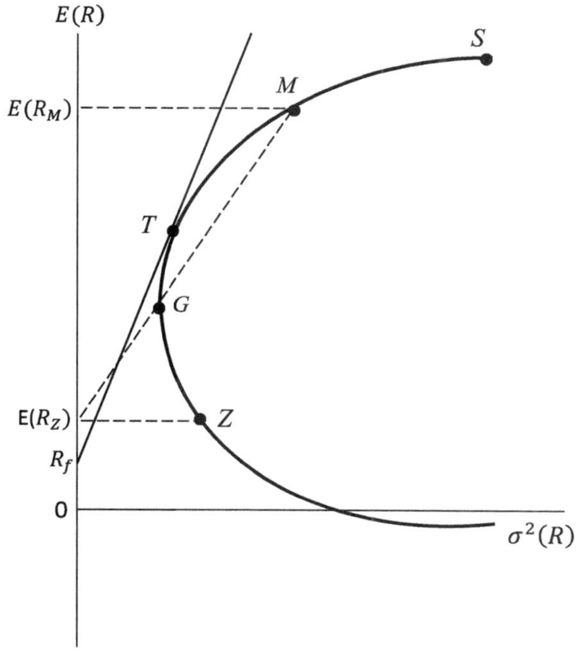


**Fig. 5.1** A graphical depiction of Black's zero-beta CAPM

where $\beta_{i,M}$ and $\beta_{i,Z}$ represent the beta risks of asset $i$ with respect to market portfolio $M$ and zero-beta portfolio $Z$, respectively. If the investor only buys market portfolio $M$, then $\beta_{i,M} = 1$ and $\beta_{i,Z} = 0$ in Eq. (5.3). On the other hand, if the investor only buys zero-beta portfolio $Z$, then $\beta_{i,M} = 0$ and $\beta_{i,Z} = 1$.

In Black's world, investors can hold different combinations of risky portfolios $M$ and $Z$ that are efficient in the sense of maximum expected return per unit variance of returns (or minimum variance for a given expected return). If they combine any risky portfolio composed of $M$ and $Z$ with the riskless asset, less risky efficient portfolios can be created. So there are now two ways for the investor to hold efficient portfolios (not simply combining the riskless asset and $M$ as in the CAPM).

Figure 5.1 shows a diagram of Black's model.[1] The risky zero-beta portfolio rate is greater than the riskless rate, or $E(R_Z) > R_f$. The investor can buy (go long) at the riskless rate and an efficient portfolio. The optimal efficient portfolio in this case is the portfolio $T$ at the tangent point to the efficient frontier. Using Roll's (1980) geometric approach, the market portfolio $M$ can be used to obtain the zero-beta portfolio rate as follows: (1) connect a ray between $M$ and $G$ (the global minimum variance portfolio, (2) extend this ray to intersect the $Y$-axis, and (3) from this point move horizontally to locate the zero-beta portfolio $Z$. The

[1] This graph is based on Figure 4 in Sharpe's (1973) conference presentation to the Midwest Finance Association.

investor has two efficient frontiers. The first part is the straight line from the riskless rate $R_f$ to efficient portfolio $T$. The second part is any efficient portfolio from portfolios $T$ to $S$ on the upper part of the efficient frontier. All portfolios between $T$ and $S$ can be constructed by the investor by means of combining portfolios $M$ and $Z$ with different weights.

Imagine that the investor holds some risky efficient portfolio denoted $I$ that is a combination of $M$ and $Z$. In this case, the zero-beta CAPM would become[2]:

$$E(R_i) - R_f = \beta_{i,I}[E(R_I) - R_f] + \beta_{i,ZI}[E(R_{ZI}) - R_f], \tag{5.4}$$

where $\beta_{i,I}$ and $\beta_{i,ZI}$ become the beta risks of asset $i$ with respect to efficient portfolio $I$ and zero-beta portfolio *ZI*, respectively. Thus, as proven by Roll (1980), the market portfolio $M$ and its zero-beta portfolio *ZM* can be replaced by any efficient portfolio $I$ and its zero-beta portfolio *ZI*. Relevant to the CAPM, any two portfolios $I$ and *ZI* can be used to construct market portfolio $M$. It should be noted that investors can use both long and short positions to construct portfolios $I$ and *ZI*. In the CAPM, only long positions can be used to construct market portfolio $M$, which is a value-weighted index of all assets.[3] However, many studies have found that short positions are needed to compute mean-variance efficient portfolios.[4] Taken together, these concepts make clear that the zero-beta CAPM is a more general equilibrium pricing model than the CAPM that depends solely on long-only market portfolio $M$.

## 5.2 Empirical Tests

There are two ways to test for the existence of the zero-beta CAPM. To see this, let's return to the Fama and MacBeth (FM) (1973) study reviewed in Chapter 4. FM proposed a two-step test procedure for the market model form of the CAPM, which can be used to test any asset pricing model and its factors. In the first step, the risk parameters of the model are estimated for test asset portfolios (e.g., beta risk or $\beta_p$). In the second step, the estimated risk parameters (or $\beta_p$s) are regressed on one-month-ahead (or out-of-sample) returns. Referring back to Eq. (4.3) in Chapter 4, the market model can be estimated in excess return form using portfolios as follows:

$$R_{pt} - R_{ft} = \alpha_0 + \beta_p(R_{mt} - R_{ft}) + e_{it}, \tag{5.5}$$

where $R_{pt} - R_{ft}$ is the excess rate of return on portfolio $p$ in time period $t$ (e.g., daily or monthly), and $R_{mt} - R_{ft}$ is the realized excess average rate of return on

[2] See equation (40) in Black (1972, p. 454).

[3] See studies by Roll (1977), Levy (1983), and Levy (2007).

[4] For example, see Pulley (1981), Kallberg and Ziemba (1983), Levy (1983), Kroll et al. (1984), Green and Hollifield (1992), Jagannathan and Ma (2003), Levy and Ritov (2010), and others.

the stock market as a whole. In the market model, if the CAPM is correct, the intercept term $\alpha_0$ should equal zero. However, if Black's zero-beta CAPM holds, then using Eq. (5.3), the intercept should be $\alpha_0 = E(R_Z) - R_f > 0$. So one way to test the zero-beta CAPM is to determine if there is a positive $\alpha_0$ term in the above market model.

Again referring back to Chapter 4, and dropping non-linear terms in our earlier Eq. (4.5), a cross-sectional regression can be estimated using market factor loadings (or $\beta_p$s for different portfolios) as follows:

$$R_{pt+1} - R_{ft+1} = \lambda_0 + \lambda_m \beta_{pt} + u_{pt+1}, \tag{5.6}$$

where $R_{pt+1} - R_{ft+1}$ is the portfolio excess return in the next out-of-sample month $t+1$, $\lambda_0$ is the intercept term not explained by the other variables in the equation, $\beta_{pt}$ is the portfolio beta estimated using monthly returns in previous years (e.g., four or five years), and $u_{pt+1}$ are independent and normally distributed error terms.

Cross-sectional regression (5.6) asks the following question: Do the estimated risk parameters for the portfolios line up with their future excess returns? The coefficient $\lambda_m$ is an estimate of the market risk premium, or $E(R_{Mt}) - R_{ft}$. According to Ferson (2019, p. 223), $\lambda_m$ can be interpreted as a zero-investment portfolio return that is long high-beta assets and short low-beta assets. Furthermore, the intercept $\lambda_0$ provides an estimate of the expected risk premium on the zero-beta portfolio, or $E(R_{Zt}) - R_{ft}$, which will also be a zero-investment long/short portfolio of assets.[5] If the CAPM holds, then $E(R_{Zt}) = R_{ft}$ and $\lambda_0$ should equal zero. Hence, a second way to test the zero-beta CAPM is to check whether the $\lambda_0$ term is positive.

It is important to recognize that the intercept term $\alpha_0$ in the time-series regression (5.5) and intercept term $\lambda_0$ in cross-sectional regression (5.6) are very different from one another. Both of these intercepts provide estimates of the expected risk premium on the zero-beta portfolio, but their estimation procedures materially affect their values. In Eq. (5.5) the intercept $\alpha_0$ is estimated in a specific estimation period (e.g., five years of monthly excess returns). By contrast, the intercept $\lambda_0$ in Eq. (5.6) is based on one-month-ahead excess returns that are out-of-sample in the sense that they are not part of the estimation period for Eq. (5.5).

Another difference in these intercept terms is that $\alpha_0$ in time-series regression (5.5) is confounded by missing factors from the right-hand-side of the equation. That is, as briefly discussed in Chapter 4, if there are missing factors that account for different systematic risks and associated returns of assets, the $\alpha_0$ term will absorb them. As such, $\alpha_0$ cannot be strictly interpreted to be an estimate of the risk premium on the zero-beta portfolio—it can be biased up by missing factor returns. Indeed, consistent with this logic and previously discussed in Chapter 4,

[5] For example, assuming all betas for assets are positive, long and short positions would be needed to get a portfolio beta equal to zero. Since it is a zero-investment portfolio like other factors, we use the notation $\lambda$ to acknowledge this fact.

Jensen (1968) argued that $\alpha_0$ can be used to test whether the market factor in the CAPM is sufficient to explain excess asset returns. If missing factors exist, so-called *Jensen's* $\alpha$ will be greater than zero. In forthcoming chapters, we will see that, based on real-world stock return data, many researchers have found that the market model can be augmented with a number of other factors that prove to have factor loadings that are significant in cross-sectional tests.

Interestingly, the confounding effect of missing factors in the market model does not necessarily contaminate the $\lambda_0$ intercept estimate in cross-sectional regression (5.6). If there are missing factor loadings in time-cross-sectional regression (5.6), this outcome will be evidenced by low goodness-of-fit as measured by estimated $R^2$ values, rather than upward bias in $\lambda_0$. For this reason, we favor cross-sectional tests of $\lambda_0$ as more reliable indicators of the existence of the risk premium on the zero-beta portfolio. Even so, the cross-sectional regression (5.6) is not without its own problems. Early researchers found that measurement errors exist in the estimated betas of individual stocks.[6] To reduce this so-called *errors-in-the-variables* problem, they recommended the use of portfolios in the estimation of betas. This recommendation led researchers to sort stocks in the U.S. and other markets into various portfolios to form test assets in empirical tests of different asset pricing models.

Fama and French (2004) have provided an excellent review of the cross-sectional regression evidence in the literature. As discussed there, in addition to our review of studies in Chapter 4, early evidence by Douglas (1969), Black et al. (1972), Miller and Scholes (1972), Blume and Friend (1973), Fama and MacBeth (1973), and Fama and French (1992) typically found that the slope $\lambda_m$ of the cross-sectional relationship between excess portfolio returns and betas is lower than predicted by the CAPM with estimated cross-sectional intercept $\lambda_0 > 0$. In their 2004 study, Fama and French repeated these tests using U.S. stock market returns from the longer sample period 1928 to 2003. The results confirmed those of earlier studies. Together, these studies' results lend some degree of support for Black's zero-beta CAPM assumption that investors borrow at a rate higher than the riskless rate in the financial market.

Lastly, both the CAPM and the zero-beta CAPM assume that the market portfolio is mean-variance efficient per Markowitz (1959). Thus, in empirical tests of these models, as Jensen recognized, there is a joint hypothesis: (1) the model is correct; and (2) the market portfolio is efficient. In cross-sectional tests of $k$ other factors that can be added to augment the market factor in the market model, the $\lambda_k$s should equal zero for the CAPM and zero-beta CAPM to hold. If these cross-sectional regression coefficients are nonzero, then not only are these models rejected but the proxy used to measure market portfolio returns is not efficient. Hence, tests of $\lambda_k$s are akin to Jensen's $\alpha$ in the sense that they test the validity of the CAPM and zero-beta CAPM and their underlying efficient market portfolio assumption.

[6] For example, see Blume (1970), Friend and Blume (1970), and Black et al. (1972).

While beyond the scope of the present book's introductory treatment of asset pricing, sophisticated econometric tests of whether all the $\alpha_0$ estimates for different portfolios (in time-series regression specifications of asset pricing models) jointly equal zero have been developed over time. As reviewed in more detail in Sect. 5.4, Gibbons et al. (1989) developed an $F$-statistic of CAPM intercepts that also tests whether the stock market index used to proxy the market portfolio is the tangency portfolio.[7] Of course, if this proxy is not efficient, according to the Roll (1977) critique mentioned in Chapter 4, the CAPM cannot be tested.

## 5.3 Connection to Later Research

As a prelude to subsequent asset pricing research to be covered in forthcoming chapters, Black's two-factor zero-beta CAPM was the seminal *multifactor model.* A multifactor model supplements the market factor with one or more other factors. Extending the BJS findings, a landmark study by Fama and French (1992) updated earlier evidence on the relationship between average returns and CAPM beta for U.S. stocks and found that it is even flatter than previously believed. Indeed, they found little or no significant relationship to support the CAPM. Moreover, they found that firm characteristics, such as size (measured by the market capitalization of stocks equal to price times outstanding shares) and value (measured by the ratio of book equity to market equity denoted BM) were significantly related to average stock returns.

Fama and French (2004) later interpreted these findings to mean that the CAPM excludes important risks that investors use to price assets in financial markets. They cited Merton's (1973) intertemporal CAPM (ICAPM) as one possible explanation, which we discuss next in Chapter 6. In brief, ICAPM investors not only are concerned about the end-of-period value of their portfolios of assets (i.e., wealth) but the ability to consume or invest their wealth. Merton introduced *state variables*, including labor income, goods prices, and portfolio opportunities, that investors use to evaluate multiple risks. According to Fama and French (1992, p. 38), investors seek efficient portfolios that are *multifactor efficient* earning the highest expected returns per unit of multiple risks associated with the state variables (or factors). The joint hypothesis is changed in this context to take into account a multifactor model with multiple beta risks and a multifactor efficient market portfolio. While Fama and French did not mention the zero-beta CAPM as justification for multifactor models, it seems logically relevant to their work, especially given that updated BJS evidence motivated Black's model.

Based on their 1992 findings, Fama and French (1993, 1995) proposed a so-called *three-factor model* that is comprised of market, size, and value factors. They documented evidence that beta coefficients associated with the size and

[7] See recent work by Ferson et al. (2019) for further discussion and citations of other studies that have progressively refined these statistical tests.

value factors are significantly related to average stock returns but not beta related to the market factor. Regarding Merton's ICAPM, they argued that the size and value factors are not ICAPM state variables themselves but are proxies for hidden (underlying) state variables. As later noted in Fama and French (2004), due to this indirect connection to state variables, their three-factor model was considered to be more consistent with the arbitrage pricing theory (APT) of Ross (1976). This theoretical model proposed that expected returns are a linear function of multiple risk factors and their associated beta coefficients. If prices diverge from the risk-adjusted price based on multiple risk factors, arbitrage by investors will buy and sell assets until the linear relation between returns and risks is established again.

The Fama and French research results on the significance of firm-level characteristics, such as size and value, in better explaining average stock returns were serious challenges to the CAPM and zero-beta CAPM. In effect, these authors take the position that the $\alpha_0$ term in time-series regressions is nonzero due to missing size and value factors.

Deviations from asset pricing models, such as a nonzero $\alpha_0$ term, that are not explained by risk factors are considered to be *market anomalies*. The size and value anomalies are not explained by CAPM beta risk. According to the efficient market hypothesis (EMH) of Fama (1970), which led to his 2013 Nobel Prize in Economics, asset prices should reflect all available information. In this world, asset pricing models should have zero $\alpha_0$s after appropriate risk adjustment. If $\alpha_0$ is nonzero, we can infer that an anomaly exists that bears explanation by a missing systematic risk factor.

However, what if investors are not always rational? Now deviations from asset pricing models could arise due to irrational investor behavior rather than an unexplained risk not yet discovered. This is where behavioralists enter the asset pricing picture. Behavioralists argue that anomalies arise due to psychological human reasons. Irrational investor responses due to overreaction, overconfidence, underreaction, overextrapolation of past performance, etc., can cause asset prices to fluctuate in ways not explained by the risk factors in asset pricing models and therefore the EMH. Good examples of behavioral research papers are by Debondt and Thaler (1985, 1987), Lakonishok et al. (1994), Barberis et al. (1998), Daniel et al. (1998), Thaler (1999, 2016), and citations therein.

Do asset pricing models misprice assets due to *bad model problems*—that is, not taking into account all the risk factors used by investors—or does this happen due to behavioral issues related to human psychology? This debate is certainly an interesting one! Continued research is needed to more fully understand why asset mispricing occurs. Perhaps both EMH and behavioral explanations are possible. In the long run after all information is revealed, the EMH should be operative. But in the short run there may be bursts of market behavior that are driven by short term, transitory risk factors, and human behavior.

As an example, on October 19, 1987, which is known as *Black Monday*, the Dow Jones Industrial Average (DJIA) experienced its largest one day loss in the history of the U.S. stock market. World stock markets plummeted also. Apparently, surging sell orders overwhelmed buy orders in stock exchanges, and this order imbalance triggered computerized trading as well as panic selling among investors. Weeks later the market more or less rebounded from the sudden downturn. While transitory structural aspects of the stock market played a central role in the collapse, market behavior due to panic no doubt was responsible also. Black Monday was a dramatic reminder of the short-run impact of temporary market risks as well as irrational market behavior on asset prices.

## 5.4 GRS Test for Portfolio Efficiency

An important theoretical implication of the CAPM is that the market portfolio $M$ is mean-variance efficient. Unfortunately, the true market portfolio is unobservable. For this reason, empirical tests of the CAPM are forced to use proxies (like the value-weighted CRSP index) for the market portfolio denoted $m$. Recognizing this shortcoming, Gibbons, Ross, and Shanken (GRS) (1989) developed a time-series regression approach to test whether any particular portfolio is ex ante mean-variance efficient (see Cochrane (2005) for an excellent discussion of the GRS test).

The GRS test utilizes the following time-series regressions of asset returns on a portfolio, or

$$r_{it} = \alpha_i + \beta_i r_{pt} + e_{it}, \tag{5.7}$$

in which $r_{it} = R_{it} - R_{ft}$ is the excess return of asset $i = 1, \ldots, N$ at time $t$, $r_{pt} = R_{pt} - R_{ft}$ is the excess return on the portfolio whose efficiency is being tested, and $e_{it}$ is the random disturbance term for asset $i$ in period $t$. The disturbances are assumed to be jointly normally distributed in each period with mean zero and covariance matrix $\Sigma$ conditional on the excess returns for portfolio $p$. It is assumed that the $N \times N$ covariance matrix is non-singular and returns are independent over time.

From general mean-variance portfolio mathematics, it follows that the first-order condition for portfolio $p$ to be mean-variance efficient (i.e., that the portfolio is on the efficient frontier spanned by assets $i = 1, \ldots, N$) is

$$E(r_{it}) = \beta_{im} E(r_{pt}) \tag{5.8}$$

for all $i = 1, \ldots, N$. Thus, testing statistically the mean-variance efficiency of portfolio $p$ reduces to testing jointly the null hypothesis

$$H_0 : \alpha_i = 0, \text{ for all } i = 1, \ldots, N. \tag{5.9}$$

A standard statistical test exists for simultaneously testing whether all observations' intercepts equal zero conditional on the excess return of portfolio $p$. The test is a generalization of the usual $t$-test, known as the Hotelling's $T^2$-test, and therefore is distinct from the single coefficient Student's $t$-test. For this particular case, in which $r_{pt}$ is a common independent variable in all regressions, the test statistic for testing null hypothesis (5.9) becomes

$$F = \frac{T - N - 1}{N} \hat{\alpha}'_p \hat{\Sigma}^{-1} \hat{\alpha}_p / (1 + \hat{\theta}_p^2), \tag{5.10}$$

where $\hat{\alpha}'_p = (\hat{\alpha}_{1p}, \ldots, \hat{\alpha}_{Np})$ is the vector of OLS estimated $\alpha_{ip}$ intercepts (the prime means vector transposition), $\hat{\Sigma}^{-1}$ is the inverse of the OLS residual covariance matrix, and $\hat{\theta}_p = \bar{r}_p / s_p$ is the Sharpe (1966) ratio of the portfolio $p$ with $\bar{r}_p$ the sample mean of the excess returns of the portfolio $p$ and $s_p$ the standard deviation of the portfolio $p$. Under the null hypothesis, the $F$-test in Eq. (5.10) has an $F$-distribution with degrees of freedom $N$ and $T - N - 1$.

Gibbons, Ross, and Shanken modified the Hotelling $T^2$-test to take into account whether portfolio $p$ lies on the efficient frontier. They showed that $\hat{\alpha}'_p \hat{\Sigma}^{-1} \hat{\alpha}_p = \hat{\theta}^{*2} - \hat{\theta}_p^2$, where $\hat{\theta}^{*2}$ is the square of the ex post maximum Sharpe ratio for the sample mean-variance efficient frontier portfolio computed using all the $N$ assets, and $\hat{\theta}_p^2$ is the square of the Sharpe ratio of portfolio $p$ defined above. As a result, the $F$-statistic in Eq. (5.10) can be written as

$$F = \frac{T - N - 1}{N} \frac{\hat{\theta}_p^{*2} - \hat{\theta}_p^2}{1 + \hat{\theta}_p^2}, \tag{5.11}$$

which gives a clear intuitive interpretation of the statistic. More specifically, it indicates whether the observed deviation of the portfolio $p$ from the efficient frontier (which is the line through the tangent point of the mean-variance frontier) can be inferred to be random noise. Also, it is notable that $\hat{\theta}^{*2} - \hat{\theta}_p^2 \geq 0$ because portfolio $p$ is included in the efficient frontier calculations.[8] We have left as an exercise for the student to show that the $F$-statistic in Eq. (5.11) can be equivalently presented as

$$F = \frac{T - N - 1}{N} \left( \left[ \frac{\sqrt{1 + \hat{\theta}^{*2}}}{\sqrt{1 + \hat{\theta}_p^2}} \right]^2 - 1 \right), \tag{5.12}$$

which is related to the form in Equation (7) of Gibbons et al. (1989, p. 1125).[9]

[8] In other words, when the riskless rate is available, $\hat{\theta}^{*2}$ is the square of the slope of the tangent line from the origin to the (ex post) efficient frontier, whereas $\theta_p^2$ is the slope of the line from the origin to portfolio $p$ in standard deviation and excess return space.

[9] The intuition of representation (5.12) is as follows. Since a line in the standard deviation ($\sigma$) mean excess return ($\mu$) space through the origin is of the form $\mu = \theta\sigma$, the square of the length of the line (by Pythagoras) is $\sigma^2 + \theta^2\sigma^2 = (1 + \theta^2)\sigma^2$. As a result, the ratio $\sqrt{1 + \hat{\theta}^{*2}} / \sqrt{1 + \hat{\theta}_p^2}$ in Eq. (5.12) is the ratio of the lengths at any $\sigma > 0$ of the tangent line with slope $\hat{\theta}^{*2}$ and the line of

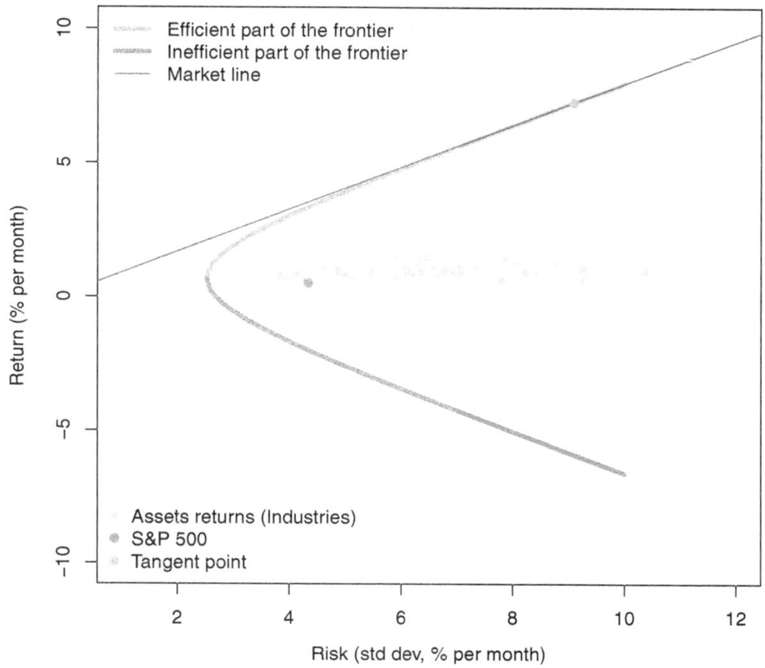


**Fig. 5.2** Industry portfolios and S &P 500 index returns with ex post efficien frontier and the market line

**Example**. To illustrate GRS testing, consider $N = 48$ industry portfolios are available on Kenneth French's data library[10] and S &P500 index returns from finance.yahoo.com. R-code for downloading needed data and computing the statistics is provided in Appendix B.

Using $T = 261$ monthly returns from January 2000 to September 2021, Figure 5.2 shows a scatter plot of average monthly returns and standard deviations of returns. Also, the ex post efficient frontier, market line, tangency portfolio (green dot), and S &P 500 (red dot) are shown in the graphs. We immediately observe that the proxy market portfolio (S &P 500) is well below the efficient frontier, including the tangency portfolio. In testing the mean-variance efficiency hypothesis in relation (5.9), we can compute from the returns $\hat{\theta}_p = (\bar{r}_{\text{sp500}} - r_f)/s_{\text{sp500}} = (0.51 - 0.13)/4.34 \doteq 0.088$. Using the fact that the Sharpe ratio of the tangency portfolio can be computed as $\hat{\theta}^* = \sqrt{\bar{r}'\hat{\Omega}^{-1}\bar{r}}$, where $\bar{r}$ is the

portfolio $p$ with slope $\hat{\theta}_p$. Therefore the ratio $[(1+\hat{\theta}^{*2})\sigma^2]/[(1+\hat{\theta}_p^2)\sigma^2] = (1+\hat{\theta}^{*2})/(1+\hat{\theta}_p^2)$ is the ratio of the squared lengths of the lines. The closer this ratio is to the lower bound of one, the closer the portfolio $p$ is to the efficient frontier.

[10] https://mba.tuck.dartmouth.edu/pages/faculty/ken.french/data_library.html.

$N+1$ vector of averages of the $N$ excess stock returns and excess return of the S &P 500 index, and $\hat{\Omega}^{-1}$ is the inverse of the sample covariance matrix of these return series, we get $\hat{\theta}^* = 0.782$. Thus, the $f$-statistic is:

$$F = \left(\frac{261-48-1}{48}\right)\left(\frac{0.782^2 - 0.088^2}{1+0.088^2}\right) \doteq 2.65.$$

where $f_1 = 212$ numerator degrees of freedom and $f_2 = 48$ denominator degrees of freedom, such that the $p$-value is zero to at least three decimal places. We infer that the null hypothesis in Eq. (5.9) is clearly rejected, which means that the S &P500 index is not an efficient frontier portfolio.

## 5.5 Summary

Early stock return evidence using the market model to estimate the CAPM found that the slope of the Security Market Line (SML) was flatter than expected and the intercept term was higher than the predicted riskless rate of interest (proxied by the government bond rate). Given this evidence, Black (1972) proposed the zero-beta CAPM in which both long and short positions in risky assets were allowed and investor borrowing could occur at rates higher than the riskless rate. His asset pricing model led to a two-factor model comprised of an efficient portfolio factor and zero-beta portfolio factor. The efficient portfolio and zero-beta portfolio are assumed to be uncorrelated (or orthogonal) to one another. Efficient portfolios are changed from those located along a single line in the CAPM (extending from the riskless rate to the tangent market portfolio on the Markowitz efficient frontier of risky assets) to two possible cases: (1) portfolios along the ray from the riskless rate to the tangent point of the efficient frontier; and (2) a segment of the efficient frontier extending from this tangent point to the end of the efficient frontier. The latter result is due to the fact that investors are not allowed to borrow at the riskless rate. The resultant zero-beta CAPM is more general than the CAPM because it holds for any two portfolios located on the efficient frontier of the mean-variance parabola and its zero-beta counterpart on the lower, inefficient boundary of the parabola.

Empirical tests of the zero-beta CAPM are based on both time-series regressions and cross-sectional regressions. The Fama and MacBeth (1973) two-step procedure combines both of these regressions in an effort to estimate the relation between betas and future returns of asset portfolios. The time-series regression of the market model for the CAPM yields an intercept known as *Jensen's* $\alpha$ which should be zero for all assets. If they are nonzero, the implication is that the zero-beta CAPM is valid; however, other missing factors could explain nonzero $\alpha$s also. The cross-sectional regression yields an intercept denoted $\lambda_0$ that measures the risk premium on the zero-beta portfolio. If $\lambda_0 > 0$, then the zero-beta CAPM's assumption that investors borrow at a rate greater than the riskless rate is supported. Also, if other risk factors than the market factor are significant in cross-sectional tests, then the zero-beta CAPM does not hold.

Research by Fama and French (1992, 1993, 1995) showed that size and value are significant firm-level characteristics that help to explain average stock returns. Thus, they rejected the zero-beta CAPM in addition to its precursor the CAPM. Because any test of the CAPM or zero-beta CAPM is a joint test that the model is valid and the portfolio proxy is an efficient portfolio, their findings suggested that efficient portfolios must be multifactor efficient in terms of multiple risk factors. By way of explanation, they cited the ICAPM of Merton (1973) and APT of Ross (1976) as theoretical models that are consistent with their three-factor model containing market, size, and value factors.

While the efficient market hypothesis (EMH) suggests that prices reflect all available information to evaluate risks in financial markets, behavioralists argue that mispricing can happen due to irrational actions of investors affected by human psychology. If behavioralists are right, then asset pricing faces serious challenges. It is likely that short-run market anomalies can occur due to irrational investor behavior as well as short run, transitory market risk factors, but long-run anomalies are attributable to unknown risk factors. Regarding the latter, if investors are rational (for the most part), asset pricing models should continue to evolve and increasingly explain the average returns of stocks (and other asset classes such as bonds, commodities, real estate, etc.) in the long run. As we will see in upcoming chapters, researchers are making progress!

In his assessment of the zero-beta CAPM, Sharpe (1973) critically commented that, given any efficient portfolio, its zero-beta portfolio is not directly identifiable. In asset pricing models, researchers typically employ proxies for the market portfolio and the riskless rate—namely, the value-weighted index of all stocks in the market and the government bond rate. However, it is not clear how to proxy the zero-beta portfolio. With no such ready proxy at hand, researchers typically do not include a zero-beta portfolio rate of return in their specifications of different models. Instead, a riskless rate proxy is almost always employed as the borrowing rate in empirical models. Circumventing the zero-beta portfolio identification problem, Chapter 10 reviews a new form the zero-beta CAPM dubbed the *ZCAPM*. The ZCAPM enables estimation of the zero-beta CAPM with readily available stock return data that does not require a proxy for the zero-beta portfolio rate.

## Questions

1. Black (1972) developed the zero-beta CAPM due to some unrealistic assumptions of the CAPM. What assumptions did he relax?
2. Black et al. (1972) found that the market model needed to be modified to better fit U.S. stock returns. What did they propose as a better fitting model?
3. Black (1972) proposed a zero-beta CAPM without and with a riskless rate. Write the equations for these two models. Can investors borrow at the riskless rate in the second model?
4. In the CAPM, the Security Market Line (SML) defines combinations of the riskless asset and market portfolio $M$ that investors can hold. By contrast, under

Black's zero-beta CAPM, what are two ways for investors to hold efficient portfolios? Draw a diagram to illustrate your answer. Where is the market portfolio $M$ in this diagram? How can the investor hold $M$. Assuming the investor holds an efficient portfolio, using your diagram, how can the uncorrelated zero-beta portfolio counterpart be located?

5. Assume that the investor holds risky efficient portfolio $I$ that is a combination of market portfolio $M$ and its uncorrelated zero-beta portfolio counterpart $ZI$. How can we write the zero-beta CAPM using these two risky portfolios?
6. Assume that you run a time-series regression of the market model. Next, you run a cross-sectional regression using one-month-ahead returns. In the cross-sectional regression, how should you interpret the estimated market prices of beta risk, or $\lambda_m$, and the intercept term, or $\lambda_0$? How is $\lambda_m$ related to the expected market risk premium in the CAPM?
7. Fama and French published a series of studies in the 1990s that are important to the validity of the CAPM and zero-beta CAPM. What did they find in these studies? What did they propose as an alternative asset pricing model?
8. What is a *market anomaly*? What might explain market anomalies? Give two explanations. What does the efficient market hypothesis (EMH) have to say about market anomalies?
9. Can financial markets be irrational? Give an example from stock market history.

## Problems

1. How can the zero-beta CAPM be empirically tested with real-world data? Discuss two tests using equations based on the market model. Which test is more reliable and why?
2. Show that the GRS statistic

$$F = \frac{T - N - 1}{N} \frac{\hat{\theta}^{*2} - \hat{\theta}_p^2}{1 + \hat{\theta}_p^2}$$

can be equivalently written as

$$F = \frac{T - N - 1}{N} \left( \left[ \frac{\sqrt{1 + \hat{\theta}^{*2}}}{\sqrt{1 + \hat{\theta}_p^2}} \right]^2 - 1 \right).$$

3. Using 12 industry portfolios from Kenneth French's data library, replicate the GRS testing for mean-variance efficiency of the market portfolio, available in FF_Research_Data_Factors_CSV. Use monthly data for the time period January 2000 to September 2021. Verify that the test statistics in Eqs. (5.10) and (5.11) produce the same results.

## Appendix A: Mathematical Derivation of the Zero-Beta CAPM

Here we provide a mathematical proof of Black's zero-beta CAPM. The derivation relies heavily on the work of Kolari et al. (Chapter 2, 2021). To begin, according to Markowitz (1959), the minimum variance of an efficient portfolio $I$ of assets with weights that sum to one and expected return $E(R_I)$ can be defined as follows:

$$\underset{\omega}{\text{Min}} \frac{1}{2}\omega'\Sigma\omega + \eta[E(R_I) - \omega'E(R)] + \kappa(1 - \omega'e), \tag{A5.1}$$

where $\omega$ is a vector of weights (with dimension $n \times 1$), $e$ is a vector of ones (with dimension $n \times 1$), $E(R) = [E(R_1), E(R_2), \cdots, E(R_n)]'$ is the expected one-period return vector for $n$ assets (with dimension $n \times 1$), and $\Sigma$ is the covariance matrix for $n$ assets (with dimension $n \times n$). First-order conditions with respect to $\omega$, $\eta$, and $\kappa$ are:

$$\begin{aligned} \Sigma\omega - \eta E(R) - \kappa e &= 0 \\ E(R_I) - \omega'E(R) &= 0 \\ 1 - \omega'e &= 0. \end{aligned} \tag{A5.2}$$

Upon solving to get the optimal weights $\omega^*$, we obtain:

$$\begin{aligned} \omega^* &= \frac{CE(R_I) - A}{BC - A^2}\Sigma^{-1}E(R) + \frac{B - \alpha E(R_I)}{BC - A^2}\Sigma^{-1}e \\ &\equiv \phi + \psi E(R_I), \end{aligned} \tag{A5.3}$$

where

$$\begin{aligned} A &\equiv E(R)'\Sigma^{-1}e \\ B &\equiv E(R)'\Sigma^{-1}E(R) \\ C &\equiv e'\Sigma^{-1}e \end{aligned} \tag{A5.4}$$

are known scalars, and

$$\begin{aligned} \phi &\equiv \frac{B\Sigma^{-1}e - A\Sigma^{-1}E(R)}{BC - A^2} \\ \psi &\equiv \frac{C\Sigma^{-1}E(R) - A\Sigma^{-1}e}{BC - A^2} \end{aligned} \tag{A5.5}$$

are known $n \times 1$ vectors. Based on these equations, the variance of efficient portfolio $I$ can be written as:

$$\sigma_I^2 = \frac{1}{C} + \frac{C\left[E(R_I) - \frac{A}{C}\right]^2}{BC - A^2}. \tag{A5.6}$$

In line with the CAPM, we can write the equation of the line through the tangent point $[E(R_M), \sigma_M]$ (i.e., market portfolio $M$) as:

$$E(R_{ZI}) - E(R_M) = \frac{BC - A^2}{C[E(R_M) - \frac{A}{C}]}\sigma_M(\sigma_{ZI} - \sigma_M), \tag{A5.7}$$

where $\frac{BC-A^2}{C[E(R_M)-\frac{A}{C}]}\sigma_M$ is the slope of the line as defined by Merton (1972, p. 1856). By replacing $E(R_{ZI})$ with the riskless rate $R_f$, we can achieve the highest (most efficient) slope of the Capital Market Line (CML) (i.e., $\sigma_{ZI} = 0$). Subsequently, we obtain the familiar slope of the CML defined as $[E(R_M) - R_f]/\sigma(R_M)$.

In Black's zero-beta CAPM, the expected return on any risky asset portfolio $P$ is a function of the expected returns on efficient portfolio $I$ and its zero-beta portfolio counterpart $ZI$. As proof, we begin by defining the covariance between the returns of portfolios $I$ and $P$ as follows:

$$Cov(R_I, R_P) = \omega^{M'}\Sigma\omega^P = [\phi + \psi E(R_I)]'\Sigma\omega^P. \tag{A5.8}$$

In terms of A, B, and C, this covariance term can be specified as:

$$\begin{aligned}
&= \left(\frac{B\Sigma^{-1}e - A\Sigma^{-1}E(R)}{BC - A^2} + \frac{C\Sigma^{-1}E(R) - A\Sigma^{-1}e}{BC - A^2}E(R_I)\right)'\Sigma\omega^P \\
&= \frac{Be'\Sigma^{-1}\Sigma\omega^P - AE(R)'\Sigma^{-1}\Sigma\omega^P}{BC - A^2} + \frac{CE(R_I)E(R)'\Sigma^{-1}\Sigma\omega^P - AE(R_I)e'\Sigma^{-1}\Sigma\omega^P}{BC - A^2} \\
&= \frac{B - AE(R_P) + CE(R_I)E(R_P) - AE(R_I)}{BC - A^2}.
\end{aligned} \tag{A5.9}$$

Solving for $E(R_P)$ yields:

$$\begin{aligned}
E(R_P) &= \frac{AE(R_I) - B}{CE(R_I) - A} + Cov(R_I, R_P)\left(\frac{BC - A^2}{CE(R_I) - A}\right) \\
&= \frac{A}{C} - \frac{BC - A^2}{C^2E(R_I) - \frac{A}{C}} + Cov(R_I, R_P)\frac{\sigma_I^2}{\sigma_I^2}\left(\frac{BC - A^2}{CE(R_I) - A}\right),
\end{aligned} \tag{A5.10}$$

where $\sigma_I^2 = \frac{1}{C} + \frac{C[E(R_I)-\frac{A}{C}]^2}{BC-A^2}$. Expanding the above equation, we get:

$$E(R_P) = \frac{A}{C} - \frac{BC - A^2}{C^2[E(R_I) - \frac{A}{C}]} + \frac{Cov(R_I, R_P)}{\sigma_I^2}\left(E(R_I) - \frac{A}{C} + \frac{BC - A^2}{C^2[E(R_I) - \frac{A}{C}]}\right). \tag{A5.11}$$

The intercept term in this equation corresponding to portfolio return $\frac{A}{C} - \frac{BC-A^2}{C^2[E(R_I)-\frac{A}{C}]}$ is orthogonal to efficient portfolio return $E(R_I)$. As such, it represents the expected return on the zero-beta portfolio or $E(R_{ZI})$. To see this, note that:

$$\omega^{ZI'}\Sigma\omega^{I} = [\phi + \psi E(R_{ZI})]'\Sigma[\phi + \psi E(R_{I})] = 0 \tag{A5.12}$$

$$B - AE(R_{ZI}) + CE(R_I)E(R_{ZI}) - AE(R_I) = 0 \tag{A5.13}$$

$$E(R_{ZI}) = \frac{AE(R_I) - B}{CE(R_I) - A} = \frac{A}{C} - \frac{BC - A^2}{C^2[E(R_I) - \frac{A}{C}]}. \tag{A5.14}$$

Finally, upon re-writing Eq. (A5.11), Black's zero-beta CAPM is obtained:

$$E(R_P) = E(R_{ZI}) + \beta_P[E(R_I) - E(R_{ZI})]. \tag{A5.15}$$

# Appendix B: R Snippet for the GRS Testing Example in Section 5.4

```
#########################################################
### Example: French data base 48 industy portfolios
### files: 48_Industry_Portfolios_CSV and
### to generate efficient frontier and using SP 500 index
### as market portfolio for GRS test for efficiency of the
### index. As of November 1, 2021.
########################################################
update.packages(repos = "https://cloud.r-project.org", ask = FALSE) # get new updates
### install.packages(pkgs = "FFdownload", repos = "https://cloud.r-project.org") # install if not installed
### install.packages(pkgs = "quantmod", repos = "https://cloud.r-project.org") # install if not installed
library(FFdownload) # package to download FF data drom French data library
library(quantmod) # package to download finance.yahoo data
tmpf <- tempfile(fileext = ".RData") # temprorary file with .RData extension for downloaded FF R-data file FFdata
FFdownload(output_file = tmpf,  # temporal output file for FF data
           tempd = tempdir(), # system specific temporal folder
           exclude_daily = TRUE, # exclude daily values to speed up process
           listsave = tempfile(fileext = ".txt"), # names of data files in French data
                                                   # library saved here to be searched by inputlist
           inputlist = c("48_Industry_Portfolios_CSV",      # select needed data files, i.e., industries
                         "F-F_Research_Data_Factors_CSV"),  # and research factors (that includes Rf)
           download = TRUE  # download the selected file given in inputlist
           )
load(tmpf) # load FF data
ls() # show object in work space
names(FFdata) # objects in FFdata
names(FFdata$x_48_Industry_Portfolios) # objects in Industry portfolios
names(FFdata$x_48_Industry_Portfolios$monthly) # objects in monthly series
names(FFdata$"x_F-F_Research_Data_Factors") # objects note, quatations needed!
names(FFdata$"x_F-F_Research_Data_Factors"$monthly) # objects note, quatations needed!
df <- merge(FFdata$x_48_Industry_Portfolios$monthly$average_value_weighted_returns,
            FFdata$"x_F-F_Research_Data_Factors"$monthly$Temp2) # merge needed data xts data frames
```

```
head(df) # six first lines
df[df %in% c(-99.99, -999)]  <- NA # replace missing values
head(df)
tail(df) # six last lines
### download SP500 form Yahoo Finance web site for the time period
sp500 <- getSymbols(Symbols = "^GSPC", env = NULL, from = "2000-01-01", to = "2021-09-30")
spret <- periodReturn(sp500) # mothly returns by default
head(spret)
index(spret) <- as.yearmon(as.Date(index(spret))) # change time index to year month format
head(spret)
df <- merge(df, spret) # merge into industry and FF factor data
df <- na.omit(df) # remove missing values
df$Sp500 <- 100 * df$monthly.returns # percentage returns
df$monthly.returns <- NULL # remove obsolete monthly.returns series
colnames(df) <- tolower(colnames(df)) # return names to lower cases for convenience
head(df) # check OK?
tail(df)
### Portfolio stats
N <- 48 # number of industries (test assets)
mu <- colMeans(df[ , c(1:N, ncol(df))]) # mean vector including sp500
Omega <- cov(df[, c(1:N, ncol(df))]) # covariance matrix of returns
### Using the Efficient Set Mathematics notations in Appenix of this chapter (Chapter 5)
### define, see equations in (A5.4)
(e <- rep(1, times = length(mu))) # vector of ones
(A <- drop(e %*% solve(Omega) %*% mu)) # i.e., sum(solve(Omega) %*% mu), solve(Omega) is the inverse of Omega
(B <- drop(mu %*% solve(Omega) %*% mu))
(C <- drop(e %*% solve(Omega) %*% e))  # i.e., sum(solve(Omega))
(D <- B * C - A^2) # define this for convenience
### Using the weight vector in eq (A5.3) and the above notations, the variance
### of the return rp of a frontier portfolio p is by equation (A5.6)
### sigma_p^2 = 1/C + (C/D) * (mu_p - A/C)^2, where
```

```
### mu_p = E[rp] from which we can solve mu_p as a function of sigma_p:
### mu_p = A/C + sqrt[(sigma_p^2 - 1/C) * (D/C)] for the upper (efficient) part of the frontier
### mu_p = A/C - sqrt[(sigma_p^2 - 1/C) * (D/C)] for the lower (inefficient) part of the frontier
###
### The following produces the upper (efficient) and lower (inefficient) frontiers
### depicted as green and red
curve(expr = A / C + sqrt((x^2 - 1 / C) * D / C), from = sqrt(1 / C), to = 10, xlim = c(1, 12),
      ylim = c(-10, 10),
      xlab = "Risk (std dev, % per month)",
      ylab = "Return (% per month)",
      lwd = 4, # line thickness
      col = "green") # upper part (efficient part of the frontier
curve(expr = A / C - sqrt((x^2 - 1 / C) * D / C), from = sqrt(1 / C), to = 10,
      col = "red", lwd = 4, # line color an thickness
      add = TRUE) # add lower part (inefficient part of the frontier)
### With riskfree rate rf, the weight vector, wq, of the tangent portfolio, q,  is
rf <- mean(df$rf) # average riskfree rate
### in matrix form: wq  <- Omega^{-1} (mu - rf) / (e'Omega^{-1} (mu - rf))
wq  <- solve(Omega) %*% (mu - rf); wq <- wq / sum(wq) # weights for the tangency portfolio
muq <- sum(wq * mu) # mean return of the tangency portfolio
sigmaq  <-  sqrt(as.double(t(wq) %*% Omega %*% wq)) # standard deviation of the tangency portfolio
abline(a = rf, b = (muq - rf) / sigmaq, col = "blue") # Mkt line
points(x = sqrt(diag(Omega)), y = mu, pch = 20, col = "orange") # returns and standard deviations
points(x = sqrt(Omega[nrow(Omega), ncol(Omega)]), y = mu[length(mu)],
      col = "red", pch = 19) # market portfolio (S&P 500)
points(x = sigmaq, y = muq, col = "green", pch = 19) # Tangency portfolio
legend("topleft",
       legend = c("Efficient part of the frontier", "Inefficient part of the frontier", "Market line"), lty = "solid",
       col = c("green", "red", "blue"), lwd = c(4, 4, 1), bty = "n")
legend("bottomleft", legend = c("Assets returns (Industries)", "S&P 500", "Tangent point"),
       col = c("orange", "red", "green"), pch = c(20, 19, 19), bty = "n")
###
### GRS test for the null hypothesis SP500 return generating process is a tangency portfolio
###
(thetap <- (mu[length(mu)] - rf) / sqrt(Omega[nrow(Omega), ncol(Omega)])) # SP600 Sharpe ratio
(thetaq <- (muq - rf) / sigmaq) # Tangency protfolio Sharpe ratio [same as sqrt(t(mu - rf) %*% solve(Omega) %*% (mu - rf))]
(Fstat <- (thetaq^2 - thetap^2) / (1 + thetap^2) * (nrow(df) - N - 1) / N) # F statistic using
(pval <- 1 - pf(q = Fstat, df1 = nrow(df) - N - 1, df2 = N)) # 0.0000633, p-value for observed F
```

## References


Barberis, M., A. Shleifer, and R. Vishny. 1998. A model of investor sentiment. *Journal of Financial Economics* 49: 307–343.

Black, F. 1972. Capital market equilibrium with restricted borrowing. *Journal of Business* 45: 444–454.

Black, F., M.C. Jensen, and M. Scholes. 1972. The capital asset pricing model: Some empirical tests. In *Studies in the Theory of Capital Markets*, ed. M.C. Jensen. New York, NY: Praeger.

Blume, M. 1970. Portfolio theory: A step towards its practical application. *Journal of Business* 43: 152–174.

Blume, M., and I. Friend. 1973. A new look at the capital asset pricing model. *Journal of Finance* 28: 19–33.

Cochrane, J.H. 2005. *Asset Pricing*. Revised. Princeton, NJ: Princeton University Press.

Daniel, K., D. Hirshleifer, and A. Subrahmanyam. 1998. Investor psychology and security market under- and overreactions. *Journal of Finance* 53: 1839–1885.

De Bondt, W.F.M., and R. Thaler. 1985. Does the stock market overreact? *Journal of Finance* 40: 793–805.

De Bondt, W.F.M., and R. Thaler. 1987. Further evidence of stock market overreaction and seasonality. *Journal of Finance* 42: 557–581.

Douglas, G.W. 1969. Risk in the equity markets: An empirical appraisal of market efficiency. *Yale Economic Essays* 9: 3–45.

Fama, E.F. 1968. Risk, return, and equilibrium: Some clarifying comments. *Journal of Finance* 23: 29–40.

Fama, E.F. 1970. Efficient capital markets: A review of theory and empirical work. *Journal of Finance* 25: 383–417.

Fama, E.F., and K.R. French. 1992. The cross-section of expected stock returns. *Journal of Finance* 47: 427–465.

Fama, E.F., and K.R. French. 1993. The cross-section of expected returns. *Journal of Financial Economics* 33: 3–56.

Fama, E.F., and K.R. French. 1995. Size and book-to-market factors in earnings and returns. *Journal of Finance* 50: 131–156.

Fama, E.F., and K.R. French. 2004. The capital asset pricing model: Theory and evidence. *Journal of Economic Perspectives* 18: 25–46.

Fama, E.F., and J.D. MacBeth. 1973. Risk, return, and equilibrium: Empirical tests. *Journal of Political Economy* 81: 607–636.

Ferson, W.E. 2019. *Empirical Asset Pricing: Models and Methods*. Cambridge, MA: The MIT Press.

Ferson, W., A.F. Siegel, and J.L. Wang. 2019. Asymptotic distributions of tests of portfolio efficiency and factor model comparisons with conditioning information. Working paper, University of Southern California and University of Washington.

Friend, I., and M. Blume. 1970. Measurement of portfolio performance under uncertainty. *American Economic Review* 60: 607–636.

Gibbons, M.R., S.A. Ross, and J. Shanken. 1989. A test of the efficiency of a given portfolio. *Econometrica* 57: 1121–1152.

Green, R.C., and B. Hollifield. 1992. When will mean-variance efficient portfolios be well diversified? *Journal of Finance* 47: 1785–1809.

Jagannathan, R., and T. Ma. 2003. Risk reduction in large portfolios: A role for portfolio weight constraints. *Journal of Finance* 58: 1651–1684.

Jensen, M.C. 1968. The performance of mutual funds in the period 1945–1964. *Journal of Finance* 23: 389–416.

Kallberg, J.G., and W.T. Ziemba. 1983. Comparison of alternative utility functions in portfolio selection problems. *Management Science* 29: 1257–1276.

Kroll, Y., H. Levy, and H. Markowitz. 1984. Mean-variance versus direct utility maximization. *Journal of Finance* 39: 47–61.

Lakonishok, J., A. Shleifer, and R.W. Vishny. 1994. Contrarian investment, extrapolation, and risk. *Journal of Finance* 49: 1541–1578.

Levy, H. 1983. The capital asset pricing model: Theory and empiricism. *Economic Journal* 93: 145–165.

Levy, M. 2007. Conditions for a CAPM equilibrium with positive prices. *Journal of Economic Theory* 137: 404–415.

Levy, M., and Y. Ritov. 2010. Mean-variance efficient portfolios with many assets: 50% short. *Quantitative Finance* 10: 1–11.

Markowitz, H.M. 1959. *Portfolio Selection: Efficient Diversification of Investments*. New York, NY: John Wiley & Sons.

Merton, R.C. 1972. An analytical derivation of the efficient portfolio frontier. *Journal of Financial and Quantitative Finance* 7: 1851–1872.

Merton, R.C. 1973. An intertemporal capital asset pricing model. *Econometrica* 41: 867–887.

Miller, M., and M. Scholes. 1972. Rates of return in relation to risk: A re-examination of some recent findings. In *Studies in the Theory of Capital Markets*, ed. M.C. Jensen, 47–78. New York, NY: Praeger.

Pulley, L.B. 1981. General mean-variance approximation to expected utility for short holding periods. *Journal of Financial and Quantitative Analysis* 16: 361–373.

Roll, R. 1977. A critique of the asset pricing theory's tests, part I: On past and potential future testability of the theory. *Journal of Financial Economics* 4: 129–176.

Roll, R. 1980. Orthogonal portfolios. *Journal of Financial and Quantitative Analysis* 15: 1005–1012.

Ross, S.A. 1976. The arbitrage theory of capital asset pricing. *Journal of Economic Theory* 13: 341–360.

Sharpe, W.F. 1966. Mutual fund performance, *Journal of Business* 39: 119–138.

Sharpe, W.F. 1973. The capital asset pricing model: Traditional and "zero-beta" versions. Presentation at the 1973 annual meetings of the Midwest Finance Association, 1–15.

Thaler, R.H. 1999. The end of behavioral finance. *Financial Analysts Journal* 55: 12–17.

Thaler, R.H. 2016. Behavioral economics: Past, present, and future. *American Economic Review* 106: 1577–1600.

# Alternative CAPM Specifications

# 6

Weak early empirical evidence with respect to the CAPM inspired a variety of alternative forms proposed by researchers to take into account realistic aspects of capital markets not considered in its original form. In the last chapter we covered Black's (1972) zero-beta CAPM allowing short sales and borrowing at rates greater than the riskless rate. Here we review further extensions of the CAPM, including the foundational and more general intertemporal CAPM (ICAPM) which spawned a number of new models such as the international asset pricing model (IAPM), consumption CAPM (CCAPM), production CAPM (PCAPM), and conditional CAPM. The latter conditional CAPM allows for time-varying risk parameters in any asset pricing model to take into account the business cycle with economic expansions and recessions. Over the years, different forms of the aforementioned models have been developed by researchers. In general, they attest to the widespread interest in the CAPM by academics and professionals in finance.

Unfortunately, the aforementioned extensions of the ICAPM did not consistently cure the weak empirical evidence problem. While they continue to draw the interest of many researchers, most asset pricing researchers nowadays emphasize multifactor models. The latter models augment the market factor by adding many new factors proposed by researchers. Multifactor models are considered to be related to the intertemporal CAPM (ICAPM) by Merton (1973) covered in this chapter in addition to the Arbitrage Pricing Model (APT) by Ross (1976) discussed in forthcoming Chapter 7. In Chapters 8 and 9 we will see that multifactor models do a better job of explaining stock returns than the CAPM and its companion models presented in this chapter. However, in Chapter 10 we return to the CAPM with an alternative form of the zero-beta CAPM dubbed the ZCAPM by

---

**Supplementary Information** The online version contains supplementary material available at https://doi.org/10.1007/978-3-031-16784-3_6.

 
J. W. Kolari and S. Pynnönen, *Investment Valuation and Asset Pricing*,
https://doi.org/10.1007/978-3-031-16784-3_6

Kolari et al. (2021). Recent empirical evidence discussed there shows that the ZCAPM outperforms popular multifactor models in cross-sectional tests. Hence, the development of alternative CAPMs continues to hold promise in asset pricing.

## 6.1 Intertemporal CAPM

The CAPM is considered to be a static model in the sense that it is based on a single-period. Considered by everyone to be a tour de force, Merton (1973) extended the CAPM to a multiperiod setting. Upon doing so, an intertemporal CAPM (ICAPM) was derived that yielded new insights into equilibrium asset prices. For example, even if no systematic market risk exists, the expected return on risky assets can exceed the riskless rate. Other factors related to state variables that shape future investment opportunities can contribute to expected returns. In the CAPM, investment opportunities are fixed and the market factor is the only risk factor.[1] Upon allowing the future opportunity set available to investors to change over time in response to state-dependent variables, Merton showed that asset pricing is more complicated than the CAPM would predict. Indeed, there are multiple potential factors associated with different state variables that can influence asset prices.

Merton examined the portfolio selection behavior of investors who maximize their lifetime consumption and trade continuously over time. He assumed that the demand function for assets by investors is affected by the possibility of uncertain changes in future investment opportunities. Changing investment opportunities are state-dependent in the ICAPM—for example, good and bad economic states related to times of prosperity versus recession.

The ICAPM makes similar assumptions to the CAPM: limited liability of assets; no transaction costs and taxes; no wealth constraints on the ability to buy and sell assets at market prices; capital markets in equilibrium, borrowing and lending at the same rate of interest, and short sales of assets (which is allowed in Black's [1972] zero-beta CAPM version of the CAPM). However, he adds a crucial new assumption: continuous trading of assets over time. This assumption allows investors to revise their portfolios over time as they learn new market information. Even daily revisions could be made by investors. Taking this logic one step further, Merton adopted a continuous-time process of asset pricing in capital markets, wherein the price process follows what is known as geometric Brownian motion.[2] This random motion implies a lognormal return distribution for asset returns. The CAPM assumes homogeneous expectations among investors about the normal joint distribution of asset returns that are unchanging over time. However, a changing investment opportunity set implies that homogeneous expectations break down. Now asset prices are untethered from a fixed return distribution.

[1] Merton cited Fama (1970), who had observed that intertemporal portfolio maximization can be treated as if the investor had a single-period utility function.

[2] Browning motion in physics is the random motion of particles.

Given the risk of a changing investment opportunity set due to underlying state variables, investors seek to hedge (or insure) against "unfavorable" shifts in such opportunities. Resultant risk hedges employed by investors give rise to new asset pricing factors unrelated to the CAPM market factor. To demonstrate these concepts, he introduced a changing riskless rate as a candidate for such a state variable. The riskless rate is known to investors in the beginning of the coming period but is changing stochastically (or randomly) thereafter over time. Due to a stochastic riskless rate, investors are exposed to possible shifts in the investment opportunity set over time. Assuming that the (stochastic) riskless rate is sufficient to describe changes in the investment opportunity set, he proposed a *three-fund theorem* with the following portfolios chosen by investors in equilibrium: (1) the riskless asset ($f$), (2) market portfolio ($M$), and (3) an asset or portfolio that is perfectly negatively correlated with the riskless rate ($N$) (i.e., hedge for the riskless asset). An example of the latter $N$ asset could be a long-term bond with returns negatively correlated to changes in short-term interest rates. Using these assumptions and capital market conditions, Merton derived a continuous-time version of the single-period CAPM or intertemporal CAPM (ICAPM):[3]

$$E(R_i) = R_f + \beta_{i,M}[E(R_M) - R_f] + \beta_{i,N}[E(R_N) - R_f], \tag{6.1}$$

where $R_i$ is the instantaneous return of stock $i$ at any instant of time $t$, $R_f$ is the instantaneous riskless rate, $R_M$ is the instantaneous market return, and $R_N$ is the instantaneous return on a portfolio that has perfect negative correlation with the riskless rate. The risk parameters in the ICAPM are defined as follows:

$$\beta_{i,M} = \frac{\sigma_i}{\sigma_M} \cdot \frac{\rho_{iM} - \rho_{iN}\rho_{NM}}{1 - \rho_{NM}^2}, \quad \beta_{i,N} = \frac{\sigma_i}{\sigma_N} \cdot \frac{\rho_{iN} - \rho_{iM}\rho_{NM}}{1 - \rho_{NM}^2} \tag{6.2}$$

with various correlations among the three portfolios in this expression of the general form $\rho_{kl} = Cor(R_k, R_l)$ for any two assets $k$ and $l$.

Equation (6.1) indicates that investors are not only compensated for bearing market risk but also for bearing the risk of unfavorable shifts in the investment opportunity set. If correlations $\rho_{iN} = 0$ for all securities $i$, then it must be true that $\rho_{NM} = 0$, where $M$ is the market portfolio containing all securities. Also, because $R_N$ is perfectly negatively correlated with $R_f$ by definition, the correlations of stocks with the future riskless rate $R_f$ would be zero. In this special case, the ICAPM reduces to the traditional CAPM in which $\beta_{i,N} = 0$ and $\beta_{i,M} = (\sigma_i/\sigma_M)\rho_{iM} = (\sigma_i\sigma_M/\sigma_M^2)\rho_{iM} = Cov(R_i, R_M)/\sigma_M^2$. Since security $N$ has a zero-beta due to zero correlation with market portfolio $M$ (or $\rho_{NM} = 0$), it is tantamount to the zero-beta portfolio of Black (1972). Notice also that, if there

[3] See equation (34) in Merton (1973, p. 882). The derivation of this model is quite complicated and beyond the scope of the present text. He utilized stochastic differential calculus, complex continuous functions, instantaneous returns (as opposed to discrete one-period returns), and optimality conditions to solve the asset pricing problem.

is no systematic market beta risk such that $\beta_{i,M} = 0 = \rho_{iM}$, but there is beta risk associated with security $N$ so that $\beta_{i,N} > 0$, the expected return on the $i$th asset will be greater than the riskless rate, unlike the traditional CAPM. Of course, in the likely case that $\rho_{iN} > 0$, asset prices are determined by all risk factors that affect changing future investment opportunities.

On a practical level, we can specify the ICAPM as a multifactor empirical model. To simplify notation, we use excess returns over the riskless rate denoted with a lowercase $r$. Following Merton, we include a number of state variables that can affect the expected excess returns of the $i$th asset:

$$r_{it} = \alpha_0 + \beta_{i,M} r_{Mt} + \beta_{i,s_1} s_{1t} + \beta_{i,s_2} s_{2t} + \cdots + \beta_{i,s_k} s_{kt} + \epsilon_{it}, \quad (6.3)$$

where there are $k$ state variables denoted $s_{jt}$, $j = 1, \ldots, k$. The multiple regression coefficients in empirical model (6.3) are beta risk measures for each asset. Each beta, or $\beta_{i,s_j}$, contains a covariance term $Cov(r_{it}, s_{jt})$, $j = 1, \ldots, k$, that determines its specific systematic risk. In place of the $k$ state variables in this equation, we equivalently could use the hedging portfolio returns for the risk associated with each state variable.

Merton leaves open the selection of state variables or definition of hedge portfolio returns in the ICAPM. His model identifies only the necessary properties for variables to qualify as state variables. As we will see, forthcoming chapters introduce various *multifactors* that augment the market factor in asset pricing models. To help visualize Merton's ICAPM, consider a two-factor model with the market factor plus a state variable denoted $s_1$. Now total systematic risk is comprised of beta coefficients$\beta_{i,M}$ and $\beta_{i,s_1}$ associated with the market factor and the state variable factor, respectively. Figure 6.1 provides a three-dimensional graph of this asset pricing model that shows the relation between expected excess returns and the two beta risks. Assets with relatively low $\beta_{i,s_1}$ risk are shown in dark dots and those with higher $\beta_{i,s_1}$ risk in gray dots (located further back in the three-dimensional space). As state variables are added to the ICAPM, more return/risk dimensions are created. How many dimensions of systematic risk do you think investors use in capital markets?

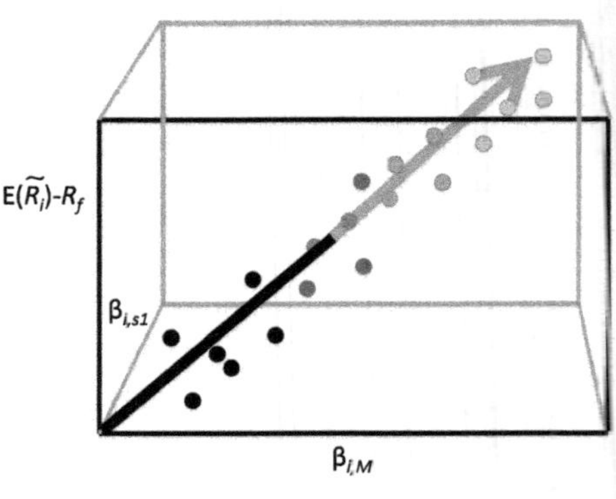


**Fig. 6.1** A three-dimensional depiction of an empirical ICAPM with two systematic beta risk factors: (1) market factor beta $\beta_{i,M}$, and (2) state variable beta $\beta_{i,s1}$

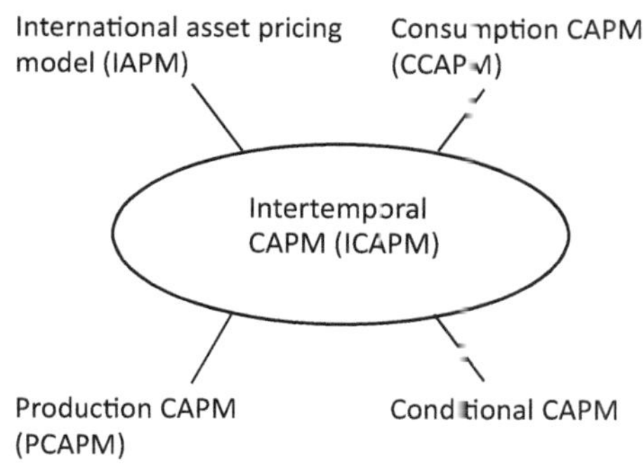


**Fig. 6.2** Alternative CAPM specifications based on the intertemporal CAPM (ICAPM)

At the end of his paper, reflecting on the ICAPM, Merton (1973, pp. 885–886) suggested future directions for research:

> The model is robust in the sense that it can be extended in an obvious way to include effects other than shifts in the investment opportunity set. Two important factors not considered are wage income and many consumption goods whose relative prices are changing over time. In a more complete model the three-fund theorem ... will generalize to an $m$-fund theory. Also, there was no discussion of the supply side, given a micro theory of the firm ... to close the model.

This forward-looking statement about the ICAPM turned out to be an accurate prediction of future equilibrium asset pricing models. As we will see in this chapter, new CAPMs were proposed by researchers that expand the breadth of the investment opportunity set to international markets (IAPM) as well as lifetime consumption behavior on the demand side of the market (CCAPM) and firm production on the supply side (PCAPM). Also, conditional CAPM methods were introduced to better capture time-varying risk parameters in asset pricing models. All these models are based on ICAPM as depicted in Fig. 6.2. The ICAPM provided a roadmap for CAPM researchers.

## 6.2 International Asset Pricing Model (IAPM)

### 6.2.1 World Market Factor

Solnick (1974a, b) extended the CAPM to an international asset pricing model (IAPM). The IAPM posits that equilibrium security prices are determined in an integrated world market comprised of different national markets. That is, capital flows move freely between different national stock markets in an inter-connected global market. By contrast, the CAPM posited a single national market, in which investors choose between the market portfolio and the riskless asset known as the *two fund theorem.* In Solnik's world market model, there is more than one riskless asset due to different interest rates in different countries. Also, there is exchange rate risk due to changes in the market values of different national currencies held by investors around the world. An international *three-fund theorem* is proposed, wherein investors can hold: (1) a world portfolio of stocks with no exchange rate risk (i.e., the market portfolio), (2) a portfolio of bonds with exchange rate risk but no market risk, and (3) the riskless asset of their own country. He derived the IAPM from the national market ICAPM of Merton (1973). Based on Merton's equilibrium pricing framework, Solnik (1974a, p. 515) specified the IAPM as follows:

$$E(R_i) - R_f = \beta_i[E(R_W) - R_B)], \tag{6.4}$$

where $R_f$ is the country riskless rate, $E(R_W)$ is the world stock market equity return (or market portfolio return), and $R_B$ is the average interest rate in the world or international bond rate. The riskless bond in a country is riskless to national investors but for foreign investors it represents a pure exchange risk asset that allows them to hedge their equity investment from exchange rate risk (i.e., a short position in the foreign bond). The $\beta_i$ coefficient measures the *international systematic risk* associated with the world stock market portfolio $W$. Bond portfolios $f$ and $B$ are different from one another. Notice that the world stock and bond portfolios are independent of investors' risk preferences and national citizenship. The risk premium of an asset in a country over its national riskless rate is proportional to its international systematic risk premium. Also, the IAPM says that all investors should buy a single world equity fund with market value weights.

Solnik (1974b, p. 541) stated the market model form of the IAPM as follows:

$$R_{it} - R_{ft} = \alpha_0 + \beta_i(R_{wt} - R_{bt}) + \epsilon_{it}, \tag{6.5}$$

where $R_{it} - R_f$ is asset $i$'s excess return over the national riskless rate at time $t$, $R_{wt} - R_{bt}$ is the international equity market excess return over the average world bond rate using proxies for $W$ and $B$, and $\epsilon_{it}$ are independent and normally distributed error terms. Solnick proceeded to test this international market model using stock returns in 10 major industrialized countries with data from March 1966 to April 1971. A value-weighted world stock market index return was constructed, whose weights were used to compute an average world bond index also. Regressing national excess market returns for each country on world excess stock market returns, the estimated $R^2$ values ranged from 14% to 52% across the 10 countries. The highest $R^2$ values were found in Switzerland and the Netherlands that are more international in scope than the other national markets. National beta estimates ranged from 0.43 to 1.30 with an average of 1.08. Hence, depending on the country, world equity market returns may or may not explain national stock market returns.

Solnik ran a cross-sectional regression on an in-sample basis as follows:

$$\bar{R}_{ct} - \bar{R}_{ft} = \lambda_0 + \lambda_w\hat{\beta}_i + u_{it}, \tag{6.6}$$

where $\bar{R}_{ct} - \bar{R}_{ft}$ is the average excess return in a country over the sample period, $\hat{\beta}_c$ is the estimated beta in Eq. (6.5) for each country in the sample period (i.e., $R_{it}$ for an individual asset is changed to $R_{ct}$ for the average stock market return for each country), and $\lambda_w$ is the estimated risk premium for international beta risk. He obtained $\lambda_w = 0.26$ with a highly significant $t$-statistic equal to 6.2. Since this is a two-week market risk premium, on an annual basis, it is fairly large at approximately 6.5% per year. These results strongly supported the IAPM. Further cross-sectional tests of individual stocks in the ten countries were conducted, but the results did not suggest that international market risk is significantly priced. To explain this finding, he cited Black et al. (1972), who recommended that portfolios should be used in cross-sectional tests to reduce or mitigate errors-in-the-variables problems in individual stock beta estimates. From these findings Solnik (1974b, p. 552) concluded that:

> Although stock prices of each country tend to move together, the international capital market seems to be sufficiently integrated and efficient to induce an inter-national pricing of risk of common stocks. While these results are in favor of the International Asset Pricing Model, they indicate that more efforts should be devoted to the study of international market structure in order to determine the stochastic process followed by security prices around the world.

Heeding this recommendation, in tests of $\alpha_0$ in time-series regression equation (6.5) using a global market factor and 13 industrialized countries, Fama and French (1998) found that the single world factor IAPM failed The intercept term was significantly greater than zero, which suggests that the model is incomplete in the sense that there is an error of omission in terms of missing factors. Confirming this problem, when they added a value factor (to be discussed in forthcoming Chapter 8) to the right-hand-side of the IAPM, the intercept was reduced to near zero in most cases. Consequently, they concluded that an " .. international two-factor model simply provides a parsimonious way to summarize the general patterns in international returns." (Fama and French 1998, p. 117) One interpretation of this finding is that the value factor captures a state variable per Merton's ICAPM that is missing from the single factor IAPM—that is, assuming that the world investment opportunity set is changing over time in response to state variables, an international IAPM exists that is comprised of a world market factor plus state variables or hedge portfolio factors.

Extending the Fama and French study, Griffin (2002) tested domestic versus global versions of the market model in the United States, United Kingdom, Canada, and Japan. Like them, they supplemented the market factor with other factors—namely, size and value factors based on firm-level characteristics. Global factors were computed as value-weighted averages of the domestic factors in the sample countries. Using stock returns from 1981 to 1995, a major finding was that domestic factors provided better goodness-of-fit to explain stock returns than global factors in the United States, Canada, the United Kingdom, and Japan.

Because tests of the $\alpha_0$ intercepts in both domestic and global models were significant in all but Japan, contrary to Fama and French, they rejected both domestic and global model specifications that contained both market and other factors.

Summarizing their findings, they inferred that stock markets around the world are not integrated with respect to risk factors that explain expected stock returns in different countries. In effect, contrary to Solnik's IAPM, stocks appear to be domestically rather than globally priced.[4] Following this study and other corroborating studies, researchers nowadays focus their investigations of asset returns and pricing factors on the national rather that global level. Apparently we will have to wait for world financial markets to become more fully integrated before Solnik's IAPM becomes a reality.

### 6.2.2 Exchange Rate Risk

Even though it is now generally accepted that assets are domestically (not globally) priced in financial markets, it is possible that the changing values of currencies can affect investors' security returns and therefore their risks. Imagine that you are a U.S. investor holding a European stock. In this case, you hold two assets: (1) the European stock, and (2) euro currency. Your return will be based on both the European stock return and the change in currency values of the dollar vis-à-vis euro. To see this, consider the following example.

1. As a U.S. investor, you exchange 100 dollars for 80 euros at the exchange rate 1 USD = 0.80 EUR or 1 EUR = 1.25 USD.
2. You buy 10 shares of a European stock for 80 euros.
3. One year later you sell the European stock for 100 euros. You earn a stock rate of return equal to $R_{iT} = (100 - 80)/80 = 25\%$ over period $T$.
4. Next, you exchange 100 euros for 130 dollars at the then exchange rate 1 USD = 0.77 EUR or 1 EUR = 1.30 USD. You earn a euro rate of return equal to $R_{xT}$ = (1.30 USD/EUR − 1.25 USD/EUR)/1.25 USD/EUR = 4.0%.
5. Your total return is $(1+R_{iT})(1+R_{xT}) - 1 = 1.25 \times 1.04 = 0.30$, or 30 %, which approximately equals the sum of the European stock return and the euro return, or 25% + 4.0% = 29.0%.

This example shows that exchange rate movements affect international investors' rates of returns on foreign assets.

A related but different question is: Do exchange rate movements affect the risk of the security investments themselves? That is, let's say that you are a U.S. investor and only buy domestic assets in the United States. Should you be concerned about how exchange risk in currency markets might affect the risks of your

---

[4] For an excellent survey of the issue of domestic (local) versus global asset pricing, see Karolyi and Stulz (2002).

U.S. investments? Given that exchange rates (e.g., USD/EUR) are more than 10 times more volatile than inflation rates based on consumer and producer prices, and most investors are concerned with inflation risk associated with potentially decreasing purchasing power, it seems likely that exchange rate risk would be an important risk factor.

To help answer the above question, Adler and Dumas (1984) defined *currency risk* as the random movement of currency values over time. Over 100 currencies exist in the world, many of which trade in currency markets on a daily basis. Indeed, the volume of currency trading on any given day exceeds that of any other asset class, including stocks, bonds, commodities, real estate, etc. The currency market is a large, inter-connected world market that is primarily managed by global corporate banks. Currencies can be classified as hard versus soft. Hard currencies are those of major industrialized countries, including the dollar, euro, pound, yen, etc. Soft currencies are those of developing countries and often are pegged to the values of hard currencies. Currency risk, as measured by the volatility of exchange rates of currencies over time, is generally higher for soft compared to hard currencies. Even so, the values of hard currencies in terms of exchange rates with other hard currencies can fluctuate considerably over time. Hence, currency risk is substantial in world currency markets.

According to Adler and Dumas, exchange rate risk is a different but related concept to currency risk that focuses on the sensitivity of a security to currency movements. More specifically, how does currency risk affect the risk of securities? Figure 6.3 illustrates the difference between currency risk and exchange rate risk. A company that is exporting its goods benefits from home currency depreciation as more foreigners would want to buy its goods, and vice versa in the case of appreciation. Also, given home currency appreciation, a goods importer experiences benefits from buying at lower costs than previously, and vice versa with depreciation. Hence, changes in exchange rates can impact the cash flows of exporting and importing firms. Since stock returns should reflect all information (in an efficient market) affecting the firm including the effects of exchange rate movements, they proposed that *exchange risk exposure* can be estimated for an investor in a home country by means of the following simple regression:

$$R_{it} = \alpha_0 + \beta_{i,x} R_{xt} + \epsilon_{it}, \qquad (6.7)$$

where $R_{it}$ is the return for the $i$th asset in the home country in time period $t$ (e.g., the dollar-denominated return for a security in the United States), and $R_{xt}$ is the rate of return on the spot exchange rate $x$ in period $t$ of dollars per euro, or $[USD/EUR_t - USD/EUR_{t-1}]/USD/EUR_{t-1}$.[5] Notice that the exchange rate $x$ is the home currency price of foreign currency (or $USD/EUR$ here). Importantly, the $\beta_{i,x}$ coefficient represents the total foreign exchange exposure of the stock as

[5] If $R_{xt} > 0$, we can infer a depreciation of the dollar against the euro, as each euro can buy more dollars at time $t$ than before at time $t-1$. If $R_{xt} < 0$, then the dollar appreciated against the euro.

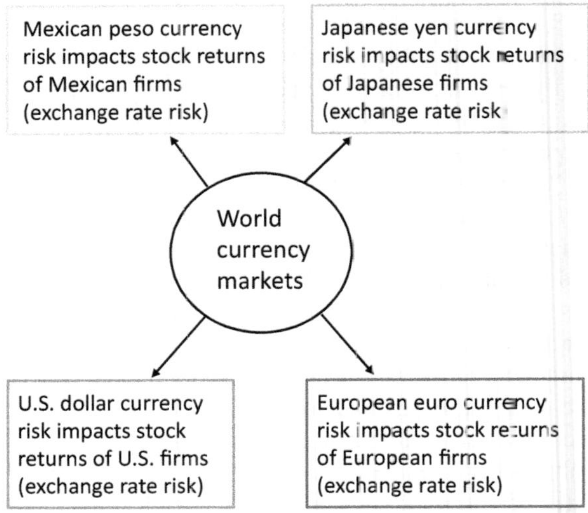


**Fig. 6.3** Currency risk in world currency markets affects the stock returns in different countries through their exchange rate risk exposure or sensitivity to national currency movements

measured by the elasticity of changes in stock prices in response to a change in exchange rates. Adler and Dumas (1984, p. 48) concluded:

> What the regression coefficient concept of exposure can provide is a single comprehensive measure that summarizes the sensitivity of the whole firm, as of a given future date, to all the various ways in which exchange rate changes can affect it.

Jorion (1990) implemented empirical tests of exchange rate risk. To do this, he modified the total exchange rate exposure equation (6.7) to take into account the market factor as follows:

$$R_{it} = \alpha_0 + \beta_{i,m} R_{mt} + \beta_{i,x} R_{xt} + \epsilon_{it}, \tag{6.8}$$

where the proxy return for the market portfolio $R_{mt}$ is augmented with exchange rate of return $R_{xt}$. He computed $R_{xt}$ as the rate of return on the USD per unit of a basket of currencies of 15 different countries (known as the Multilateral Exchange Rate Model or MERM of the International Monetary Fund).[6] Using U.S. returns in the sample period 1971 to 1987 when exchange rates were allowed to freely float in world currency markets, he found that most exchange risk coefficients, or $\beta_{i,x}$, were insignificant. In this period only 15-out-of-287 sample firms had significant exposure coefficients at the five percent level. Looking more closely at 40 large multinational firms that actively engage in international trade activities, he

[6] A more widely used currency basket by the IMF is the Special Drawing Right (SDR) consisting of currencies in the United States, Europe, Japan, and the United Kingdom. The Federal Reserve in the United States constructs a number of other currency baskets. In general, currency baskets are formed using trade weights of the different exchange rates.

detected significant exposure coefficients. Further tests confirmed that firms with more foreign sales as a percentage of total sales had larger foreign exchange risk exposure coefficients.

We can summarize the early empirical evidence on foreign exchange risk and valuation as mixed. Most stocks' returns do not appear to be exposed to foreign exchange risk. However, the values of multinational firms and firms with relatively high foreign sales are significantly affected by foreign exchange risk. Many other researchers have investigated the exposure of stocks to currency movements. Due to the lack of exposure for most companies despite volatile movements in exchange rates over time, many researchers consider this weak evidence to be one of the most perplexing puzzles in modern asset pricing.

## 6.3 Consumption CAPM

Seminal work by Lucas (1978) and Breeden (1979) proposed a consumption CAPM (CCAPM) version of the CAPM. Both authors employed the ICAPM framework of Merton (1973). Instead of a market beta related to the expected excess return on the market portfolio, a consumption beta was proposed. Also, while the CAPM is a one-period model based on the mean and variance of returns, the CCAPM is an intertemporal model in which investors maximize expected lifetime utility. Consumers buy and sell financial assets over time to smooth their consumption of goods. For example, they sell (buy) assets when times are bad (good) to maintain their consumption needs.

Lucas derived the CCAPM under simple assumptions about the economy. There is one consumer (a representative agent) that seeks to maximize their expected lifetime utility from one good. The consumer can buy dividend-paying shares in companies that make the good in the financial market to form a portfolio of financial assets. Stock prices fluctuate over time with the state of the economy. The consumer seeks to optimize their holdings of both the good and portfolio over time to maximize their lifetime expected utility. A key insight is that the marginal rate of substitution of current for future consumption by the consumer is equivalent to the rate of return on a stock. This means that consumption is equivalent to dividends over time.

Lucas posited that intertemporal patterns of consumption and financial asset transactions exist. The consumer will seek assets with negative covariances with their consumption, which results in low risk premiums for these assets. They will sell financial assets when the economy is in a recession to supplement their consumption which has decreased due to lower income at such times. Conversely, assets with positive covariances with their consumption pattern (i.e., low values when consumption is lower) will not be desired by investors and, therefore, will have higher risk premiums to get people to hold them. In good economic times, consumers will buy financial assets as incomes are higher to meet consumption needs. Hence, as shown in Fig. 6.4, the lifetime pattern of consumption is smoothed by means of buying and selling financial assets over time.

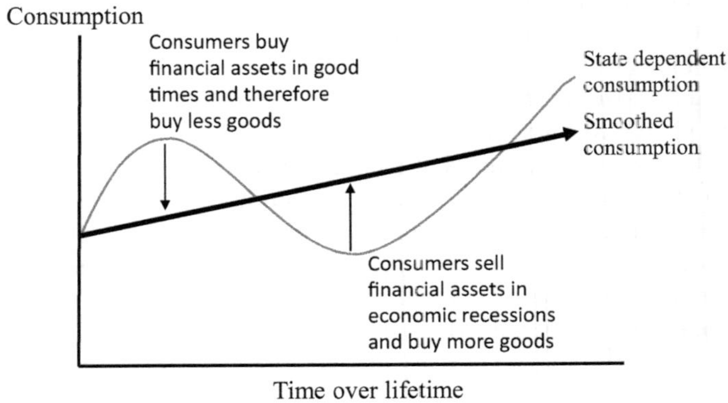


**Fig. 6.4** Consumers buy and sell financial assets over time to smooth consumption in the consumption CAPM (CCAPM)

In his model, the expected return on asset $i$ at time $t$ is generally expressed as:

$$E(R_{it}) - R_{ft} = -\frac{1}{E[U(C_t)]} Cov[U(C_t), R_{it}], \tag{6.9}$$

where $E[U(C_t)]$ is the expected utility from consumption (i.e., its expected value to the consumer), and $Cov[U(C_t), R_{it}]$ is the covariance of consumption utility and asset returns related to systematic risk that cannot be diversified away by the consumer. In this context, $\beta_i$ is represented by the right-hand-side term. Assets with negative covariance have higher risk premiums, and positive covariance assets have lower risk premiums. Negative covariance assets offer insurance against bad times and therefore tend to smooth consumption, whereas positive covariance assets do not smooth consumption at such times.

Breeden (1979, p. 266) proposed a CCAPM that closely follows the Lucas model:

> ... it is shown that Merton's multi-beta pricing equation can be collapsed into a single-beta equation, where the instantaneous expected excess return on any security is proportional to its 'beta' (or covariance) with respect to aggregate consumption alone.

Since the CCAPM focuses on an easily identified variable (viz., aggregate consumption) rather than a number of unspecified variables (e.g., the difficult to proxy market portfolio in the CAPM), he argued that it can be readily implemented and tested. Assuming there is an asset with returns perfectly correlated with aggregate consumption over time, he specified excess asset returns as follows:

$$E(R_{it}) - R_t = -\beta_C[E(R_{Ct}) - R_t], \tag{6.10}$$

where $E(R_C) - R_t$ is the excess return on aggregate consumption of the perfectly correlated asset (e.g., over the riskless rate or zero-beta portfolio rate), and $\beta_C$ is the consumption beta at each instant in time $t$. As in Lucas, asset values are negatively related to their covariance with respect to aggregate consumption. Higher (lower) expected returns on assets are related to larger (smaller) covariances with aggregate consumption. He contended that wealth in the CAPM was not a sufficient measure of the marginal utility of a dollar to the investor. There can be states of the world when wealth is low but the marginal utility of a dollar could be low also. However, it is always true that, when the marginal utility of a dollar is high, consumption is low in that state, and vice versa. Due to this rationale, he claimed that the CCAPM using consumption beta was more appropriate than the CAPM market beta in the determination of equilibrium expected rates of return. Hence, from a theoretical perspective, consumption beta is more justified than market beta.

According to Breedon, one potential problem in empirically testing the CCAPM is that consumption is measured with error in the real world. Despite this issue, he asserted that measured consumption reflects a greater fraction of total consumption than proxies used for the market portfolio that typically only include stocks (for example) to the exclusion of other asset classes (e.g., bonds, commodities, real estate, etc.). In other words, empirical proxies for aggregate consumption in the CCAPM enable better tests of the theory than those used to test the CAPM. As discussed in Chapters 4 and 5, consistent with the Roll (1977) critique, it could be that evidence against the CAPM is due to bad proxies for the market portfolio.

Breeden et al. (1989) provided an early test of the CCAPM. In the period 1959 to 1982, they measured aggregate consumption in two ways: (1) quarterly changes in nondurable goods and services, and (2) a stock portfolio with maximum correlation with the growth in aggregate consumption. Also, the CAPM was comparatively tested using the CRSP value-weighted index to proxy for the market portfolio. Their results showed that market betas and consumption betas are highly correlated at 0.96 and 0.94 for the two consumption proxies respectively.

Using estimated betas, the authors conducted cross-sectional Fama and MacBeth (1973) tests of the CCAPM. Test assets included 17 portfolios comprised of 12 industry stock portfolios, four bond portfolios, and the CRSP value-weighted index. In summary, they found the following results.

1. Plots of expected returns and estimated consumption betas revealed relatively flat lines consistent with early tests of the CAPM. Given the high correlation between market and consumption betas, this finding is not surprising.
2. The significance of the market price of consumption risk (as measured by estimated $\lambda_C$ coefficients on estimated betas) was mixed for different sample periods. In some samples, consumption risk is priced, but in others it is not.
3. Cross-sectional regression models had small estimated intercept terms $\lambda_0$. This finding was interpreted as more consistent with a riskless rate than a zero-beta portfolio borrowing rate.
4. Both the CRSP value-weighted index and maximum correlation portfolio with consumption (which were highly correlated with one another) were not mean-variance efficient. This inference was based on joint tests that rejected all $\alpha_0$

terms in a time-series regression model equaled zero. Their results indicated weak cross-sectional evidence for both the CAPM and CCAPM.

In later tests of the CCAPM by other researchers, similar findings have been reported. For this reason, as new asset pricing models evolved, especially multi-factor models covered in forthcoming Chapters 8 and 9, most researchers augment the market factor with other proposed factors. As we will see, multifactor models were a major advance over the CAPM in terms of their ability to explain average stock returns.

## 6.4 Production CAPM

Cochrane (1991) developed a production CAPM (PCAPM) that is based on producers and production functions instead of consumers and consumption functions in the CCAPM. He observed that stock returns are generally accepted to be forward looking in that they forecast future economic activity, including business investment and GNP growth. More specifically, the PCAPM links asset returns to the production function—high expected returns are explained by high business investment growth. Firms put to work labor and capital to produce consumption goods. Similar to the logic of the CCAPM, investment returns on capital (used in private firm production) equal the return on a portfolio of assets over time (e.g., stock returns). Figure 6.5 gives an example of this proposition with forecasts of stock returns and capital investment returns that are highly correlated over time. Thus, both the PCAPM and CCAPM connect real economic activity (and associated macroeconomic risks) and expected stock returns. We can think of the CCAPM as a demand side theory (consumers) and the PCAPM as a supply side theory (producers). In equilibrium, given the law of one price for each asset, these two theories are flip sides of the same coin.

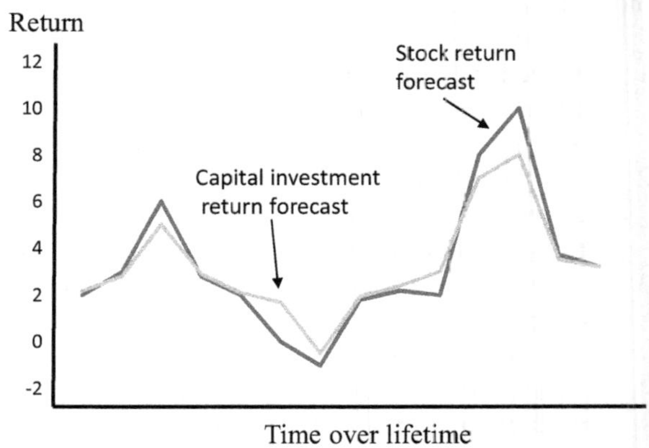


**Fig. 6.5** Close relation between stock return and capital investment forecasts in the production CAPM (PCAPM)

A model of the form of CCAPM relation (6.10) can be specified to represent the PCAPM. Rather than using the growth rate of aggregate consumption, Cochrane constructed an investment/capital ratio $(I/k)_t$ at time $t$. Quarterly data series were computed from 1947 to 1987. Based on a variety of tests, among other findings, he found a positive correlation between forecasts of capital/investment ratios and stock returns. This time-series evidence provided some support for the PCAPM.

In a second paper, Cochrane (1996) published more in-depth cross-sectional asset pricing tests of the PCAPM. Because the tests did not explicitly model a pure production model, he referred to the empirical specification as an investment-based model. In this indirect test of the PCAPM, he hypothesized the following single factor model:

$$R_{it} - R_{ft} = \alpha_0 + \beta_i(R_{It} - R_{ft}) + \epsilon_{it}, \tag{6.11}$$

where $R_{It}$ is the investment return equal to the extra output sold by the firm upon investing in an additional unit of capital, $R_{ft}$ is the riskless rate, and $\beta_i$ is the investment beta. Here investment returns represent an asset pricing factor for asset returns. His analyses employed investment returns for both nonresidential and residential gross investments on a quarterly basis in the United States. Using 10 portfolios sorted into size deciles as test assets, cross-sectional regression $\lambda$ estimates were not significant for the nonresidential investments factor but negatively significant for the residential investments factor.

Further tests conditioned these investment factors on market variables—namely, the term premium and dividend/price ratio of a stock market index—to allow for time variation in the beta loadings or coefficient estimates over time. In the next subsection, we overview conditional asset pricing models. On a conditional basis, both investment factors were significant. Also, he tested the CAPM and CCAPM and found that the investment-based CAPM performed similar to the CAPM but outperformed the CCAPM.[7] Cochrane (1996, p. 615) concluded that:

> The simple investment return model performs surprisingly well. The investment return factors significantly price assets, the model is not rejected, and it is able to explain a wide spread in expected returns ...

The PCAPM draws an important link between investment in the real sector of the economy and asset returns in the financial sector. The fact that the conditional model improved its performance suggests that risk parameters are time-varying over the business cycle. Good and bad economic times are relevant to asset pricing. We next take a closer look at conditional models and their empirical setup.

---

[7] Also, he tested a five-factor model by Chen et al. (1986) that contains the growth in industrial production and some inflation and interest rate variables. Like the CAPM, the performance of this multifactor model was similar to the PCAPM.

## 6.5 Conditional CAPM

The CAPM and its companion models are unconditional models that normally assume that expected returns are constant, the market factor and other factors can be measured, and assets' betas are fairly constant (or stationary) over time. Cross-sectional tests of asset pricing models regress unconditional expected returns on unconditional betas. However, considerable research has shown that expected returns and estimated betas of stocks vary considerably over time. That is, beta moves up and down in the financial market. Why does this happen? One explanation is that beta risk could change over the business cycle. In a recession, when economic activity is depressed and the risk of business failure is higher than normal, beta risks of companies prone to bankruptcy (e.g., due to high debt on their balance sheet) are likely to be higher than otherwise.

The unconditional CAPM implies that expected excess returns are proportional to market beta:

$$E(r_{it}) = \frac{E(r_{mt})}{\sigma^2(r_{mt})} Cov(r_{it}, R_{mt}), \tag{6.12}$$

where lowercase $r$ denotes excess returns $E(R_{it}) - R_{ft}$, and the familiar unconditional beta is defined as $\beta_i = Cov(R_{it}, R_{mt})/\sigma^2(R_{mt})$. Recognizing the contributions of numerous authors, including Hansen and Hodrick (1983), Gibbons and Ferson (1985), Ferson et al. (1987), Harvey (1989), and Shanken (1990), we follow Harvey by writing the conditional form of this expression as follows:

$$E(r_{it}|I_{t-1}) = \frac{E(r_{mt}|I_{t-1})}{\sigma^2(r_{mt}|I_{t-1})} Cov(r_{it}, r_{mt}|I_{t-1}), \tag{6.13}$$

where expected excess returns and the covariance of excess returns with excess market returns are conditional on previous information $I_{t-1}$ in the financial markets, and the conditional beta is $\beta_{it} = Cov[r_{it}, r_{mt}|I_{t-1}]/\sigma^2(r_{mt}|I_{t-1})$. In line with this logic, a conditional CAPM can be specified as:

$$E(r_{it}|I_{t-1}) = \beta_{it} E(r_{mt}|I_{t-1}), \tag{6.14}$$

where $\beta_{it}$ has a time subscript to indicate variation over time.

Following Cochrane (1996) discussed in the previous section,[8] factors can be scaled with instruments that are related to financial market variables. This instrumental approach is consistent with the ICAPM of Merton, who proposed that the investment opportunity set of investors changes over time conditional on time-varying state variables. For example, we can scale the market factor (or any risk

---

[8] See also Cochrane (2005, Section 8.4).

factor) by specifying a conditional (time-varying) beta as a linear function[9]:

$$\beta_{it} = \beta_{0i} + \beta_{1i} I_{t-1}, \tag{6.15}$$

where $\beta_0$ is the unconditional CAPM beta, and $I_{t-1}$ is a time-varying financial market variable that scales beta to different values over time. The lagged variable $I_{t-1}$ is known as an *instrument* to help capture the time-varying conditional beta. If we also assume that the intercept term is conditional, so that $\alpha_{it} = \alpha_{0i} + \alpha_{1i} I_t$, the conditional form of the market model can be estimated as:

$$r_{it} = (\alpha_{0i} + \alpha_{1i} I_{t-1}) + (\beta_{0i} + \beta_{1i} I_{t-1}) r_{mt} + \epsilon_{it} \tag{6.16}$$

$$r_{it} = \alpha_{0i} + \alpha_{1i} I_{t-1} + \beta_{0i} r_{mt} + \beta_{1i} (r_{mt} I_{t-1}) + \epsilon_{it}. \tag{6.17}$$

Here $\alpha_{0i}$ and $\beta_{0i}$ are the unconditional alpha and beta denoted earlier as $\alpha_i$ and $\beta_i$, respectively. The new intercept $\alpha_1 I_{t-1}$ varies over time with $I_{t-1}$. Also, the new beta estimate $\beta_{1i}$ relates excess turns to the interaction variable $r_{mt} I_{t-1}$, which is computed as excess market returns $r_{mt}$ times variable $I_{t-1}$ at time $t$.

In effect, the conditional approach changes the single factor market model into a multifactor model with a market factor plus an interaction factor. As an example, Petkova and Zhang (2005) used a variety of financial market variables, including default premiums on bonds, dividend yields, Treasury bill rates, and the term premiums on bonds, as instruments in a conditional CAPM. In this regard, any variable that could affect market risk over time is a feasible instrument.

Does time variation in beta explain the weak evidence for the CAPM? Research evidence appears to be mixed in this regard. For example, Lettau and Ludvigson (2001) compared both unconditional and conditional versions of the CAPM and CCAPM to the three-factor model of Fama and French (1992, 1993, 1995). They instrumented betas with the aggregate consumption/wealth ratio in the United States computed quarterly from 1968 to 1998. The three-factor model is a multifactor model covered in Chapter 8 that has proven to better explain average stock returns than the CAPM. It is comprised of market, size, and value factors, where the latter two factors are based on firm characteristics. In cross-sectional tests, the authors found that the conditional CCAPM performed as well as the three-factor model, which supports the conditional approach.

By contrast, other research by Lewellen and Nagel (2006) did not find support for the conditional CAPM. Since it is not known what instruments a researcher should use in the conditional CAPM, they estimated beta over a large number of short intervals of time to capture its time variation and that of alpha terms also.

[9] Beyond the scope of the present discussion, a first-order Taylor series can be used to approximate the potentially complex effects of an instrument on factor loadings. Taylor series are well known in the sciences and represent an infinite sum of derivatives of a mathematical function at a single point.

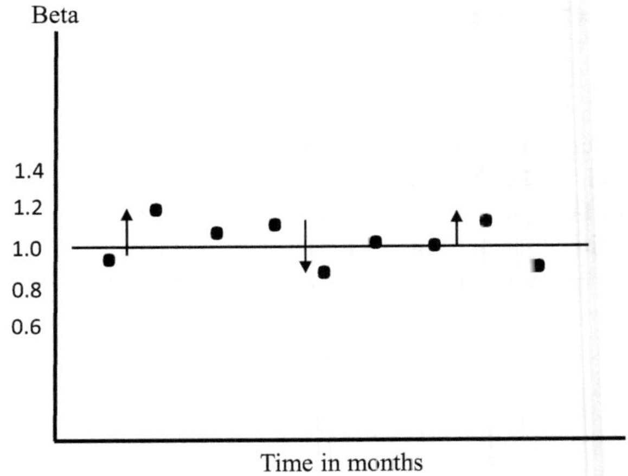


**Fig. 6.6** Beta estimates for the market factor tend to vary randomly over time consistent with the unconditional CAPM but contrary to the conditional CAPM

Using U.S. stock returns from 1964 to 2001, they reported that betas change over time but not sufficiently to explain weak evidence for the CAPM. Also, beta variation over time could not account for the size and value factors of Fama and French or the momentum factor is to be discussed in Chapter 8.

Figure 6.6 gives an illustration of beta for a factor varying considerably over time in a random fashion. Here beta is not moving in a regular pattern that would suggest an underlying state variable (e.g., macroeconomy, firm characteristic, etc.). Consistent with this observation, Lewellen and Nagel found that the conditional CAPM did not improve upon the unconditional CAPM in time-series intercept ($\alpha_0$) tests as well as modifications of Lettau and Ludvigson cross-sectional tests. Similar inferences were made in comparisons of the conditional and unconditional consumption CAPM (CCAPM). Because conditional alphas ($\alpha_0$s) were large and significant, they concluded that the conditional CAPM did not hold.[10] This evidence suggests that business cycle effects in asset pricing models are not sufficiently large to invalidate unconditional models.

Nowadays, most asset pricing studies do not incorporate the business cycle in their analyses. Long periods of time are used that contain a number business cycles with economic expansions and recessions. Of course, results of different models can vary over time and this may indeed be due to the influence of a business cycle in the sample period used by a researcher. Nonetheless, regardless of the economic state, a valid asset pricing model should do a good job of measuring returns with respect to various systematic risks.

[10] Simin (2008) also found that conditional versions of the CAPM and Fama and French three-factor model did not outperform their unconditional versions in terms of one-month-ahead cross-sectional tests of their predictive ability.

## 6.6 Summary

Early evidence that weakly supported the CAPM sparked researchers to develop alternative specifications in an effort to be more compatible with real-world conditions in capital markets. Merton's (1973) famous intertemporal CAPM (ICAPM) extended the single-period or static CAPM to multiple periods. Investors make decisions about their future wealth over their lifetime and even beyond to their heirs. In this more realistic situation, the investment opportunity set facing investors can change over time. He believed that state variables explain the shifting opportunity set, which itself introduces new risks for investors. Investors can form hedge portfolios to manage risks associated with state variables. These portfolios are factors not taken into account by the single market factor CAPM. His three-fund theorem introduced a third asset or portfolio that is perfectly negatively correlated with the riskless rate (i.e., the CAPM's two-fund theorem includes the market portfolio and riskless asset). Practically speaking, the ICAPM can be empirically modeled by adding multifactors beyond the market factor to the market model. Unfortunately, the ICAPM does not identify the state variables that investors use in the real world to price assets.

Merton's landmark ICAPM stimulated the development of CAPM variants. The international asset pricing model (IAPM) of Solnik (1974a, 1974b) broadened the scope of the CAPM from a single national market to an integrated world market with inter-connected national markets. Now investors face exchange rate risk associated with currency movements that was not present in the CAPM. Solnik's IAPM specifies excess returns of assets as a function of beta times of the world stock market premium over the average interest rate on a global portfolio of bonds. Cross-sectional tests of 10 countries supported the IAPM in terms of a significant world market price of risk (or $\lambda_w$). He concluded that national stock markets are integrated globally. However, later evidence by Fama and French (1998) and Griffin (2002) did not support the IAPM due to significant $\alpha_0$ intercept terms greater than zero in the time-series regression estimation of the empirical IAPM. Even though national stock markets are not internationally integrated, and asset pricing is therefore domestic (or local) rather than global in nature, currency risk related to volatile exchange rates can affect stock returns. Adler and Dumas (1984) advocated that exchange rate exposure of stocks can influence returns. Empirical tests by Jorion (1990) confirmed this conjecture but with mixed evidence. Primarily stocks of large multinational firms engaged in international trade activities were affected by exchange rate movements but not most other stocks. Due to the general insensitivity of most stocks to fairly volatile currency movements over time, an exchange rate risk puzzle persists.

Another extension by Lucas (1978) and Breeden (1979) used the ICAPM to derive a consumption CAPM (CCAPM). In this model, beta is related to consumption rather than the market portfolio in the CAPM. Investors seek to maximize their expected lifetime utility of consumption. By buying and selling financial assets, they smooth their consumption over time. This consumption smoothing behavior causes investors to prefer assets with negative covariances between returns and consumption (which benefits them in bad states such as an economic recession), thereby reducing risk premiums on these assets. By contrast, positive covariance assets have relatively higher risk premiums. In general, systematic risk for assets is dependent on the state of the economy over time and related consumption behavior. Despite some empirical advantages of the CCAPM, such as the ability to obtain better proxies for aggregate consumption than the CAPM's market portfolio, stock market tests by Breeden et al. (1989) showed that the CCAPM did not provide a better fit to returns than the CAPM. Again, a relatively flat relation between expected returns and estimated consumption betas was obtained. This finding is not surprising in view of the very high correlation between market betas and consumption betas.

Related to the CCAPM with consumers and consumption functions, Cochrane (1991) proposed the production CAPM (PCAPM) based on producers and production functions. Stock returns are forward-looking forecasts of future economic activity and the related production function. While the CCAPM focuses on the supply side (consumers) in the economy, the PCAPM takes a demand side (producers) perspective. He showed that the investment/capital ratio is positively correlated with stock returns. Also, he tested an investment-based version of the PCAPM that performed similar to (better than) the CAPM (CCAPM) in cross-sectional tests.

Lastly, the conditional CAPM was developed by numerous authors to take into account time-varying risk parameters in asset pricing models (or betas). In this regard, it is reasonable to believe that risk parameters will change in response to the business cycle with economic expansions and recessions. To model time-varying risk parameters, lagged instrumental variables are introduced that model beta coefficients as a function of financial market variables. In this way, the unconditional CAPM is extended to conditional state variables consistent with the ICAPM. Evidence by Lettau and Ludvigson (2001) supported the conditional CAPM in cross-sectional tests. However, Lewellen and Nagel (2006) later conducted direct tests of betas in short intervals of time and found that betas did not change sufficiently over time to justify the conditional CAPM.

Overall, the ICAPM and its derivative CAPMs have enhanced our understanding of asset pricing. No doubt these models will play an important role in future research and development.

## Questions

1. Merton (1973) developed the intertemporal CAPM (ICAPM). What is different about the ICAPM compared to the CAPM? What new assumption does it make?
2. In the ICAPM, how do investors respond to unfavorable shifts in future investment opportunities? What are state variables?
3. In the ICAPM, what is the three-fund theorem? In view of this theorem, write the equation for the ICAPM.

4. In the ICAPM, if correlations $\rho_{iN} = 0$ for all securities *i*, which also implies that $\rho_{NM} = 0$ (where *M* is the market portfolio), but $r_N$ is perfectly negatively correlated with $R_f$ (which is true by definition), the correlations of stocks with the future riskless rate would be zero. What happens to the ICAPM is this special case? What is the beta of security *N* in this case? Is *N* related to the zero-beta portfolio of Black in this case? If the market beta $\beta_{i,M} = 0$ but $\beta_{i,N} > 0$, is the expected return on the *i* asset equal to the riskless rate?
5. Solnik (1974) proposed an international asset pricing model (IAPM) based on an international three-fund theorem. What is this theorem and how does it change the CAPM? Write the equation for the IAPM and discuss Solnik's model.
6. How did Adler and Dumas (1984) define currency risk? How is currency risk different than exchange rate risk? How did they propose to measure the exchange risk exposure of a security? Write an equation that can be used to measure this exposure.
7. Jorion (1990) investigated the exchange risk exposure of U.S. stocks. He modified the total exchange risk exposure equation of Adler and Dumas (1984) in what way? What did he find?
8. Lucas (1978) and Breeden (1979) proposed the consumption CAPM (CCAPM) using the ICAPM framework of Merton (1973). In this model, consumers buy and sell financial assets over time to smooth consumption and maximize lifetime expected utility. What assets will consumers seek? Why? How does it affect the risk premiums on these assets? What happens to other assets?
9. Breeden (1979) specified a CCAPM that collapses the multi-beta Merton (1973) ICAPM into a single-beta equation. Write this model and define its variables and parameters. Why did he believe that the CCAPM was a better model than the CAPM from a theoretical perspective as well as in terms of empirical testing? Later work by Breeden et al. (1989) conducted empirical tests of the CCAPM. What did they find?
10. Cochrane (1991, 1996) created a production CAPM (PCAPM). How is the PCAPM different from the consumption CAPM (CCAPM)? He tested it using a single factor model. Write the equation for this model and discuss his results. What did he conclude?
11. Assume that we scale the market factor with an instrumental lagged variable denoted as $I_{t-1}$. Write a conditional (time-varying) linear function for beta and define its terms. Assuming that the alpha term is conditional also, incorporate this instrument into the market model and discuss the parameters in this conditional form of the market model.
12. Does time-variation in beta explain the weak evidence for the CAPM? Discuss empirical results of studies testing conditional CAPMs.

## Problems

1. Write the ICAPM as a multifactor model with state variables. What could be used to proxy for the state variables?
2. Write the market model form of Solnik's IAPM. Solnik ran this model on 10 major industrialized countries from 1966 to 1971. What did he find? What did cross-sectional regression tests find? What did later authors find in testing the IAPM?
3. Assume that you are a U.S. investor buying a European stock:
   1. You exchange 100 dollars for 90 euros at the exchange rate 1 USD = 0.90 EUR or 1 EUR = 1.11 USD.
   2. You buy 10 shares of a European stock for 90 euros.
   3. One year later you sell the European stock for 100 euros. You exchange the 100 euros for 120 dollars at the exchange rate 1 USD = 0.83 EUR or 1 EUR = 1.20 USD.

   What is your stock rate of return? What is your euro rate of return? What is your total return?

## References


Adler, M., and D. Bernard. 1984. Exposure to currency risk: Definition and measurement. *Financial Management* 13: 41–50.

Black, F. 1972. Capital market equilibrium with restricted borrowing. *Journal of Business* 45: 444–454.

Black, F., M.C. Jensen, and M. Scholes. 1972. The capital asset pricing model: Some empirical tests. In *Studies in the Theory of Capital Markets*, ed. M.C. Jensen. New York, NY: Praeger.

Breeden, N.D. 1979. An intertemporal asset pricing model with stochastic consumption and investment opportunities. *Journal of Financial Economics* 7: 265–296.

Breeden, N.D., M.R. Gibbons, and R.H. Litzenberger. 1989. Empirical tests of the consumption-oriented CAPM. *Journal of Finance* 44: 231–262.

Chen, N., R. Roll, and S.A. Ross. 1986. Economic forces and the stock market. *Journal of Business* 59: 383–404.

Cochrane, J.H. 1991. Production-based asset pricing and the link between stock returns and economic fluctuations. *Journal of Finance* 46: 209–237.

Cochrane, J.H. 1996. A cross-sectional test of an investment-based asset pricing model. *Journal of Political Economy* 104: 572–621.

Cochrane, J.H. 2005. *Asset Pricing*. Revised. Princeton, NJ: Princeton University Press.

Fama, E. F. 1970. Multiperiod consumption-investment decisions. *American Economic Review* 60: 163–174.

Fama, E.F., and K.R. French. 1992. The cross-section of expected stock returns. *Journal of Finance* 47: 427–465.

Fama, E.F., and K.R. French. 1993. The cross-section of expected returns. *Journal of Financial Economics* 33: 3–56.

Fama, E.F., and K.R. French. 1995. Size and book-to-market factors in earnings and returns. *Journal of Finance* 50: 131–156.

Fama, E.F., and K.R. French. 1998. Value versus growth: The international evidence. *Journal of Finance* 53: 1975–1999.

Fama, E.F., and J.D. MacBeth. 1973. Risk, return, and equilibrium: Empirical tests. *Journal of Political Economy* 81: 607–636.

Jorion, P. 1990. The exchange-rate exposure of U.S. multinationals. *Journal of Business* 63: 331–345.

Ferson, W.E., S. Kandel, and R.F. Stambaugh. 1987. Tests of asset pricing with time-varying expected risk premiums and market betas. *Journal of Finance* 42: 201–220.

Gibbons, M.R., and W.E. Ferson. 1985. Testing asset pricing models with changing expectations and an unobservable market portfolio. *Journal of Financial Economics* 14: 217–236.

Griffin, J.M. 2002. Are the Fama French factors global or country specific? *Review of Financial Studies* 15: 783–803.

Hansen, L.P., and R.J. Hodrick. 1983. Risk averse speculation in the forward foreign exchange market: An econometric analysis of linear models. In *Exchange Rates and Iinternational Macroeconomics*, ed. J.A. Frenkel. Chicago, IL: University of Chicago Press.

Harvey, C.R. 1989. Time-varying conditional covariances in tests of asset pricing models. *Journal of Financial Economics* 24: 289–317.

Karolyi, G.A., and R.M. Stulz. 2002. Are financial assets priced locally or globally?’. In *The Handbook of the Economics of Finance*, ed. G. Constantinides, M. Harris, and R. Stulz. Amsterdam, Netherlands: North Holland Publishing Co.

Kolari, J.W., W. Liu, and J.Z. Huang. 2021. *A New Model of Capital Asset Prices: Theory and Evidence*. Cham, Switzerland: Palgrave Macmillan.

Lettau, M., and S. Ludvigson. 2001. Resurrecting the (C)CAPM: A cross-sectional test when risk premia are time-varying. *Journal of Political Economy* 109: 1238–1287.

Lewellen, J., and S. Nagel. 2006. The conditional CAPM does not explain asset pricing anomalies. *Journal of Financial Economics* 82: 289–413.

Lucas, R.E. 1978. Asset prices in an exchange economy. *Econometrica* 46: 1429–1445.

Merton, R.C. 1973. An intertemporal capital asset pricing model. *Econometrica* 41: 867–887.

Petkova, R., and L. Zhang. 2005. Is value riskier than growth? *Journal of Financial Economics* 78: 187–202.

Roll, R. 1977. A critique of the asset pricing theory’s tests, part I: On past and potential future testability of the theory. *Journal of Financial Economics* 4: 129–176.

Ross, S.A. 1976. The arbitrage theory of capital asset pricing. *Journal of Economic Theory* 13: 341–360.

Shanken, J. 1990. Intertemporal asset pricing: An empirical investigation. *Journal of Econometrics* 45: 99–120.

Simin, T. 2008. The poor performance of asset pricing models. *Journal of Financial and Quantitative Analysis* 43: 335–380.

Solnik, B.H. 1974a. The international pricing of risk: An empirical investigation of the world capital market structure. *Journal of Finance* 29: 365–378.

Solnik, B.H. 1974b. An international market model of security price behavior. *Journal of Financial and Quantitative Analysis* 9: 537–554.

# 7 The Arbitrage Pricing Theory Model

One of the most controversial assumptions of the CAPM is that returns are normally distributed, which implies that agents have quadratic utility functions. This assumption guarantees the mean-variance efficiency of the market portfolio. Also, it leads to a linear equilibrium relation between the expected return on an asset and its sensitivity to the expected market premium (i.e., beta risk). This implied linear relation is widely accepted due to its sound intuition and easy empirical specification.

Taking linearity as a starting premise, Ross (1971, 1974, 1976) developed the *arbitrage pricing theory* (APT).[1] The APT depends on no-arbitrage conditions in the financial market. The underlying intuition is that the total variation of the return on a single asset stems from a (small) number of common factors and a random idiosyncratic residual term. Although the APT is based on the similar intuition of linearity in the CAPM, it is much more general. This chapter discusses briefly the concept of no arbitrage, introduces the basic idea of Ross's APT model, and reviews empirical tests of the model. Huberman and Wang (2017) give an excellent overview of the APT and its practical applications.

[1] See also Huberman (1982).

**Supplementary Information** The online version contains supplementary material available at https://doi.org/10.1007/978-3-031-16784-3_7.



J. W. Kolari and S. Pynnönen, *Investment Valuation and Asset Pricing*,
https://doi.org/10.1007/978-3-031-16784-3_7

## 7.1 APT Model

### 7.1.1 Assumptions

The key assumption of the *arbitrage pricing theory* (APT) is the absence of arbitrage opportunities. Another important assumption is that there are common risk factors that are linearly related to individual asset returns. Other assumptions, including the normality of returns that implies investors have quadratic utility functions, are similar to the CAPM. Summarizing these starting conditions, the APT assumes : (1) risk-averse investors; (2) investors can hold long and short positions including borrowing and lending at the same rate; and (3) capital markets are perfectly competitive and frictionless. The most important distinction between the APT and CAPM is replacing the CAPM assumption of homogeneous expectations about the distribution of assets' returns with homogeneous beliefs about the linear factor model of returns. Because the CAPM leads to a linear relationship between expected returns and the market portfolio with completely diversifiable return-specific idiosyncratic risk, the CAPM meets the no-arbitrage condition of the APT and, therefore, can be considered as a special case of APT.

### 7.1.2 Theoretical Model

We can introduce the basic idea of the APT model in terms of a single factor model with the following return generating process:

$$R_i = E(R_i) + \beta_i F + \epsilon_i, \tag{7.1}$$

where $R_i$ is the random rate of return on the $i$th asset, $E(R_i)$ is the expected return on the $i$th asset, $\beta_i$ is the sensitivity of the $i$th asset's return with respect to a factor, $F$ is a random common factor with respect to all returns with $E(F) = 0$, and $\epsilon_i$ is the random error term idiosyncratic to the $i$th asset that is not correlated with $F$ or the error terms of other assets, and $i = 1, \ldots, n$ assets which is assumed to be a large number.

The no-arbitrage condition has two main features: (1) no wealth; and (2) no risk must earn zero return on average. These features are easy to understand in terms of riskless returns. If $R_f$ and $R_f^*$ are two riskless rates that differ, then borrowing at the lower rate and investing in the higher rate would generate a possibility to earn unlimited riskless returns generated by the interest rate difference. As another example, Fig. 7.1 shows how to arbitrage riskless profits by buying underpriced assets and selling overpriced assets.

Arbitrage portfolios are portfolios that involve no wealth, which is known as *zero-investment portfolios*. In this respect, buying assets in a long portfolio is financed by selling short other assets (i.e., selling borrowed assets).

How to arbitrage riskless profits – assume there is a portfolio with assets that are correctly priced.

| Asset price too low | Asset price too high |
|---|---|
| • Short sell your portfolio of assets<br>• Buy the underpriced asset with the funds from this sale | • Short sell the overpriced asset<br>• Buy a portfolio of assets with funds from this sale |
| **Later reverse these positions** | **Later reverse these positions** |
| • Sell the previously underpriced asset<br>• Buy back your portfolio of assets | • Sell the portfolio<br>• Buy back the previously overpriced asset |
| **Gain on arbitrage** | **Gain on arbitrage** |
| • The underpriced asset will rise in price as this trading occurs<br>• Earn a capital gain on the difference in buy and sell prices of asset. | • The underpriced asset will fall in price as this trading occurs<br>• Earn a capital gain on the difference in sell and buy prices of asset |

**Fig. 7.1** Arbitraging riskless profits by buying and selling mispriced assets (*Source* Adapted from Wikipedia [https://en.wikipedia.org/wiki/Arbitrage_pricing_theory])

Mathematically, such a zero-investment portfolio satisfies the following condition:

$$\sum_{i=1}^{n} w_i = 0, \tag{7.2}$$

where $w_i$ are the amounts invested in asset $i$.

In developing the APT it is assumed that the portfolio weights $w_i$ are of order $1/n$ to guarantee a well-diversified zero-investment portfolio. This assumption allows us to utilize the law of large numbers in probability theory to eliminate idiosyncratic risks from the portfolio. Given that returns to satisfy the representation in Eq. (7.1), the arbitrage portfolio becomes

$$\begin{aligned} R_p &= \sum_{i=1}^{n} w_i R_i \\ &= \sum_{i=1}^{n} w_i E(R_i) + \sum_{i=1}^{n} w_i \beta_i F + \sum_{i=1}^{n} w_i \epsilon_i . \end{aligned} \tag{7.3}$$

In order to make this a zero risk arbitrage portfolio, we should be able to eliminate the last two terms in the second line of the equation. That is, the systematic risk component $\sum_i w_i \beta_i F$ and the residual idiosyncratic risk $\sum_i w_i \epsilon_i$ drop out. The latter is eliminated by the independence assumptions of random error terms $\epsilon_i$ from common factor $F$ and the error terms of different assets. These assumptions combined with the assumption that $w_i \approx \pm 1/n$ imply that the last term is zero, or $\sum_i w_i \epsilon_i \approx 0$ for large $n$ as idiosyncratic risks are diversified away. Subsequently, for large $n$ we can discard the error from (7.3) and approximate the portfolio by

$$R_p = \sum_{i=1}^{n} w_i E(R_i) + \sum_{i=1}^{n} w_i \beta_i F. \tag{7.4}$$

Note that $\sum_i w_i \beta_i F = F \sum_i w_i \beta_i$. Under the zero-investment restriction in Eq. (7.2), we can always select weights $w_i$ such that

$$\sum_i w_i \beta_i = 0. \tag{7.5}$$

With these weights, all the risks from the arbitrage portfolio become eliminated so that

$$R_p = \sum_{i=1}^{n} w_i E(R_i), \tag{7.6}$$

which is a riskless, zero-investment portfolio. Therefore, because the zero-investment portfolio is riskless, the no-arbitrage condition implies that we must have $R_p = 0$, or

$$\sum_{i=1}^{n} w_i E(R_i) = 0. \tag{7.7}$$

Given that this must hold for *all* zero-investment portfolios with $\sum_i w_i = 0$ and $\sum_i w_i \beta_i = 0$, pure linear algebra implies that the expected return, or $E(R_i)$, is a linear combination of a constant and the asset's beta. This insight yields the APT model for the expected return on each asset of the form:

$$E(R_i) = \gamma_0 + \gamma_1 \beta_i, \tag{7.8}$$

where $\gamma_0$ and $\gamma_1$ are common to all stocks, and $\beta_i$ is the stock's sensitivity to the risk factor.

It should be noted that, because all arbitrage portfolios are not necessarily well diversified, Eq. (7.8) may hold only approximately. Taking the approximation as a starting point, Huberman (1982) provided an interesting approach to derive the APT model. Using purely the no-arbitrage argument and without explicit reference to the meaning of *well diversified*, we can utilize linear algebra to write:

$$E(R_i) = \gamma_0 + \gamma_1 \beta_i + \alpha_i \tag{7.9}$$

wherein alpha ($\alpha_i$) is orthogonal to both the vector of ones and betas. Huberman and Wang (2017) refer to Eq. (7.9) as an *approximate* APT model and Eq. (7.8) as an *exact* APT model. Even though the representation in Eq. (7.9) is purely a mathematical identity, the way it is constructed makes $\alpha_i$ satisfy the zero-investment arbitrage portfolio restrictions in Eqs. (7.2) and (7.5), which can be utilized as a basis for defining a zero-investment portfolio. With this convention, Huberman derived the main result of the APT theory that, if there is no arbitrage, the deviations, or $\alpha_i = E(R_i) - (\gamma_0 + \gamma_i \beta_i)$, must be negligible as the number of stocks $n$ grows, i.e., the representation of the expected return $E(R_i)$ in Eq. (7.8) is essentially accurate.[2] Of course, from a financial economics perspective, the $\alpha_i$ parameter in equation (7.9) can be interpreted as a pricing error.

These results must hold for all assets. In particular, if there exists a riskless asset with return $R_f$ whose sensitivity to the common risk factor $F$ is zero by definition, Eq. (7.8) yields for the riskless asset $R_f = \gamma_0$. Therefore if a riskless rate exists, the APT model becomes

$$E(R_i) - R_f = \gamma_1 \beta_i. \tag{7.10}$$

Alternatively, setting $\lambda = \gamma_1 + R_f$, we can re-write Eq. (7.10) in the commonly expressed form

$$E(R_i) - R_f = (\lambda - R_f)\beta_i, \tag{7.11}$$

which is known as the APT model for asset returns. The difference $\lambda - R_f$ is common to all stocks as the factor risk premium, and $\lambda$ is the expected value of the common risk factor. Finally, if $F$ is the market portfolio, the APT model reduces to the CAPM.

**Example:** Assume that the common factor in the APT model is the market portfolio with expected return $\lambda = E(R_m)$. Let $R_p$ be the return of a well-diversified portfolio such that

$$R_p^e = \alpha_p + \beta_p R_m^e,$$

where $R_p^e = R_p - R_f$ is the excess return of the portfolio, and $R_m^e = R_m - R_f$ is the market excess return. If $\alpha_p \neq 0$, there is an arbitrage opportunity. The general recipe is that, if $\alpha_p$ is positive, short the market, and if $\alpha_p$ is negative, short the portfolio.

More precisely, as $\alpha_p = R_p - \beta_p R_m - (1 - \beta_p)R_f$, then if $\alpha_p > 0$, the sign in front of each return gives the long (+) versus short (−) position. That is, for a desired riskless arbitrage income of $\alpha_p \times x$ dollars, multiply both sides by $x$. This would result in buying portfolio $p$ with $x$ dollars, selling short the market portfolio with $\beta_p x$ dollars, and borrowing/lending $(1 - \beta_p) \times x$ dollars (borrowing if $\beta_p < 1$, lending if $\beta_p > 1$, and neither if $\beta_p = 1$). If $\alpha_p < 0$, the strategy is simply reversed.

[2] See also Ingersoll (1984) for a generalization of this approach.

The single factor model can be easily extended to multiple factors, wherein the single factor $F$ in Eq. (7.1) is replaced by $K$ common factors denoted $F_1, F_2, \ldots, F_K$ with slope coefficients $\beta_{i1}, \beta_{i2}, \ldots, \beta_{iK}$, respectively. Each factor is orthogonal to (or uncorrelated with) all other factors. Then the multifactor model becomes:

$$R_i = E(R_i) + \beta_{i,1} F_1 + \cdots + \beta_{i,K} F_K + \epsilon_i. \tag{7.12}$$

In this case the equilibrium relation in Eq. (7.10) generalizes to the following form:

$$E(R_i) - R_f = \beta_{i,1}\gamma_1 + \cdots + \beta_{i,K}\gamma_K, \tag{7.13}$$

where $\gamma_1, \ldots, \gamma_K$ are risk premiums associated with the $K$ common factors.

The arbitrage portfolio is again selected to diversify away asset-specific idiosyncratic risk. Similarly, the weights $w_i$ can be selected similar to the single factor case such that $\sum_{i=1}^{n} w_i \beta_{i,k} = 0$ for all $k = 1, \ldots, K$. Finally, it is notable that the APT applies even if some of the error terms are correlated within some clusters of assets, like industries, provided that the error terms are independent between the clusters and the number of clusters is large. In this case the number of clusters takes care of the diversification effect.

Unlike the CAPM mean-variance theory, which implies a linear relation with the market portfolio, the APT neither identifies the number of factors nor what the factors are. This generality is one of the main weaknesses of the APT model. In the next section we discuss attempts by researchers to empirically identify the number of factors in the APT.

## 7.2 Empirical Testing

Even though the market portfolio of the CAPM is unobservable, the procedures for empirically testing the CAPM are fairly clear. Testing the APT is more elusive as theory does not identify the number of factors or their identity. That said, the Achilles' heel of the CAPM is the unobservability of the market portfolio. Because the APT does not require the measurement of the market portfolio, Roll and Ross (1980) argued that the APT is more readily testable. Even so, substantial debate surrounds the testability of the APT. Shanken (1982) and Dybvig and Ross (1985) have exchanged different views on the testability of the APT. Also, Dhrymes, Friend, and Gultekin (1984) have questioned the empirical relevance of the model.

In an effort to test the APT, Roll and Ross (1980) used daily U.S. stock returns from July 3, 1962 to December 31, 1972. For computational reasons to extract the underlying factors, return series were divided alphabetically into 42 groups of 30 securities each. For each group: (1) a $30 \times 30$ covariance matrix was computed from the return time series; (2) a maximum likelihood *factor analysis* was used to estimate the number of factors and the factor loadings; (3) and estimates of cross-sectional regressions were used to measure the significance of risk premiums associated with different estimated factors.

Before discussing their results, we should mention that factor analysis is a statistical method that seeks to find the number of dimensions in sample data observations. In our daily lives, we normally think in terms of length, width, and depth dimensions. Of course, time is a fourth dimension. In the present instance, the data are stock returns over time for 42 groups of securities. We do not know how many risk dimensions are present within these stock returns. The factor analysis seeks to identify how many factors exist within the data. Each factor derived by the factor analysis corresponds to an orthogonal risk dimension. Using statistical methods, the factor analysis generates the factors in rank order from most to least important.

In their factor analysis, which was used for identifying and estimating factors, the authors over-fitted the model to include a few extra factors. Using these factors, they estimated a time-series regression model. Next, based on the estimated loadings in the time-series model, they estimated Fama and MacBeth (1973) cross-sectional regressions of the form:

$$\bar{R}_{it} - R_f = \gamma_{1t}\hat{\beta}_{i1} + \cdots + \gamma_{Kt}\hat{\beta}_{iK} + u_{it}, \tag{7.14}$$

where $\hat{\beta}_{ij}$ are estimated loadings corresponding to the factors, $i = 1, \ldots, n$ (number of stocks), $j = 1, \ldots, K$ (number of factors), $\gamma_{jt}$ is the risk premium associated with factor $j$ estimated at each time point $t = 1, \ldots, T$, and $u_{it}$ is the regression error term. The final estimates of the factor risk premiums, or $\gamma_j$, $j = 1, \ldots, K$, were obtained by averaging the respective cross-sectional estimates for the $n$ stocks. Insignificance of the estimated premiums of extra factors would serve to double check the inference of the most likely number of the underlying true return generating factors generated by the factor analysis.

Using these procedures, Roll and Ross determined that there were five factors in the factor analysis. The two extra factors were found to be insignificant in the cross-sectional regression tests. On the basis of their empirical results, Roll and Ross concluded that: "... at least three factors are important for pricing, but it is unlikely that more than four are present ..." (Roll and Ross (1980, p. 1092). They concluded that the evidence supported the APT.

While evidence of several priced factors is consistent with the APT, Roll and Ross tested further whether there might be other variables, not related to undiversifiable risk, that were priced. If such variables exist, the APT would be rejected. To do this, the authors investigated the total variance or "own" variance of individual stock returns. It is well known that total variance is positively correlated with the sample mean return.[3] The initial results from cross-sectional regressions augmented with the standard deviation of returns as an additional explanatory variable

[3] For example, see Miller and Scholes (1972).

turned out to be ambiguous. The authors suspected that the explanatory power of "own" variance may be spurious due to the high serial correlation of squared returns. Therefore, to eliminate possible spuriousness, the authors used days 1, 7, 13, ...for estimated returns, observations 3, 9, 15, ...for loadings, and 5, 11, 17, ...for standard deviations. This approach reduced the sample size for estimation from the initial 2,619 observations down to 436. With these changes, in 9-out-of-42 groups of stocks, the "own" variance was statistically significant. Upon implementing the Fama–MacBeth procedure with the above sampling conventions, just 3-out-of-42 groups had significant "own" variance. Hence, consistent with the APT, these results suggested that *own variance* does not explain expected asset returns.

Another study by Chen (1983) conducted a similar study of the APT by making comparisons to the CAPM. Using daily returns in the period 1968 to 1978, they used factor analysis to identify five asset pricing factors in U.S. stock returns. Cross-sectional tests were made using these factors' beta loadings. Breaking their sample period into four subperiods, they found that the five APT factors were significantly priced. In other tests, the CAPM appeared to be misspecified, as mispricing was captured by the APT. Also, own variance and size did not improve upon the factor loadings based on the APT. Consistent with Roll and Ross, based on these and other findings, he concluded that the evidence supported the APT over the CAPM.

While the empirical evidence supports the notion of multiple factors in asset pricing models in line with the APT, the identification of the macro variables associated with systematic risks is problematic. What variables should be used? Is there precedent in the literature for using specific variables? Taken together, could the multiple factors in the APT be proxies for the unobservable theoretical market portfolio in the CAPM? Due to these questions, the APT remains controversial.

## 7.3 Summary

Ross (1971, 1974, 1976) developed the arbitrage pricing theory (APT) as a new general equilibrium framework grounded in a linear relation between expected returns on assets and their risks. A no-arbitrage condition is assumed in which no wealth is required due to long/short portfolios held by investors. Investors earn zero returns for zero risk in well-diversified portfolios with no asset-specific idiosyncratic risk. Ross showed that the CAPM is a special case of the APT with a single market factor. More generally, the APT can have multiple orthogonal factors that investors use to arbitrage away any excess risk-adjusted return in the market. However, Ross did not specify the number of factors or their identity in the APT.

To empirically test the APT, Roll and Ross (1980) used the statistical method of factor analysis in combination with cross-sectional regression analyses to show that at least three factors exist in U.S. stock returns. Further tests of own variance as a factor were insignificant in line with the APT. Another factor analysis study by Chen (1983) found five significant factors in cross-sectional tests. The empirical findings of these studies supported the APT.

In sum, the APT provides a general framework for linear factor pricing models. Researchers building multifactor models in forthcoming chapters often cite the APT as a theoretical justification for their specifications. Due to their widespread acceptance among both academic researchers and investment professionals, multifactor models have become popular over the past 30 years.

## Questions

1. In the CAPM, one of the assumptions is that investors have common (homogeneous) beliefs about the return distribution of assets. What is the common assumption about the asset return generating process in the APT theory?
2. What are the major strengths and weaknesses of the APT in relation to the CAPM?
3. In the single factor case, given that $R_i = E(R_i) + \beta_i F + \epsilon_i$, the APT model specified as $E(R_i) = \gamma_0 + \gamma_i \beta$ is called the *exact* APT model by Huberman and Wang (2017). Huberman (1982) considers the representation $E(R_i) = \gamma_0 + \gamma_1 \beta_i + \alpha_i$, which Huberman and Wang refer to as an *approximate* APT model. Here it is assumed that $\sum_{i=1}^{n} \alpha_i = 0$ and $\sum_{i=1}^{n} \alpha_i \beta_i = 0$. How can $\alpha_i$s be interpreted in economic terms?

## Problems

1. Consider the following APT model:

$$E(R_i) - R_f = \gamma_1 \beta_{i,1} + \gamma_2 \beta_{i,2}. \tag{7.15}$$

Suppose that the riskless rate $R_f = 5\%$, and we have the following data for three stocks.

| Stock $i$ | $E(R_i)$ | $\beta_{i1}$ | $\beta_{i2}$ |
|---|---|---|---|
| 1 | 10.1 | 1.5 | 0.4 |
| 2 | 8.9 | 1.2 | 0.2 |
| 3 | 11.0 | 1.0 | |

(a) What are the risk premiums of the factors, i.e., $\gamma_1$ and $\gamma_2$?
(b) What are the expected values of the factors?
(c) What is the stock risk premium for each stock?
(d) What is $\beta_{3,2}$?

2. Form the equal-weighted portfolio of the stocks in problem 1
(a) Compute $\beta_{i,1}$ and $\beta_{i,2}$ for the portfolio.

   (b) Compute the expected return of the portfolio.
   (c) Compute the portfolio's risk premium.
3. Suppose the expected market return $E(R_M)$ equals 8%.
   (a) Compute CAPM betas for the stocks in problem 1.
   (b) Are the data in problem 1 consistent with both the CAPM and the APT?

## References

Chen, N.-F. 1983. Empirical tests of the theory of arbitrage pricing. *Journal of Finance* 33: 1393–1414.

Connor, G., and R. Korajzyck. 1985. Risk and return in equilibrium APT: Theory and tests. Banking Research Center Working paper 129, Northwestern University.

Connor, G., and R. Korjzyck. 1986. Performance measurement with the arbitrage pricing theory. *Journal of Financial Economics* 15: 373–394.

Dhrymes, P., I. Friend, and N.B. Gultekin. 1984. A critical reexamination of the empirical evidence on the arbitrage pricing theory. *Journal of Finance* 39: 703–738.

Dybvig, P., and S.A. Ross. 1985. Yes, the APT is testable. *Journal of Finance* 40: 1173–1188.

Fama, E.F., and J.D. MacBeth. 1973. Risk, return, and equilibrium: Empirical tests. *Journal of Political Economy* 38: 607–636.

Huberman, G. 1982. A simple approach to arbitrage pricing theory. *Journal of Economic Theory* 28: 183–191.

Huberman, G., and Z. Wang. 2017. Arbitrage pricing theory. In *The New Palgrave Dictionary of Economics*, ed. M. Vernengo, E.P. Caldentey, and B.J. Rosser Jr. London, UK: Palgrave Macmillan.

Ingersoll, J.E. 1984. Some results in the theory of arbitrage pricing. *Journal of Finance* 39: 1021–1039.

Miller, M.H., and M. Scholes. 1972. Rates of return in relation to risk: A re-examination of recent findings. In *Studies in the Theory of Capital Markets*, ed. M.C. Jensen. New York, NY: Praeger.

Roll, R., and S.A. Ross. 1980. An empirical investigation of the arbitrage pricing theory. *Journal of Finance* 35: 1073–1103.

Ross, S.A. 1971. The general validity of the mean variance approach in large markets. Discussion paper no. 12–72. Rodney L, White Center for Financial Research, University of Pennsylvania.

Ross, S.A. 1974. Return, risk, and arbitrage. In *Risk and Return in Finance*, ed. I. Friend and J. Bicksler. New York, NY: Heath Lexington.

Ross, S.A. 1976. The arbitrage theory of capital asset pricing. *Journal of Economic Theory* 13: 341–360.

Shanken, J. 1982. The arbitrage pricing theory: Is it testable? *Journal of Finance* 37: 1129–1140.

# Multifactor Models

# 8

In 1990 William Sharpe was awarded the Nobel Prize in Economics for the CAPM along with Harry Markowitz for portfolio diversification and Merton Miller for corporate valuation.[1] The Swedish industrialist Alfred Nobel (inventor of dynamite) dedicated a foundation to recognize discoveries that benefit humankind. The gold standard for intellectual achievement, the Nobel Prize is conferred on a person after the true significance of their discoveries, research, and writings are known. The CAPM and mean-variance portfolio diversification had become the centerpieces of modern finance.

Unfortunately, the leading role of the CAPM in asset pricing was cut short by soon-to-be-published studies. In 1992 Fama and French published the first in a series of papers that showed the CAPM did not work in the real world. They documented extensive evidence that there was no relationship between beta risk and average U.S. stock returns over long periods of time. Upon reviewing their accumulating evidence in a number of papers, they concluded that the CAPM was *dead*. In its place, they proposed a *three-factor model* comprised of the market factor plus two factors based on the firm characteristics of size (i.e., small and large firms) and book equity/market equity ratios (i.e., value and growth firms). Their empirical tests showed that this new *multifactor* model substantially improved the goodness-of-fit of the CAPM to stock returns. Not surprisingly, some degree of

[1] See their original works, especially Sharpe (1964), Markowitz (1959), and Modigliani and Miller (1958, 1963). With respect to the CAPM, both Lintner (1965) and Mossin (1966) had died by 1990 and Treynor (1961, 1962) had not never published his CAPM papers, such that these authors were not eligible for the prize.

**Supplementary Information** The online version contains supplementary material available at https://doi.org/10.1007/978-3-031-16784-3_8.



J. W. Kolari and S. Pynnönen, *Investment Valuation and Asset Pricing*,
https://doi.org/10.1007/978-3-031-16784-3_8

controversy was sparked by the three-factor model. In this chapter we review the three-factor model and resultant controversy in the asset pricing literature.

## 8.1 What Explains Stock Returns?

If CAPM beta does not explain stock returns very well, what does? Fama and French (1992) set the stage for their later multifactor models by showing that two simple firm characteristics—size and book-to-market equity—can help to explain the cross-section of average stocks returns in the United States. They cited earlier research to support their findings. The size effect on stock returns goes back to Banz (1981), who found that small (large) firms had average returns that were too high (low) based on their betas. Statman (1980) and Rosenberg et al. (1985) found that stock returns were related to the ratio of book equity to market equity (denoted hereafter as BM). Other researchers detected relations between stock returns and other firm characteristics, including financial leverage and earnings/price ratios.[2]

To prove the relation of stock returns to size and BM characteristics of firms, Fama and French collected U.S. stock returns from 1963 to 1990. Stocks were formed into 10 deciles in terms of size (as measured by market capitalization equal to stock price times number of shares outstanding) as well as BM. Also, they formed decile portfolios of stocks using estimated market model betas. In the sample period, average betas ranged from 0.87 for the low decile to 1.72 for the high decile. This range of beta values is representative of the population of U.S. stocks in their sample period. The corresponding average returns for these low and high beta deciles were 1.34% per month and 1.14%, respectively, which is opposite of CAPM theory with expected returns increasing as beta increases.

While beta did not appear to explain stock returns in a reliable manner, size and BM did. Table 8.1 documents selected results reported by Fama and French (1992, Table V, p. 446). Looking at the columns in the table, at any given BM ratio, with the exception of the low decile (high growth) stocks in the column on the left, average returns per month (in percent) tend to decrease as size increases from the low decile (small stocks) to the high decile (big stocks). Also, referring to the rows, for any given size, average returns tend to increase as BM increases from the low decile (growth stocks) to the high decile (value stocks). The highest earnings stocks are small, growth stocks in the upper right-hand corner of the table (e.g., a maximum average return of 1.92% for stocks that are in the low decile by size and high decile by BM). Again, high growth stocks in the low BM decile do not follow the return pattern of other stocks. Nonetheless, the size and BM returns patterns in Table 8.1 are quite convincing. Simple sorts on size and BM firm-level characteristics tell the story—stock returns are related to size and BM.

[2] See Basu (1977), Lakonishok and Shapiro (1986), and Bhandari (1988). Fama and French (2004) have provided an excellent survey of the CAPM and these contradictory studies.

**Table 8.1** Average monthly returns for U.S. stock portfolios sorted by size and book-to-market equity (BM) from July 1963 to December 1990 in the Fama and French (1992) study

| | Book-to-market equity (BM) | | | | |
|---|---|---|---|---|---|
| Size | Low decile | Decile 3 | Decile 5 | Decile 7 | High decile |
| Small decile | 0.70 | 1.20 | 1.56 | 1.70 | 1.92 |
| Decile 3 | 0.56 | 1.23 | 1.36 | 1.30 | 1.60 |
| Decile 5 | 0.88 | 1.08 | 1.13 | 1.44 | 1.49 |
| Decile 7 | 0.95 | 0.99 | 0.99 | 0.99 | 1.47 |
| Big decile | 0.89 | 0.84 | 0.79 | 0.81 | 1.18 |

This table reports the average monthly returns (in percent) for U.S. stock portfolios sorted into deciles by size and book-to-market equity (BM). Size is measured by the market capitalization of stocks (i.e., stock price times shares outstanding). The sample period is July 1963 to December 1990. The selected results shown below are based on Fama and French (1992, Table V, p. 446)

Next, the authors ran formal statistical tests using Fama and MacBeth (1973) cross-sectional regressions using different models. The time-series models contained a number of variables, including the market factor, size, BM, leverage, and the earnings/price ratio. The market price of risk for CAPM beta ($\lambda_m$) was insignificant. However, the market prices of beta coefficients associated with size and BM (or loadings) were very significant. Their market prices were $-0.15\%$ and 0.50% per month with significant $t$-statistics equal to $-2.58$ and 5.71, respectively. These results confirmed that bigger stocks have lower returns than smaller stocks (i.e., the negative price of risk), and that high BM (value) stocks have higher returns than lower BM (growth) stocks (i.e., positive price of risk). Also, loadings for leverage and the earnings/price ratio were not significant when size and BM beta loadings were included in the model. Therefore, they inferred that these firm characteristics were absorbed (or accounted for) by the size and BM variables. From these findings, the authors concluded that size and BM beta risk loadings help to explain stock returns but not CAPM beta. In their final remarks concerning the CAPM, they commented:

> Black et al. (1972) and Fama and MacBeth (1973) find that, as predicted by the model, there is a positive simple relation between average return and market $\beta$ during the years (1926-1968) ... we find that this simple relation between $\beta$ and average return disappears during the more recent 1963-1990 period. (Fama and French 1992, p. 449)

This sensitivity of the CAPM to the sample period was observed by Jagannathan and McGrattan (1995) also. In the U.S. stock market, they found a noticeable relation between average returns and beta in the long sample periods of 1926 to 1975 and 1926 to 1991 but not in the shorter periods 1976 to 1980 and 1981 to 1991. In the latter periods, size and BM factors did better than the market factor at explaining cross-sectional variation in average stock returns. Thus, the CAPM does not consistently hold over time, which implies that it should be supplemented with other factors.

The 1992 Fama and French study is an important landmark in the asset pricing literature because it set the stage for multifactors that better fit stock return data. One year later, Fama and French would propose their seminal multifactor model.

## 8.2 Fama and French Three-Factor Model

Akin to the APT of Ross (1976) and Fama and French (1993) utilized size and BM variables to construct long/short portfolios as *factors*. These long/short or zero-investment portfolios are also called *mimicking portfolios*. The betas or loadings on these factors measure the sensitivity of asset returns to the factors. They sort stocks into six portfolios in a 2×3 matrix by size and value (BM) as shown in Fig. 8.1. The *size factor* is defined as the average of the three small (blue) portfolios' returns minus the three big (red) portfolios' returns. The *value factor* is the average of the two value (green) portfolios' returns minus the two growth (brown) portfolios' returns. They used more value than size portfolios due to the stronger relation of BM to stock returns than size in their 1992 paper. They denoted the size factor as *SMB* for small minus big and the value factor as *HML* for high minus low BM. Both factors were computed using value-weighted (not equal-weighted) returns on a monthly basis.

Together with the market factor, they proposed a three-factor model with the added *multifactors* of size and value. The market factor was the value-weighted excess return computed as the average CRSP stocks' return minus the Treasury bill rate each month. The CRSP market index contains all U.S. stocks in the database created by the Center for Research in Security Prices at the University of Chicago. The three-factor model is:

$$R_{it} - R_{ft} = \alpha_i + \beta_{i,m}(R_{mt} - R_{ft}) + \beta_{i,S} SMB_t + \beta_{i,V} HML_t + e_{it}, \quad (8.1)$$

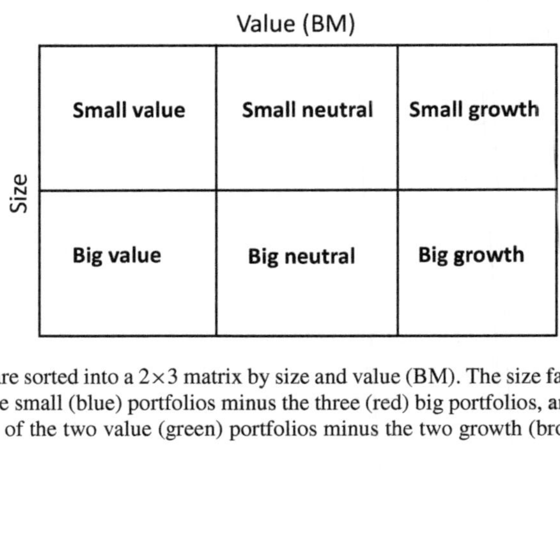


**Fig. 8.1** Stocks are sorted into a 2×3 matrix by size and value (BM). The size factor is the average returns of the three small (blue) portfolios minus the three (red) big portfolios, and the value factor is average returns of the two value (green) portfolios minus the two growth (brown) portfolios

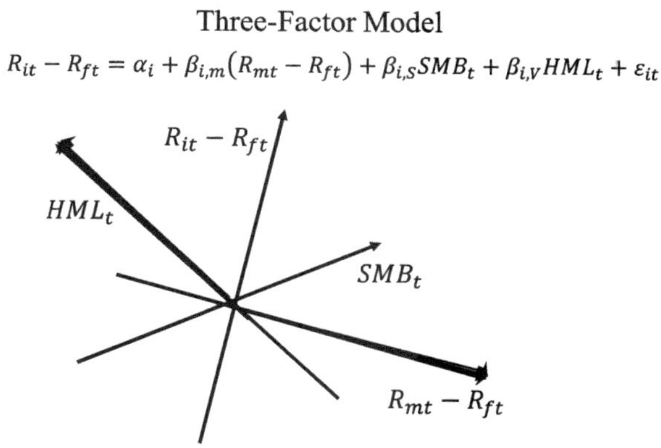


**Fig. 8.2** The Fama and French three-factor model with excess returns a function of market, size, and value factors takes into account four dimensions in return/risk space

where $\beta_{i,S}$ and $\beta_{i,V}$ estimate the sensitivity of excess returns of the *i*th stock or stock portfolio to the size and value factors, respectively, and other notation is as in previous chapters. Figure 8.2 gives a four-dimensional visualization of the model in risk/return space. Each axis in this figure is perpendicular (or orthogonal) to all the other coordinate axes.[3]

To estimate the three-factor model, dependent variable excess returns on the left-hand-side of Eq. (8.1) were based on 25 portfolios sorted on size and BM (similar to the six size/BM portfolios in their factors). Value-weighted returns were again computed on a monthly basis. These portfolio returns are the test assets. In the sample period 1963 to 1991, they found that the market risk premium was 0.43% per month compared to the size risk premium (or *SMB* return) of 0.27% and the value risk premium (or *HML* return) of 0.40%. Hence, the value factor was larger in magnitude than the size factor.

Fama and French estimated the three-factor model using monthly U.S. stock returns in the period July 1963 to December 1991. The results strongly supported their model. The beta coefficients denoted $\beta_{i,m}$, $\beta_{i,S}$, and $\beta_{i,V}$ corresponding to the market, size, and value factors, respectively, were all highly statistically significant with very high *t*-statistics in most of the 25 size and BM portfolios. The magnitudes of the beta coefficients followed definite patterns: (1) small stocks had larger coefficients $\beta_{i,S}$ related to the size factor *SMB* than big stocks; and (2) high

[3] We cannot visualize four-dimensional objects as humans, but a multivariate regression model enables a mathematical realization of *N* dimensions corresponding to *N* variables including both the dependent and independent variables. Interestingly, Einstein's theory of General Relativity argued that a space-time continuum exists with 3 dimensions of space and 1 dimension of time. He thought that there is curvature in space-time due to gravity. Could the return-risk space be curved also? Is there a unifying force like gravity that links returns and risk in financial markets? Perhaps it can bend return-risk space much as gravity can bend light as it travels through space.

BM (value) portfolios had larger coefficients $\beta_{i,V}$ related to value factor *HML* than low BM (growth) portfolios. These patterns suggest that small (value) stocks have relatively higher returns than big (growth) stocks on average. It is important to mention that the size and value factors were uncorrelated with one another for the most part, but both had some correlation with the market factor. The latter is not surprising as the size and value portfolios are comprised of stocks that represent large components of the market portfolio. Hence, there could be some amount of multicollinearity in the three-factor model, which can lead to unstable regression parameter estimates as discussed in Chapter 4.

To measure the goodness-of-fit of different models, $R^2$ estimates were computed. Table 8.2 summarizes their findings. In Panel A of this table, we see that the CAPM has fairly strong goodness-of-fit with $R^2$ values in the range of 61% to 92%. There is a tendency for $R^2$ values to be higher for low BM (growth) and big size stocks than other stocks. Looking at Panel B with three-factor model results, the $R^2$ values are relatively higher in the range of 79% to 97%. Indeed, 20-out-of-25 $R^2$ values exceed 90%, and 10-out-of-25 are equal to or greater than 95%. The relatively high and in many cases near perfect goodness-of-fit of these size and BM sorted portfolios suggests that the model is empirically valid with respect to the 25 size and BM test asset portfolios.

They also tested a bond market model using government bond portfolios with maturities from 1-to-10 years and five corporate bond portfolios with different Moody's credit ratings. A term-to-maturity risk factor denoted *TERM* was defined

**Table 8.2** Goodness-of-fit $R^2$ estimates for 25 U.S. stock portfolios sorted on size and book-to-market equity (BM) from July 1963 to December 1991 in the Fama and French (1993) study

| | Low BM | Quintile 2 | Quintile 3 | Quintile 4 | High BM |
|---|---|---|---|---|---|
| Panel A. CAPM $R^2$ estimates | | | | | |
| Small size quintile | 0.67 | 0.70 | 0.68 | 0.65 | 0.61 |
| Quantile 2 | 0.79 | 0.79 | 0.76 | 0.76 | 0.71 |
| Quantile 3 | 0.84 | 0.84 | 0.80 | 0.79 | 0.74 |
| Quantile 4 | 0.89 | 0.90 | 0.87 | 0.80 | 0.76 |
| Big size quintile | 0.89 | 0.92 | 0.84 | 0.79 | 0.69 |
| Panel B. Three-factor model $R^2$ estimates | | | | | |
| Small size quintile | 0.94 | 0.96 | 0.97 | 0.97 | 0.96 |
| Quantile 2 | 0.95 | 0.96 | 0.95 | 0.95 | 0.96 |
| Quantile 3 | 0.95 | 0.94 | 0.93 | 0.93 | 0.93 |
| Quantile 4 | 0.94 | 0.93 | 0.91 | 0.89 | 0.89 |
| Big size quintile | 0.94 | 0.88 | 0.90 | 0.79 | 0.83 |

This table reports the $R^2$ estimates for the CAPM and Fama and French three-factor model using U.S. stock portfolios sorted into quintiles by size and book-to-market equity (BM). Size is measured by the market capitalization of stocks (i.e., stock price times shares outstanding). The sample period is July 1963 to December 1991. The selected results shown below are based on Fama and French (1993, Tables 4 and 6, pp. 20 and 24)

as the long-term bond return minus one-month Treasury bill rate. A default risk factor denoted *DEF* was the differenced returns of long-term corporate bonds minus long-term government bonds. As we have seen, the three-factor model performed well for the 25 stock portfolios, but this feat was not repeated for the bond portfolios. Likewise, the bond factors were significant for bond portfolios but not stock portfolios. Since the bond factors tended to be explained by the market factor, once the market factor was added to the stock model, there was little support for the bond factors. Of course, the market factor contains the Treasury bill rate, which likely explains the weak effect of bond factors.

To cross-sectionally test their three-factor model, the intercepts ($\alpha$s) for different models were estimated for the 25 size and BM portfolios. Citing Merton's (1973) ICAPM paper, Fama and French argued that a well-specified model should have intercepts equal to zero (i.e., no mispricing error). Table 8.3 summarizes some of their $\alpha$ test results.

In Panel A of Table 8.3, we see the results for the CAPM. The $\alpha$ estimates for the portfolios using the market factor alone produced positive and significant intercepts. For example, the small size quintile and high BM quintile portfolio has a monthly $\alpha$ equal to 0.92%, which is highly significant at the 1% level and therefore different from zero. This $\alpha$ corresponds to a very large mispricing error of about 11% per year. Except for low BM (growth) stocks, the $\alpha$ estimates for most

**Table 8.3** Intercept or $\alpha$ estimates for 25 U.S. stock portfolios sorted on size and book-to-market equity (BM) from July 1963 to December 1991 in the Fama and French (1993) study

| | Low BM | Quintile 2 | Quintile 3 | Quintile 4 | High BM |
|---|---|---|---|---|---|
| Panel A. CAPM $\alpha$ estimates | | | | | |
| Small size quintile | 0.31 | 0.62* | 0.71** | 0.80*** | 0.92*** |
| Quintile 2 | 0.35 | 0.63* | 0.77*** | 0.75*** | 0.93*** |
| Quintile 3 | 0.34 | 0.58** | 0.60** | 0.73*** | 0.89*** |
| Quintile 4 | 0.41 | 0.27 | 0.49** | 0.69*** | 0.96*** |
| Big size quintile | 0.34 | 0.30 | 0.25 | 0.50** | 0.53** |
| Panel B. Three-factor model $\alpha$ estimates | | | | | |
| Big size quintile | −0.34*** | −0.12 | −0.05 | 0.01 | 0.00 |
| Quintile 2 | −0.11 | −0.01 | 0.08 | 0.03 | 0.02 |
| Quintile 3 | −0.11 | 0.04 | −0.04 | 0.05 | 0.05 |
| Quintile 4 | 0.09 | −0.22*** | −0.08 | 0.03 | 0.13 |
| Big size quintile | 0.21*** | −0.05 | −0.05 | −0.05 | −0.17 |

This table reports the monthly $\alpha$ estimates (in percent) for the CAPM and Fama and French three-factor model using U.S. stock portfolios sorted into quintiles by size and book-to-market equity (BM). Size is measured by the market capitalization of stocks (i.e., stock price times shares outstanding). The sample period is July 1963 to December 1991. The selected results shown below are based on Fama and French (1993, Table 9a, pp. 36–37)

*Note* Asterisks indicate that the $\alpha$ estimate is statistically different from zero at the *−10%, **−5%, and ***−1% levels

portfolios are significantly greater than zero. When they repeated these tests using only the *SMB* and *HML* factors in a two-factor model, the $\alpha$ estimates were again very positive and significant with a high of 0.79% per month, or about 9.5% per year.

In stark contrast to the CAPM and two-factor model with size and value factors, as shown in Panel B of Table 8.3, upon combining the market factor with *SMB* and *HML* factors in the three-factor model, the intercepts became close to zero. With the exception of only 3-out-of-25 portfolios, the intercepts were not significantly different from zero. These results strongly support the three-factor model.

The bond factors *TERM* and *DEF* did not further reduce the intercepts for stock portfolios but did so for bond portfolios. Based on these and other tests, Fama and French (1993, p. 41) inferred that "... the three-factor model does a good job on the cross-section of average stock returns." They interpreted the size and value factors as proxies for risk factors associated with these firm-level characteristics (akin to the CRSP excess return serving as a proxy for the true market factor in the CAPM).

In their paper Fama and French conjectured that Merton's (1973) ICAPM and Ross' (1976) APT provided some theoretical support for their three-factor model. Recall that these theoretical models proposed multiple risk factors to price assets in equilibrium. In this regard, the three-factor model is mainly justified on empirical grounds—that is, it noticeably improves the goodness-of-fit to stock return data compared to the CAPM. In their paper entitled "The CAPM is Wanted, Dead or Alive," Fama and French (1996) argued that the failures of the CAPM to explain expected returns motivate the investigation of return anomalies which can be taken into account by multifactor ICAPM and APT models. In their view, the CAPM was *dead*.

Summarizing their new long/short zero-investment portfolio, multifactor model approach to asset pricing, Fama and French were mindful of the questions left unanswered. In their words,

> ... our work leaves many open questions. Most glaring, we have not shown how the size and book-to-market factors in returns are driven by the stochastic behavior of earnings ... Can specific fundamentals be identified as variables that lead to common variation in returns that is independent of the market and carries a different premium than general market risk? These and other interesting questions are left for future work. (Fama and French 1993, p. 55)

Returning to the above question of the role of earnings, Fama and French (1996) published another paper in which they considered the following dual hypotheses: (1) size and value factors are related to some common factor; and (2) size and value patterns are related to the behavior of earnings which affects stock prices. They contended that high BM (value) ratios with low relative stock prices signal low earnings and possible financial distress, and vice versa for low BM (growth) ratios with high relative stock prices. Moreover, holding BM constant, small companies tend to have lower earnings than big companies. While it is possible that small companies' earnings fluctuate with the business cycle and exceed those of big companies at times, in the long run small companies underperform big companies in terms of profits over time.

To investigate these dual research hypotheses, Fama and French collected data on size, BM, earnings, and stock returns for U.S. companies in the period 1963 to 1992. Using simple descriptive analyses, they documented that size and BM factors based on companies' earnings were similar to those computed using stock returns. In other words, common factors in earnings and returns were found. However, while market and size factors in earnings were linked to the market and size factors in returns, the BM factor in returns did not appear to be closely associated with the BM factors in earnings. Contrary to their hypothesis, equity returns were not related to the BM factor in earnings.

In sum, there is some evidence to support the notion that common variations in returns are related to common factors in earnings. As such, they concluded by posing the following questions for future research:

> (i) What are the underlying state variables that produce variation in earnings and returns related to size and BE/ME?
>
> (ii) Do these unnamed state variables produce variation in consumption and wealth that is not captured by the overall market factor and so can explain the risk premiums associated with size and BE/ME? (Fama and French 1996, p. 154)

Unfortunately, given that state variables are proxied by macro level information (e.g., gross national product (GNP), aggregate wealth and consumption, employment, etc.), they were doubtful about the prospects of finding state variable determinants or drivers of earnings and returns. This pessimistic assessment of finding empirical models in the true spirit of the ICAPM and APT laid down a clear challenge to the asset pricing world. A challenge that many researchers accepted as we will see in the next chapter.

## 8.3 Three-Factor Controversy

Black (1993, p. 75) later criticized the three-factor model on a number of grounds. First, Black complained of potential *data mining*. This problem is a result of researchers exploring many different independent variables on the right-hand-side of the time-series regression equation, different time periods, and alternative combinations of variables in different models. Eventually, if you run enough data, you will find something that looks statistically significant and then report those results to the exclusion of all the other insignificant results. This kind of *data snooping* could produce results that are entirely accidental or random. He singled out anomalies in finance literature as a classic example of this problem. The size effect in the Fama and French (1992) study was an anomaly that disappeared in the 1981 to 1990 period with little or no impact on stock returns. Also, there is no clear explanation for why size and expected returns or BM ratios and expected returns are related to one another. For these reasons, he commented: "Lack of theory is a tipoff: watch out for data mining!" Black concluded that it was premature to claim the death of beta and the CAPM.

In a short paper, Black (1995) observed that theory posits at least one priced factor. Everyone agrees (including Fama and French) that the expected excess return in the market as a whole is positive. He reasoned that, if the relation between expected returns and beta was flat, then the expected return on the second factor related to the zero-beta portfolio in his zero-beta CAPM must be large. Interestingly, due to the fact that size and BM ratios sometimes are not related to expected returns and lack theoretical foundations as discussed above, he referred to the size and value factors as third and fourth factors, respectively. He believed these multifactors were of lesser importance than his zero-beta factor.[4]

An often-cited study by Kothari et al. (1995) published findings that contradicted Fama and French. Using annual (not monthly) U.S. stock returns for the longer sample period 1927 to 1990, they found that the annual contribution of beta risk was 8.9% to 11.7% for the equally weighted stock market index and 6.2% to 8.9% for the value-weighted stock market index. Note here that the equal-weighted index weights small stocks more heavily, as the value-weighted index weights them less than big stocks. So a size effect is apparent, with small stocks having higher returns than big stocks. Time-series regression was used to estimate betas over the sample period, and then the market price of beta was estimated using in-sample cross-sectional regression. This two-step Fama and MacBeth procedure was used on both a monthly and annual basis by rolling forward one month and one year at a time. Cross-sectional regressions were estimated using both monthly and annual returns as dependent variables and betas estimated using annual returns for the entire sample period as the independent variable. The average of these estimated $\lambda_m$s over the entire sample period had $t$-statistics greater than 2.50 in a number of different test asset portfolios. Thus, beta risk loadings were priced in the cross-section of average stock returns for annual betas. They repeated these analyses in the subperiod 1941 to 1990 with similar results. Thus, based on annual returns to estimate market beta instead of monthly returns, their empirical tests supported the CAPM.

Using industry portfolios as test assets, the value factor was only weakly related to average stock returns. In this regard, the stocks used in the Fama and French tests were suspected of *survivor bias* as firms in financial distress were dropped from their analyses. Value firms with high book-to-market equity ratios were less likely to survive over time and therefore be included in sample data. Consequently, they argued that Fama and French results refuting the CAPM were subject to some degree of sample period selection as well as sample stock selection. Betas estimated using annual (not monthly) returns and broader samples including industry

---

[4] In Chapter 10 we cover the ZCAPM of Kolari et al. (2021), which is based on Black's (1972) zero-beta CAPM. Consistent with Black's (1995) comments about a large second factor, empirical tests of the ZCAPM have revealed a highly significant, large second factor (viz.,cross-sectional returncross-sectional return dispersion in the market).

portfolios appeared to better support the CAPM and somewhat diminish support for the size and value factors.[5] Kothari et al. (1995, p. 221) concluded:

> Finally, we emphasize that the failure of a significant relation between B/M and return to emerge for the S &P industry portfolios ... poses a serious challenge to the B/M "empirical asset pricing model" ... A useful pricing model must be trusted to work under a wide variety of conditions and not just for a limited set of portfolios.

Echoing this concern, researchers have contended that an *endogeneity problem* arises when the test assets used to test the size and value factors are themselves based on size and value firm-level characteristics. In the extreme, if you regress $Y$ on $Y$, a perfect goodness-of-fit will be achieved.[6] Similar to Kothari, Shanken, and Sloan, a number of authors, including Lewellen et al. (2010), Daniel and Titman (2012), and others, have recommended that the test assets should be expanded to include portfolios that are less strongly correlated with proposed factors. Industry portfolios are considered to be a good choice due to being exogenous (or external) to various factors for the most part.

It was not long before Fama and French (1996) responded to these criticisms. They countered that: (1) beta is insufficient to fully explain average stock returns; and (2) size and BM are uncorrelated to beta but add more significantly to explaining returns than beta. Even if beta is significant in some instances, empirical tests suggested that multifactor forms of the ICAPM and APT were superior to the CAPM. It is important to recognize that Fama and French did not say that the market factor is useless; rather, the market factor must be augmented with other factors to more fully account for average stock returns. Their main argument was that the CAPM does not hold—multifactor models are needed in asset pricing. Consistent with this argument, in another study of 12 different countries plus the United States, Fama and French (1998) presented corroborating evidence that the three-factor model outperformed the CAPM.

As recognized by Fama and French, it is possible that the CAPM fails due to poor (inefficient) proxies for the true (efficient) market portfolio. In Chapter 4 we cited Roll's (1977) critique that the CAPM cannot be tested without an efficient empirical proxy $m$ for the theoretical market portfolio $M$. In the words of Fama and

---

[5] See also Hsia et al. (2000), who used annual returns to compute moving-average betas and better take into market anomalies. Their results supported a positive relation between average returns and beta risk also. Additionally, a study of U.K. stock market returns by Clare et al. (1998) found that the beta was not dead. Using a somewhat different method of estimating the cross-sectional relation between expected returns and factor loadings, market beta risk was significantly priced in their tests. However, their study only employed 100 U.K. stocks with data available from 1980 to 1993. Thus, their results were somewhat limited in scope.

[6] In time-series regressions of the three-factor model, information in the size and value test asset portfolios (and even residual errors for these portfolios) will naturally have information related to the size and value factors. In this respect, recall from Chapter 4's discussion of the market model and underlying statistical assumptions, the error terms should be uncorrelated with the independent variables.

French (1996, p. 1957): "... valid applications of the CAPM await the coming of *M*." They later commented in a 2004 survey article on the CAPM that "... If betas do not suffice to explain expected returns, the market portfolio is not efficient, and the CAPM is dead in its tracks" (Fama and French 2004, p. 36). In other words, even if the market premium is significant, other factors such as size and value are needed to more fully explain expected returns.

Fama and French (1996) inferred from their empirical evidence that either multifactor ICAPM and APT models explain the failure of the CAPM or investors are irrational. The former possibility arises from the reasonable inference that investors are concerned with more than beta risk associated with the market factor. Risk-averse investors could plausibly care about a number of different risks that exist in the market. The latter possibility relates to the *behavioral school* for explaining asset pricing anomalies such as size, value, etc. that the CAPM failed to explain (see Chapter 2). For example, investors price growth firms with low BM ratios at too high a stock price that results in low returns; conversely, value firms with high BM values are distressed and therefore priced too low by investors that result in high returns. If indeed irrational market behavior based on emotional investor responses is important in financial markets, then the efficient markets assumption of asset pricing models is weakened. In either (or both) case(s), asset pricing is more complex than originally conceived by Markowitz, Sharpe, Black, Merton, Ross, and many others.

In search of better models, researchers began to explore long/short zero-investment portfolios to see if other significant factors might exist. The hunt was on—the search for anomalies in stock returns accelerated in the years to come in efforts to identify new factors. Forthcoming Chapter 9 reviews some of the most prominent of these factors and models.

## 8.4 Summary

After extensive tests using U.S. stock returns over many years, Fama and French (1996) declared the CAPM *dead*. Little or no relation between U.S. stock returns and beta risk led them to propose a new multifactor model. In their papers, Fama and French (1992, 1993, 1995, 1996) introduced a three-factor model, which proved to boost the empirical fit to stock returns of the CAPM's market factor by using the firm characteristics of size and value (i.e., book-to-market equity ratios denoted BM). A major innovation consistent with Ross' (1976) APT was the construction of long/short zero-investment factors—for example, long small stocks and short big stocks as well as long high BM stocks and short low BM stocks. These so-called *size* and *value* factors in combination with the market factor substantially lowered intercept ($\alpha$) estimates that reflect mispricing in the time-series regression estimation of asset pricing models. Related loosely to the theoretical ICAPM and APT models of Merton (1973) and Ross (1976), respectively, the three-factor model is foundational in the evolution of asset pricing. In an effort to link their three-factor model to economic fundamentals, they showed that the size and value factors in stock returns have some relationship to size and value factors in firm earnings. However, the identification of ICAPM and APT state variables that drive the linkage between size plus BM firm characteristics and returns/earnings was left an unanswered question for future research.

Controversy surrounding the three-factor model started with Black's (1993) criticism that it was a product of data mining rather than theory. While it improved the empirical fit of the CAPM to stock return data, the state variables underlying the size and value factors were unknown. Also, Black (1995) reasoned that, given positive expected excess returns in the market over time, if the return/beta relation is flat, then the zero-beta factor from his zero-beta CAPM must be large to explain market returns. The size and value factors were not always present in different sample periods and, more importantly, lacked theory. A well-known study by Kothari et al. (1995) found evidence that annual stock returns over long periods of time were consistent with a linear relation between market beta and the cross-section of average stock returns. Fama and French (1996) countered that the CAPM failed in some periods but worked in others; in both cases, the size and value factors boosted the explanatory power of the CAPM. Kothari et al. also argued that the value factor did not work well with industry portfolios and that survivor bias exists among high book-to-market equity ratio firms that are distressed and can drop out of data samples in some time periods. Relatedly, some researchers have cited an endogeneity problem wherein the test asset portfolios' returns (i.e., the dependent variable in an asset pricing model) are closely related by construction to the factors (i.e, the independent variables in a model). Naturally the model would fit this data quite well. Hence, Lewellen et al. (2010), Daniel and Titman (2012), and others have recommended that other test assets portfolios exogenous to the factors should be used to investigate the validity of an asset pricing model. Industry portfolios were believed to be good exogenous portfolios.

Fama and French (1996, 2004) defended the three-factor model due to the failure of the CAPM. According to their logic, the market portfolio is not efficient which means the CAPM is dead. Two possibilities help to explain this failure: (1) other factors exist as theorized by the ICAPM and APT; and (2) investors can be irrational at times that causes anomalies in asset returns unrelated to risk as proposed by the behavioral school. The ensuing search for multifactors and anomalies in stock returns triggered a revolution in asset pricing that continues today. As we will see in forthcoming Chapter 9, many new long/short factors have been proposed by researchers that go well beyond the prototypical three-factor model.

## Questions

1. If CAPM beta does not explain stock returns, what does? In this regard, Fama and French (1992) found that stock returns were related to two firm characteristics. What are these characteristics and briefly discuss what they found.

2. Fama and French (1993) used the size and BM variables to construct zero-investment factors. Define these factors and write the equation for their resultant three-factor model. What are the multifactors in this model?
3. Fama and French (1993) conducted tests of their proposed three-factor model. What were the test asset portfolios? What did they find? Discuss the results for estimated beta coefficients and goodness-of-fit of their model.
4. How did Fama and French (1993) cross-sectionally test the three-factor model? What did they find in test results?
5. Fama and French (1993) specified and tested a bond model. What did their results show?
6. If the CAPM is dead, and asset prices are better explained by multiple factors, what theoretical support for multifactor models exists?
7. Fama and French (1996) argued that size and value factors are linked to economic fundamentals such as earnings within the firm. What were their arguments in this regard?
8. Did Fama and French (1996) find evidence to support a link between earnings and the size and value factors? Review their findings. What are the underlying state variables that produce variation in earnings and stock returns related to size and BM ratios?
9. Controversy surrounded the three-factor model due to skepticism by researchers. Black (1993, 1995) said that the model had two problems. Discuss these two potential problems.
10. Kothari, Shanken, and Sloan (1995) found evidence to support the CAPM. Also, they criticized the Fama and French studies. Review these issues in their study.
11. What is a possible endogeneity problem in the Fama and French asset pricing tests of the three-factor model? How can we reduce this problem in asset pricing tests?
12. How did Fama and French (1996) counter criticisms of their three-factor model? Do you think that multifactor models are needed to more fully price assets or are investors irrational leading to anomalous returns in the market not explained by the CAPM market factor?

## Problems

1. Assume that stocks are sorted into a 2×3 matrix of size and value (BM). How did Fama and French (1993) use this matrix to create their size and value factors?
2. Draw a diagram that depicts Fama and French's three-factor model. How many dimensions are there in your drawing?

## References


Banz, R.W. 1981. The relationship between return and market value of common stocks. *Journal of Financial Economics* 9: 3–18.

Basu, S. 1977. Investment performance of common stocks in relation to their price-earnings ratios: A test of the efficient market hypothesis. *Journal of Finance* 12: 129–156.

Bhandari, L.C. 1988. Debt/equity ratio and expected common stock returns: Empirical evidence. *Journal of Finance* 43: 507–528.

Black, F. 1972. Capital market equilibrium with restricted borrowing. *Journal of Business* 45: 444–454.

Black, F. 1993. Beta and return. *Journal of Portfolio Management* 20: 8–18.

Black, F. 1995. Estimating expected return. *Financial Analysts Journal* 49: 36–38.

Black, F., M.C. Jensen, and M. Scholes. 1972. The capital asset pricing model: Some empirical tests. In *Studies in the Theory of Capital Markets*, ed. M.C. Jensen. New York, NY: Praeger.

Clare, A.D., R. Priestley, and S.H. Thomas. 1998. Reports of beta's death are premature: Evidence from the UK. *Journal of Banking and Finance* 22: 1207–1229.

Daniel, K., and S. Titman. 2012. Testing factor-model explanations of market anomalies. *Critical Finance Review* 1: 103–139.

Fama, E.F., and K.R. French. 1992. The cross-section of expected stock returns. *Journal of Finance* 47: 427–465.

Fama, E.F., and K.R. French. 1993. The cross-section of expected returns. *Journal of Financial Economics* 33: 3–56.

Fama, E.F., and K.R. French. 1995. Size and book-to-market factors in earnings and returns. *Journal of Finance* 50: 131–156.

Fama, E.F., and K.R. French. 1996. The CAPM is wanted, dead or alive. *Journal of Finance* 51: 1947–1958.

Fama, E.F., and K.R. French. 1998. Value versus growth: The international evidence. *Journal of Finance* 53: 1975–1999.

Fama, E.F., and K.R. French. 2004. The capital asset pricing model: Theory and evidence. *Journal of Economic Perspectives* 18: 25–46.

Fama, E.F., and J.D. MacBeth. 1973. Risk, return, and equilibrium: Empirical tests. *Journal of Political Economy* 81: 607–636.

Gibbons, M.R., S.A. Ross, and J. Shanken. 1989. A test of the efficiency of a given portfolio. *Econometrica* 57: 1121–1152.

Gordon, M.J. 1962. *The Investment, Financing, and Valuation of the Corporation*. Homewood, IL: R.D Irwin.

Hsia, C.-C., B.R. Fuller, and B.Y.J. Chen. 2000. Is beta dead or alive? *Journal of Business Finance and Accounting* 27: 283–311.

Jagannathan, R., and E.R. McGrattan. 1995. The CAPM debate. *Quarterly Review* 19 (4, Fall): 2–17. Federal Reserve Bank of Minneapolis.

Kolari, J.W., W. Liu, and J. Huang. 2021. *A New Capital Asset Pricing Model: Theory and Evidence*. New York, NY: Palgrave Macmillan.

Kothari, S.P., J. Shanken, and R.G. Sloan. 1995. Another look at the cross-section of expected stock returns. *Journal of Finance* 50: 185–224.

Lakonishok, J., and A.C. Shapiro. 1986. Systematic risk, total risk, and size as determinants of stock market returns. *Journal of Banking and Finance* 10: 115–132.

Lakonishok, J., and A. Shleifer. 1984. Stock returns, beta, variance and size: An empirical analysis. *Financial Analysts Journal* 40: 36–41.

Lewellen, J., S. Nagel, and J.A. Shanken. 2010. A skeptical appraisal of asset pricing tests. *Journal of Financial Economics* 96: 175–194.

Lintner, J. 1965. The valuation of risk assets and the selection of risky investments in stock portfolios and capital budgets. *Review of Economics and Statistics* 47: 13–37.

Markowitz, H.M. 1959. *Portfolio selection: Efficient diversification of investments*. New York, NY: Wiley.

Merton, R.C. 1973. An intertemporal capital asset pricing model. *Econometrica* 41: 867–887.

Modigliani, F., and M.H. Miller. 1958. The cost of capital, corporation finance and the theory of investment. *American Economic Review* 48: 261–297.

Modigliani, F., and M.H. Miller. 1963. Corporation income taxes and the cost of capital: A correction. *American Economic Review* 53: 433–443.

Mossin, J. 1966. Equilibrium in a capital asset market. *Econometrica* 34: 768–783.

Roll, R. 1977. A critique of the asset pricing theory's tests, part I: On past and potential future testability of the theory. *Journal of Financial Economics* 4: 129–176.

Rosenberg, B., K. Reid, and R. Lanstein. 1985. Persuasive evidence of market inefficiency. *Journal of Portfolio Management* 11: 9–17.

Ross, S.A. 1976. The arbitrage theory of capital asset pricing. *Journal of Economic Theory* 13: 341–360.

Sharpe, W.F. 1964. Capital asset prices: A theory of market equilibrium under conditions of risk. *Journal of Finance* 19: 425–442.

Statman, D. 1980. Book values and stock returns. *The Chicago MBA: A Journal of Selected Papers* 4: 25–45.

Treynor, J. L. 1961. Market value, time, and risk. Unpublished manuscript.

Treynor, J. L. 1962. Toward a theory of market value of risky assets. Unpublished manuscript.

# 9 Anomalies and Multifactor Models

Fama and French (1992, 1993, 1995, 1996) published a series of papers in the 1990s that replaced the CAPM with a three-factor model containing size and value factors. Their innovative long/short zero-investment factors based on firm characteristics of size and book-to-market equity ratios sparked a revolution in asset pricing. Loosely grounded in Merton's (1972) ICAPM and Ross' APT (1976) theoretical multifactor asset pricing models, the three-factor model became the foundation for many new factors and models that continue to be proposed by researchers.

In this chapter we highlight some of the most popular multifactor models in the field of asset pricing. Carhart (1997) added a momentum factor to create a four-factor model for studying mutual fund performance. Fama and French (2015, 2018) extended their three-factor to five- and six-factor models. Other researchers, such as Hou et al. (2015) as well as Stambaugh and Yuan (2017) proposed alternative four-factor models. In a major departure from previous multifactor models, Fama and French (2020), Lettau and Pelger (2020), and others began using machine learning and artificial intelligence (AI) to create multifactors driven by stock return data instead of researcher judgment. In general, asset pricing models can be classified into those based on theoretical, discretionary, and machine learning methods. Due to the increasing diversity of asset pricing models, a new problem has arisen. Cochrane (2011), a *factor zoo* exists with hundreds of different factors. Which factors should be used? Which combinations of factors yield the best model? These questions are new challenges facing the field of asset pricing.

---

**Supplementary Information** The online version contains supplementary material available at https://doi.org/10.1007/978-3-031-16784-3_9.

 
J. W. Kolari and S. Pynnönen, *Investment Valuation and Asset Pricing*,
https://doi.org/10.1007/978-3-031-16784-3_9

## 9.1 Carhart Four-Factor Model

*Momentum* is an old anomaly that goes back centuries in early financial markets around the world. The idea is simple—winner stocks (or assets) will continue or persist to win and losing stocks will continue to lose in the near future. Jegadeesh and Titman (1993) showed that momentum exists for U.S. stocks in the period 1965–1989. They formed momentum portfolios that are long stocks in the top decile of returns in the past year and short stocks in the bottom decile of returns in the past year (see the illustration in Fig. 9.1). This kind of *relative strength* trading strategy is well known to professional investment managers. Long/short momentum portfolios earned relatively high returns. For example, holding this portfolio for three months yielded between 1.3 and 1.5% per month or about 16 or 17% per year! Over time these momentum profits disappear and eventually reverse with negative earnings. Are these return patterns due to behavioral investor responses or systematic market risk? The authors left this question for further study.

Carhart (1997) investigated momentum profits in mutual funds holding diversified equity portfolios. Do mutual fund managers use momentum persistence in stock returns to outperform other mutual funds? To answer this question, he modified the three-factor model by incorporating a momentum factor. His four-factor model is:

$$R_{it} - R_{ft} = \alpha_i + \beta_{i,m}(R_{mt} - R_{ft}) + \beta_{i,S} SMB_t + \beta_{i,V} HML_t + \beta_{i,MOM} MOM_t + e_{it}, \tag{9.1}$$

where $MOM_t$ is the Jegadeesh and Titman momentum factor that has low correlation with the $SMB_t$ and $HML_t$ factors. Using mutual funds as the test assets on the left-hand-side of Eq. (9.1) and the sample period 1963–1993, the time-series regression model had very high $R^2$ values typically over 90% and

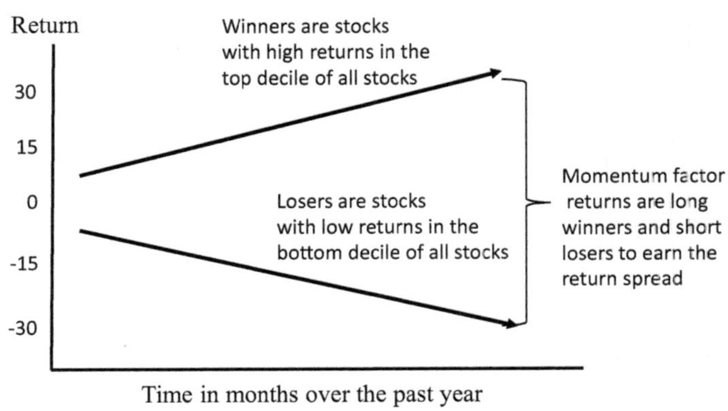


**Fig. 9.1** Momentum factor returns are long/short zero-investment portfolio returns

relatively low $\alpha_i$ values for the *i*th mutual fund. Hence, the model explained differences in mutual funds' returns. A number of interesting findings were revealed by Carhart's analyses.

1. The top (bottom) decile performing mutual funds in the past year have returns that were positively (negatively) correlated with the momentum factor.
2. An investor that buys last year's top decile funds and sells the bottom decile funds earned about 8% per year.
3. Funds with high $\alpha_i$s (or mispricing errors) tended to have above average alphas in the near future.
4. Mutual fund management expenses, turnover (i.e., buying and selling activity), and load fees (i.e., sales charges on investors to invest in a fund) lowered fund returns. Due to the latter finding, no load mutual funds with no sales charges that are passively managed (e.g., hold the S &P 500 index) outperformed load mutual funds that are actively managed.
5. High performing positive $\alpha_i$ funds (i.e., high risk-adjusted abnormal returns) tended to have high investment expenses that offsets their higher gross returns before expenses for the most part. More generally, most funds actually underperformed risk-adjusted returns after taking into account their investment expenses.

Table 9.1 reports selected results from the Carhart study on the relation between mutual fund performance and their operating characteristics. Mutual funds in the low return decile in the sample period had relatively high expense ratios and turnover compared to most other funds. Other characteristics, such as age and size of funds, did not explain the difference between high and low return mutual funds. Based on these and other findings, Carhart (1997, p. 81) made the following investment recommendations:

> (1) Avoid funds with persistently poor performance;
> (2) funds with high returns last year have higher-than-average expected returns next year, but not in years thereafter; and
> (3) the investment costs of expense ratios, transactions costs, and load fees all have a direct, negative impact on mutual fund performance.

An important takeaway for investors is to buy passive mutual funds rather than actively managed funds to earn higher risk-adjusted long-run returns. The Carhart study demonstrates that asset pricing models can be used as practical investment tools. Due to this study, many later models have included a momentum factor to better explain stock returns.

Of course, a criticism of momentum, like the size and value factors, is the lack of theory. Why do relative strength measures explain stock returns? They are so simple and widely used in investment practice that investors should have arbitraged away any momentum profits in an efficient market (e.g., buy underpriced winners and sell overpriced losers). Since momentum consistently is significant in

**Table 9.1** The relation between mutual fund performance and their operating characteristics in the Carhart (1997) study

| | Age of firm | Net assets | Expense ratio | Turnover | Maximum load |
|---|---|---|---|---|---|
| High return decile | 14.1 | 128.7 | 1.22 | 92.9 | 4.18 |
| Decile 3 | 17.3 | 194.3 | 1.10 | 76.3 | 4.72 |
| Decile 5 | 18.3 | 185.9 | 1.09 | 68.4 | 4.71 |
| Decile 7 | 18.3 | 169.7 | 1.14 | 62.2 | 4.50 |
| Low return decile | 13.6 | 77.1 | 1.92 | 81.4 | 4.38 |

This table reports selected results from Carhart (1997). Based on the returns of U.S. equity mutual funds, mispricing error is regressed on different operating characteristics of mutual funds. The dependent variable in these time-series regressions is monthly mispricing error or $\alpha$ on an out-of-sample basis. More specifically, the four-factor model is estimated for a mutual fund using three previous years of monthly returns. Alpha is estimated in the next month using the factor loadings of the model from the previous three years multiplied by the four factors in the next month. This out-of-sample monthly alpha is regressed on mutual fund characteristics. The average results for over 1,800 mutual funds are shown in the table by mutual fund returns sorted into deciles from high to low returns. The results shown below are based on Carhart (1997, Table IV, p. 66)

explaining stock returns, there must be a risk story. What is the underlying equilibrium process in a mean-variance investment opportunity world that accounts for its persistence as a significant asset pricing factor? In this regard, it is worth noting that momentum is considered by many researchers to be the foremost anomaly or puzzle in asset pricing.

Another problem is that *momentum crashes* sometimes occur. Research by Barroso and Santa-Clara (2015), Daniel and Moskowitz (2016), and others has shown that the momentum factor becomes negative at times, especially is down market states related to an economic recession when market volatility is high. For this reason they scale (or divide) investments in momentum portfolios using measures of market volatility to decrease the magnitude of momentum portfolio return crashes. Perhaps researchers should scale the momentum factor in asset pricing models to take into account market conditions. More generally, given that factor returns can dramatically change over time from economic boom times to slowdowns in recessions, it seems reasonable to infer that the performance of asset pricing models can be affected by the business cycle. In one sample period a model may more significantly price assets compared to another period due to fluctuating economic and related financial market conditions. In our opinion, robust asset pricing factors and models should significantly price assets under different economic and market conditions.

## 9.2 Fama and French Four- and Five-Factor Models

Building on their three-factor model, Fama and French (2015) argued that stock returns related to BM can be linked to the operating profit and capital investment characteristics of firms. High BM (value) firms tend to have low profit and investment, and vice versa for low BM firms.[1] As theoretical justification, they cited the dividend discount model[2] in which the value of a share of stock is:

$$P_{it} = \sum_{\tau=1}^{\infty} \frac{E(D_{t+\tau})}{(1+R)^{\tau}}, \tag{9.2}$$

where expected future dividends per share (over an infinite time horizon) are discounted at the required rate of return $R$ by investors. Assuming two stocks have the same expected dividends, stocks with higher prices have lower discount rates over time. As risk increases, the discount rate $R$ increases and thereby lowers the stock price (i.e., risk-averse investors will buy a stock at a lower price as compensation for higher risk, all else the same). They reasoned that the expected dividends in the numerator are a function of firm cash flows, equity earnings available to shareholders, and changes in the book value of equity.

Based on these basic concepts, they specified the following five-factor model:

$$\begin{aligned} R_{it} - R_{ft} = \alpha_i &+ \beta_{i,m}(R_{mt} - R_{ft}) + \beta_{i,S} SMB_t + \beta_{i,V} HML_t \\ &+ \beta_{i,R} RMW_t + \beta_{i,C} CMA_t + e_{it}, \end{aligned} \tag{9.3}$$

where $RMW_t$ is of the robust profit minus weak profit factor, $CMA_t$ is the conservative minus aggressive capital investment factor, and other notation is as before. These new multifactors are formed by using four sorts: two size groups, two BM groups, two operating profit groups, and two capital investment groups. The intersection of these four sorts gives 16 value-weighted portfolios. For example, the size factor is long the eight small size portfolios and short the eight big portfolios. Similarly, value, profit, and investment factors are constructed. Fama and French were careful to point out that, in the context of the ICAPM, the four multifactors measure sensitivities to unknown state variables. Despite not knowing the underlying state variables, the factors capture their effects on expected stock returns.

In the sample period 1963–2013, the average monthly risk premiums for their five factors were as follows: $R_m - R_f = 0.50\%$, $SMB = 0.30\%$, $HML = 0.30\%$, $RMW = 0.25\%$, and $CMA = 0.14\%$. The correlations between the multifactors were relatively low, which means that each of their factors accounts for different information in the market. They compared the five-factor model to different combinations of factors in three- and four-factor models (or seven models altogether). In addition to 25 size and BM sorted portfolios as test assets, they formed 25 size and operating profit, 25 size and capital investment (denoted Inv), 32 size and BM and operating profit, 32 size and BM and capital investment, and 32 size and operating profit and capital investment portfolios. They did not use industry portfolios in their tests. Next, Gibbons, Ross, and Shanken (GRS) (1989) tests of

[1] Novy-Marx (2013) also found that stock returns are related to expected profits.
[2] Gordon (1962) is famous for this simple valuation model.

the joint hypothesis that all $\alpha_i$s equal zero for each set of test asset portfolios were conducted. They found that:

1. average intercepts for the five-factor model were lower than the three-factor model; and
2. the five-factor model performance was similar to a four-factor model that drops the $HML$ factor.

Given these findings, they dropped the $HML$ value factor and proposed the following more parsimonious four-factor model:

$$\begin{aligned} R_{it} - R_f = \alpha_i + \beta_{i,m}(R_m - R_{ft}) + \beta_{i,S}SMB_t + \beta_{i,R}RMW_t \\ + \beta_{i,C}CMA_t + e_{it}. \end{aligned} \tag{9.4}$$

They did not add a momentum factor due to correlations between other multifactors. Also, more or less than four factors appeared to diminish the performance of the multifactor model. Lastly, Fama and French (1995, p. 21) mentioned that their model had difficulty pricing some portfolios:

> The portfolios of small and big stocks in the lowest B/M quartile and highest Inv (growth stocks that invest a lot) produce intercepts more than 3.5 standard errors from zero but of opposite sign – (-0.20% per month, $t = -4.18$) for small stocks and positive (0.37%, $t =$ 5.39) for big stocks.

Hence, these portfolios are not priced by their four-factor model, which suggests that a missing factor is needed to price these test assets.

## 9.3 Hou, Xue, and Zhang Four-Factor Model

Hou et al. (2015) developed a model that is very close to the Fama and French four-factor model. Here we see an example of research similarities between independent researchers. They contended that the three-factor model was not able to account for a number of asset pricing anomalies. To price stock portfolios associated with these anomalies, the following four-factor model was proposed:

$$\begin{aligned} R_{it} - R_{ft} = \alpha_i + \beta_{i,m}(R_{mt} - R_{ft}) + \beta_{i,S}ME_t + \beta_{i,R}ROE_t \\ + \beta_{i,C}IA_t + e_{it}, \end{aligned} \tag{9.5}$$

where $ME$ is equity market capitalization, $ROE$ is return on equity, $IA$ is the investment to assets ratio of the firm, and other notation is as before. Their conceptual framework is the production (Cochrane 1991). An investment-based asset pricing model is built on the $q$-theory of investment, which predicts that firms with high investment/asset ratios (profit/assets ratios) should earn higher stock returns than those with low investment/asset (profit/asset) ratios. As Fama and French

(2015) argued, it seems natural that capital investment and profitability impact firm cash flows and dividends and, in turn, stock returns.

Using U.S. stock return data from the period 1972 to 2012, their so-called *q-factor model* explained many different anomalies in stock returns (i.e., their test asset portfolios), including momentum, value versus growth, capital investment, profitability, intangibles (e.g., corporate governance), and trading frictions (e.g., illiquidity, idiosyncratic volatility, short-term reversal, etc.). Of almost 80 anomalies, about one-half had insignificant average returns, which means that these anomalies were not present in their data. Among 35 anomalies that had significant average returns, the *q*-factor model had lower average intercept ($\alpha_i$) terms based on Eq. (9.5) than the Fama and French three-factor model as well as Carhart four-factor model—namely, 0.20%, 0.55%, and 0.55% for these models, respectively. Only 5-out-of-35 anomalies had significant alphas (at the five percent level) compared to 19 for the Carhart model and 27 for the Fama and French model. They inferred that their model did a better job of explaining anomalies than these other popular models. They did not test the Fama and French five-factor model that appeared in the literature at the same time in 2015.[3] Hou et al. (2015, p. 685) concluded:

> Many seemingly unrelated anomalies turn out to be different manifestations of the investment and profitability effects. These empirical findings highlight the importance of understanding the driving forces behind the *q*-factors and their broad empirical power in the cross-section.

## 9.4 Stambaugh and Yuan Four-Factor Model

Multifactor models continued to evolve. Stambaugh and Yuan (2017) developed a new four-factor model as follows:

$$R_{it} - R_{ft} = \alpha_i + \beta_{i,m}(R_{mt} - R_{ft}) + \beta_{i,S} SMB_t + \beta_{i,MT} MGMT_t + \beta_{i,P} PERF_t + e_{it}, \tag{9.6}$$

where $MGMT$ is a management factor, $PERF$ is a performance factor, and other notation is as before. The latter $MGMT$ and $PERF$ factors were constructed from stocks' rankings with respect to a number of asset pricing anomalies. They grouped 11 well-known anomalies[4] into two clusters. Next, these clusters were

---

[3] In a later study by Barillas and Shanken (2018), various factors and models in previous studies were tested. Using novel tests of the relative performance of different models, in both in-sample and out-of-sample tests, they found that a six-factor model containing market, size, value, profit, investment, and momentum factors outperformed other possible models.

[4] The 11 anomalies were: net stock issues, equity issuance, accruals, net operating assets, asset growth, investment to assets, financial distress, O-score of distress, momentum, gross profitability, and return on assets.

**Table 9.2** Intercept or $\alpha$ estimates for selected anomaly portfolios from January 1967 to December 2013 in the Stambaugh and Yuan (2017) study

| | Anomaly return | FF 3-factor | FF 5-factor | HXZ 4-factor $q$ | SY 4-factor |
|---|---|---|---|---|---|
| Net stock issues | 0.56*** | 0.66*** | 0.32*** | 0.37*** | 0.06 |
| Accruals | 0.43*** | 0.51*** | 0.56*** | 0.65*** | 0.31** |
| Asset growth | 0.52*** | 0.32*** | 0.06 | 0.08 | −0.22** |
| Distress | 0.44 | 1.21*** | 0.62** | 0.20 | −0.16 |
| Momentum | 1.26*** | 1.59*** | 1.35*** | 0.48 | 0.12 |
| Gross profitability | 0.28* | 0.69*** | 0.35*** | 0.39** | 0.27 |
| Book-to-market | 0.43** | −0.20** | −0.14 | −0.03 | −0.17 |

This table reports selected results from Stambaugh and Yuan (2017). Based on U.S. stock returns, monthly $\alpha$ estimates (in percent) are shown. These mispricing errors are estimated for the following models: Fama and French three- and five-factor models, Hou, Xue, and Zhang four-factor $q$ model, and Stambaug and Yuan four-factor model. The sample period is January 1967–December 2013. Anomaly returns are long-short portfolio returns using high and low decile returns. The results shown below are based on Stambaugh and Yuan (2017, Table 4, p. 1287)
*Note* Asterisks indicate that the $\alpha$ estimate is statistically different from zero at the
* = 10%, ** = 5%, and *** = 1% levels

used to define two long/short zero-investment portfolios (viz., *MGMT* and *PERF*), which they called *mispricing factors.* Unlike other models, their size factor is not based on a two-way sort on size and BM. Departing from previous researchers, they drop stocks contained in their two mispricing factors' portfolios and create a small-minus-big size factor. These stocks are less mispriced than other stocks. Further departing from other models, they do not include a value factor (*HML*). They found that their mispricing factors *MGMT* and *PERF* priced BM portfolios such that the value factor was redundant in their model.

Using the sample period 1967–2013 and U.S. stock returns, they tested alternative models using the anomalies in Hou et al. (2015). Table 9.2 shows some selected results from their study. In the left-hand column of numbers the table gives the average anomaly return computed as long minus short portfolio returns using high and low decile returns for each anomaly. They compared the multifactor model in Eq. (9.6) with the Fama and French three- and four-factor models and Hou, Xue, and Zhang four-factor $q$-factor model. Notice that estimated alphas ($\alpha_i$s) tend to be lower in magnitude and significance (indicated by asterisks) for the Hou, Xue, and Zhang $q$-factor model as well as Stambaugh and Yuan four-factor models compared to the Fama and French three- and four-factor models. Also, comparing the four-factor models in the last two columns, their performance is somewhat similar, but the Stambaugh and Yuan model outperforms the $q$-factor model in terms of smaller and less significant mispricing error.

The authors reported further evidence that their four-factor model did a better job of pricing factors in the other models. That is, they used the factors in other models as anomaly portfolios or test assets. In view of these and other tests, they concluded that, instead of constructing each factor from a single anomaly, multi-factor models can be improved by developing factors from multiple anomalies. In this way each factor has a broader ability to price a wider array of stocks manifesting different anomalies. This innovative multifactor approach has the advantage of reducing the number of factors in asset pricing models. With so many factors being proposed by researchers that are associated with different anomalies, Stambaugh and Yuan (2017, p. 1307) observed:

> In this sense, while parsimonious factor models are appealing and useful, there are limits to their abilities to explain expected returns. Nevertheless, among such models, those with mispricing factors appear to have greater ability than prominent alternatives.

As additional proof, they constructed a single mispricing factor from the 11 anomalies and found that a three-factor model with market, size, and the mispricing factor outperformed the Fama and French five-factor model. In other words, the value, profit, and capital investment factors can be collapsed into one mispricing factor using their methods. This multiple mispricing approach to constructing factors therefore can help to reduce the number of factors to develop more parsimonious asset pricing models.

## 9.5 Fama and French Six-Factor Model

Continuing to build on their earlier empirical work, Fama and French (2018) added the momentum factor (*MOM*) as in Carhart (1997) to their five-factor model to form a six-factor model[5]:

$$\begin{aligned} R_{it} - R_{ft} = \alpha_i &+ \beta_{i,m}(R_{mt} - R_{ft}) + \beta_{i,S} SMB_t + \beta_{i,V} HML_t \\ &+ \beta_{i,R} RMW_t + \beta_{i,C} CMA_t + \beta_{i,M} MOM_t + \varepsilon_{it}, \end{aligned} \tag{9.7}$$

where notation is as before. Moreover, they tested other value, profitability, and capital investment factors by further sorting each factor into a small and big factor (e.g., small stocks with high BM returns minus small stocks with low BM returns $= HML_S$ and big stocks with high BM returns minus big stocks with low BM returns $= HML_B$). Using sorts on size with the other factors (not just BM as in the past), a number of different size factors were created also. Altogether, excluding the market factor, they considered 48 multifactors!

The empirical analyses sought to determine which configuration of factors provided the best model. To do this, various tests of the intercepts ($\alpha_i$s) were conducted using U.S. stock returns from 1963 to 2016. The winner model among

---

[5] As cited in footnote 3, Barillas and Shanken (2018) tested this model also.

different models was the one with the smallest squared Sharpe ratio for the intercepts.[6] Different versions of their three-, five-, and six-factor models were tested using various combinations of multifactors. They found that the winner was a six-factor model comprised of market and size factors plus small stock factors for the value, profitability, capital investment, and momentum factors. Other tests rejected the CAPM as well as three- and five-factor models.[7] With so many factors and contender models, it seems reasonable to ask: How should researchers choose factors and models? To avoid potential data snooping (or dredging), Fama and French (2018, p. 247) gave the following cautionary advice:

> We suggest that model comparisons in any paper should be limited by theory, even an umbrella theory like the dividend discount model, and by evidence on model robustness out-of-sample (different time periods and markets).

As mentioned before, intercept tests are typically in-sample, not out-of-sample tests in which the model is estimated in a sample period and then tests are conducted on returns in the subsequent period.[8] For out-of-sample tests, Fama and MacBeth (1973) two-step regression tests are needed. We will return to this discussion shortly.

## 9.6 Fama and French Cross-Section Factors

Recently, Fama and French (2020) proposed modified versions of their models in which the multifactors are replaced by long/short mimicking portfolios estimated from a cross-sectional regression. As observed by Ferson (2019, p. 223) and others, estimated coefficients (or $\lambda_k$s) in a Fama and MacBeth cross-sectional regression are long/short portfolios (e.g., long high BM stock returns and short low BM stock returns for the market price of risk associated with value factor loadings). Given this fact, Fama and French used these mimicking portfolios as the factors in their five-factor model in Eq. (9.3). Let's take a closer look at their methods.

In one version of their new model, using a cross-sectional regression with tests asset portfolios, they regress portfolios' returns in month $t$ (e.g., 25 size and BM

[6] Beyond the scope of the present introductory text, this squared Sharpe ratio test of intercepts was based on work by Barillas and Shanken (2018), who developed the performance metric for comparing competing asset pricing models.

[7] Barillas and Shanken (2018) tested different factors and models and found that a six-factor model with market, size, value, profit, investment, and momentum factors outperformed other models in both in-sample and out-of-sample tests.

[8] Fama and French (2018) conducted a different kind of out-of-sample test for models by using a subsample of returns in the sample period for in-sample test statistics and then using the remaining returns in the same sample period for out-of-sample test statistics.

portfolios) on lagged firm characteristic values at time $t - 1$ as follows:

$$R_{it} = R_{zt} + R_{MCt}MC_{it-1} + R_{BMt}BM_{it-1} + R_{OPt}OP_{it-1} + R_{INVt}INV_{it-1} + e_{it}, \tag{9.8}$$

where $MC_{it-1}$, $BM_{it-1}$, $OP_{it-1}$, and $INV_{it-1}$ are observed values of size, the book-to-market ratio, operating profitability, and the rate of growth of assets. The intercept $R_{zt}$ was named the *level return* not explained by these firm characteristic variables. In this equation, the corresponding $\lambda_k$ coefficients (associated with the $k$ factor loadings) are denoted $R_{MCt}$, $R_{BMt}$, $R_{OPt}$, and $R_{INVt}$, respectively. These $\lambda_k$s are the mimicking portfolio returns or so-called *cross-section factors*. They then created a new five-factor model by substituting these cross-section factors into their original time-series five-factor model in Eq. (9.3) as follows:

$$R_{it} - R_{ft} = \alpha_i + \beta_{i,m}(R_{mt} - R_{ft}) + \beta_{i,S}R_{MCt} + \beta_{i,V}R_{BMt} + \beta_{i,R}R_{OPt} + \beta_{i,C}R_{INVt} + e_{it}, \tag{9.9}$$

where their long/short factors $SMB$, $HML$, $RMW$, and $CMA$ are replaced by the cross-section factors.

Previous studies by Back et al. (2013, 2015) showed that this cross-sectional regression approach is a way to let the data itself (i.e., accounting variables for firms) determine multifactors rather than constructing them using $2 \times 3$ size and BM sorts (see Fig. 8.1) that are ad hoc or subjective in terms of using researcher judgment. We can consider this new five-factor model a machine learning competitor of their original five-factor model that was based on researcher judgment.

In another twist, they proposed a *mathematical four-factor model* as follows:

$$R_{it} - R_{zt} = MC_{it-1}R_{MCt} + BM_{it-1}R_{BMt} + OP_{it-1}R_{OPt} + INV_{it-1}R_{INVt} + e_{it}, \tag{9.10}$$

where there is no intercept mispricing term, and the "coefficients" are the accounting variables lagged one period. You can see that there are no regression coefficients in this model. It is simply a mathematical model with time-varying loadings (accounting variables) in place of constant beta coefficients. The cross-section factors are the multifactors. There is no market factor which would require a regression coefficient to be estimated if it were in the model. The average of the error terms $e_{it}$ over $t$ time periods becomes the mispricing alpha in this model.[9]

The advantage of the mathematical model, in the spirit of conditional models discussed in Chapter 6, is that the risk loadings are allowed to vary over

[9] In regression models with an intercept term, OLS fits the model such that the average of the residuals, or $E(e_{it})$, approximately equals zero. Without an error term in model (9.10) the average of the residual terms will not be zero and, therefore, is a good proxy for the mispricing alpha.

time. Recall earlier that, since we know that beta risks vary over time, it was hoped that conditional models could strengthen the CAPM and other models. However, research showed that the improvement was not sufficient to save the CAPM or materially improve the results of other models. Perhaps this new conditional model using time-varying accounting variables could revive the conditional approach.

Fama and French specified a second conditional model with time-varying risk loadings using their five-factor model:

$$\begin{aligned} R_{it} - R_{ft} = {} & \alpha_i + \beta_{i,m}(R_{mt} - R_{ft}) + \beta_{i,S}SMB_t + \beta_{i,V}HML_t + \beta_{i,R}RMW_t \\ & + \beta_{i,C}CMA_t + \beta_{i,S2}MC_{it-1}SMB_t + \beta_{i,V2}BM_{it-1}HML_t \\ & + \beta_{i,R2}OP_{it-1}RMW_t + \beta_{i,C2}INV_{it-1}CMA_t + e_{it}, \end{aligned} \tag{9.11}$$

where the interaction terms (e.g., $MC_{it-1} \times SMB_t$) allow for conditional time variation in the regression coefficients. The accounting variables $MC$, $BM$, $OP$, and $INV$ are the instruments in this regression model. They did not instrument the intercept, which therefore is constant over time. Will this model perform as well as the conditional mathematical model?

U.S. stock returns from 1963 to 2018 were employed in their analyses. They used joint tests that the intercepts ($\alpha_i$s) equal zero.[10] The main findings of their study were:

1. conditional models (9.10) and (9.11) outperformed the other models with constant risk loadings over time;
2. conditional mathematical model (9.10) outperformed conditional model (9.11) with instruments;
3. cross-section factor model (9.9) (with constant coefficient loadings) outperformed conditional model (9.11) with instruments to allow time-varying risk loadings; and
4. cross-section factor model (9.9) (with constant coefficient loadings) outperformed their original five- and six-factor models but only by a small or marginal amount.

From these results, Fama and French (2020, p. 1915) concluded:

> Simply substituting CS (cross-section) factors for TS (time-series) factors in regression models ... doesn't improve much on the descriptions of average returns.

In other words, the cross-section factors did not improve their original time-series models enough to warrant their use. However, using cross-section factors

[10] As in their 2015 study of the six-factor model, they applied maximum squared Sharpe ratio tests of the intercepts also (see footnote 6).

in combination with firm characteristics (or accounting variables) in the conditional mathematical model improved upon time-series models using researcher definitions of factors based on firm characteristics as in their original models.

A drawback of the conditional mathematical model is that no out-of-sample Fama and MacBeth tests are possible. The intercept tests performed in their study are entirely in-sample tests. Simin (2008) has argued that step ahead (e.g., one-month-ahead that are out-of-sample) Fama and MacBeth tests avoid a number of model evaluation problems, such as data snooping. Also, Ferson et al. (2013) have recommended that the practical value of asset pricing models should be evaluated based on out-of-sample tests.

An important point here is that model tests should be *investable*. For example, an investor picks stocks based on the estimation of their risk and then subsequently tracks their return performance in the future. Fama–MacBeth tests first estimate model parameters from available historical data. In the second step, returns in the next (out-of-sample) month are regressed on previously estimated parameters (beta loadings). There is no possibility of cheating in this setup. The model that performs best in the second step dominates the other models. Note that some researchers use an in-sample Fama–MacBeth approach. Model parameters are estimated with monthly returns over many years in a sample period. Then returns in each month within the sample period are regressed on the model parameters in the second step. But this method is not investable. Investors could not rely on this kind of analysis to guide them concerning the relation between past risk and future returns. They want models that give estimates of risk parameters that are related to returns in the future rather than the past. The Fama and French conditional mathematical model (using time-varying firm characteristics as risk loadings and cross-section factors) proved itself to be a dominant model using in-sample tests. However, out-of-sample tests are needed to assess its practical use as an investable strategy.

## 9.7 Lettau and Pelger Latent Five-Factor Model

In light of the growing number of possible factors in asset pricing models, Lettau and Pelger (2020) proposed a method for finding the most important factors. Their method identifies latent asset pricing factors using Principal Component Analysis (PCA). PCA is a statistical method that can reduce the information contained in sample observations (e.g., stock portfolios' returns) into a select few components that summarize all of the sample information.

Each factor in an asset pricing model can be considered a risk dimension. The CAPM is a single risk dimension (market factor) model. The three-factor Fama and French model has three-dimensional risk. If say 50 different stocks are input into a PCA (i.e., we start with 50 dimensions), the PCA seeks to reduce the dimensions down to a smaller set that explains the data. In this way PCA is very similar to factor analysis covered in Chapter 7's discussion of empirical tests of Ross' (1976) APT. It is reasonable to believe that some of the stocks' returns are correlated with one another. For example, 10 stocks' returns could be highly correlated and therefore are combined into one dimension. The first dimension in PCA has higher explanatory power in terms of stock returns than other dimensions. In their study, they found that stock returns could be explained by a five-dimensional space. The sixth dimension and higher dimensions were dropped because they did not significantly help to explain the data observations (or stock returns).

Since the dimensions are not readily observable, they are referred to as *latent* or *hidden*. Each component is constructed by PCA to be orthogonal (or uncorrelated) with other components. For this reason, PCA has some connection to the intertemporal CAPM (ICAPM) of Merton (1972) and arbitrage pricing theory (APT) of Ross (1976) which assume orthogonal asset pricing factors.

PCA is a machine learning technique that has been applied in many fields of study, including finance and economics. Rather than use researcher judgment to form factors, computer algorithms within the PCA software let the data select the factors based on correlation patterns in stock returns. In Fama and French's (2020) study of cross-section factors, they let the data compute these factors from cross-sectional regressions. PCA is another example of machine learning in factor construction. According to Lettau and Pelger, PCA analyses yielded five systematic factors.

In the sample period 1963–2017, the authors gathered U.S. stock returns for 370 portfolios sorted on size, BM, accruals, investment, profitability, momentum, volatility measures, and other characteristics of firms. In-sample intercept ($\alpha_i$) tests of mispricing errors were performed on different models. Some out-of-sample intercept tests were conducted also (i.e., factor loadings were estimated and then average pricing errors were computed in the step ahead period).

Table 9.3 summarizes selected results in their paper. They compared their PCA model (denoted LP-PCA) to standard PCA methods as well as the Fama and French three- and five-factor models. The root mean square of alpha ($\alpha$) estimates, or $RMS_\alpha$, was used to measure mispricing error in the sample period

**Table 9.3** Mispricing error of different models in the Lettau and Pelger (2020) study

| | In-sample | Out-of-sample | In-sample | Out-of-sample |
|---|---|---|---|---|
| Model | 370 portfolios | 370 portfolios | 270 stocks | 270 stocks |
| LP-PCA | 0.16 | 0.15 | 0.27 | 0.43 |
| PCA | 0.22 | 0.19 | 0.28 | 0.41 |
| FF three-factor | 0.31 | 0.25 | 0.43 | 0.43 |
| FF five-factor | 0.26 | 0.19 | 0.39 | 0.42 |

This table reports selected results of mispricing error tests in Lettau and Pelger (2020). Average mispricing error is measured by the root mean square of alpha pricing error computed as follows: $RMS_\alpha = (\hat{\alpha}^T \hat{\alpha}/N)^{1/2}$, where $\alpha$ is mispricing error for $T$ months, and $N$ is the number of portfolios or stocks. There are four models: the Lettau-Pelgar five-factor PCA model, five-factor PCA model based on previous methods, and Fama and French three- and five-factor models. In-sample and out-of-sample $RMA_\alpha$ estimates are shown for 370 stock portfolios and 270 individual stocks. The sample period is from November 1963 to December 2017 ($T = 650$). The results shown below are based on Lettau and Pelger (2020, Table 2, p. 2297) comprised of 650 months. Root mean square error (*RMSE*) is a common measure used in statistics to compare the forecasting errors of different models. Using 370 stock portfolios, mispricing errors were smaller for the Lettau and Pelger PCA model (LP-PCA) than the other models both in- and out-of-sample (e.g., 0.16 and 0.15, respectively, compared to 0.26 and 0.19 for the Fama and French five-factor model). Using 270 individual stocks, LP-PCA outperformed the other models in terms of in-sample mispricing error but had similar out-of-sample mispricing error. Summarizing their results, the evidence indicated that the proposed latent five-factor PCA model had smaller pricing errors compared to other models.

Interestingly, the five PCA latent factors identified by Lettau and Pelger were correlated with well-known multifactors, including market, value, and momentum factors. For example, the first latent factor was highly correlated with the value-weighted CRSP market index. This correlation evidence suggests that the latent factors are related to the same systematic risk factors as popular multifactors. Lettau and Pelger (2020, p. 2274) inferred that:

> Our factors imply that a significant amount of characteristic information is redundant.

In other words, machines can do a good job of capturing underlying risk factors in stock returns. As such, researcher judgment is not needed about which firm characteristics should be used in multifactor models. For interested readers, another recent study using PCA is Kozak et al. (2020), who employed portfolios based on firm characteristics to choose a few principal component factors that achieved good out-of-sample performance. While PCA methods yield significant factors, the sources of economic risk underlying machine-made factors can be difficult to discern.

## 9.8 Rise of the Machines

Cross-section factor models in Fama and French (2020) and latent factor models in Lettau and Pelger (2020) and others break new ground in asset pricing. Both types of models employ a machine learning approach to develop empirical asset pricing models. Less researcher judgment and subjective factor construction is used in these mechanical types of models. Large amounts of data are mined by fairly sophisticated computer algorithms and statistical programs in an effort to detect useful patterns in asset pricing. The computer essentially constructs factors by analyzing large amounts of data, thereby moving asset pricing closer to artificial intelligence (AI). Previous multifactor models utilized what we can refer to as *discretionary methods* that depend on human judgment rather than *machine learning methods*. Figure 9.2 summarizes the multifactor models (i.e., discretionary methods). Figure 9.3 reviews the machine learning models (i.e., AI methods).

A missing link in both discretionary and machine learning methods is theory. The CAPM, its companion models, and the APT relied heavily on efficient markets, equilibrium pricing, and portfolio diversification. These traditional *theoretical*

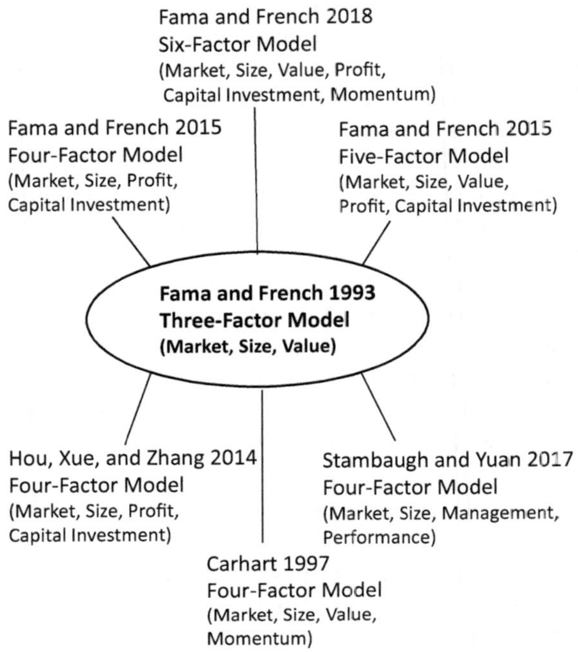


**Fig. 9.2** Multifactor models extensions of the original Fama and French three-factor model using discretionary methods

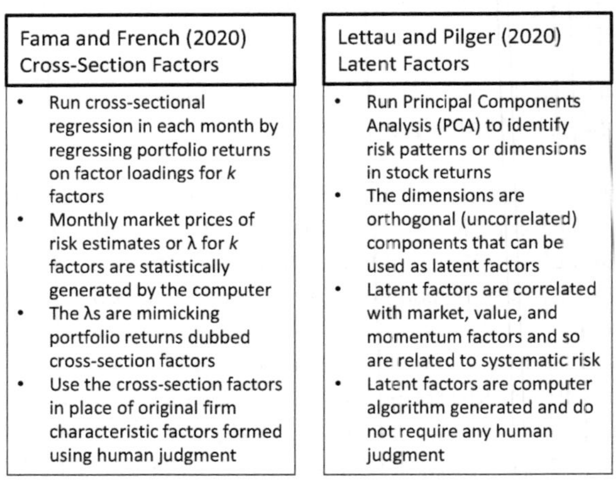


**Fig. 9.3** Machine learning methods based on artificial intelligence (AI) models rather than human judgment

*methods* have been supplanted by contemporary discretionary and machine learning methods due to their better data fitting ability with respect to stock returns. In the next chapter, we will review a new model dubbed the *ZCAPM* that falls within the wheelhouse of theoretical methods. As we will see, the ZCAPM appears to be a serious contender in the pantheon of asset pricing models due to its strong empirical ability to explain the cross-section of average stock returns. Also, it provides a missing link that grafts discretionary and machine learning methods onto the traditional theoretical branch of asset pricing methods.

## 9.9 Summary

After extensive tests using U.S. stock returns over many years, Fama and French (1996) declared the CAPM *dead*. Little or no relation between U.S. stock returns and beta risk led them to propose new multifactor models. In their papers, Fama and French (1992, 1993, 1995, 1996) introduced a three-factor model, which proved to boost the empirical fit to stock returns of the CAPM's market factor by using the firm characteristics of size and value (i.e., book-to-market equity ratios denoted BM). A major innovation was the construction of long/short zero-investment factors—for example, long small stocks and short big stocks as well as long high BM stocks and short low BM stocks. These so-called *multifactors* triggered a revolution in asset pricing.

The multifactor movement resulted in many new long/short factors proposed by researchers. Carhart (1997) added a momentum factor to the three-factor model to make a four-factor model. The momentum factor is long stocks with high past returns in the last year and short stocks with low past returns. This new factor was helpful in explaining the returns on mutual funds, which are portfolios of securities. Practical implications for investment were gained, such as to buy funds with higher-than-average performance in the recent past. Also, buy passively managed index funds rather than actively managed funds with higher operating expenses. Fama and French (2015) augmented their three-factor model with two more factors—namely, profit and capital investment factors—to make a five-factor model. These additional long/short factors further boosted the empirical fit and suggested that the value factor could be dropped.

Other researchers began to enter the multifactor competition. Hou et al. (2015) advanced a four-factor model with the market factor plus new size, profit, and capital investment factors. They linked their model to production CAPM models by means of the *q*-theory of investment. According to this theory, firms with high investments and profits should tend to earn higher stock returns and vice versa for those with low investments and profits. They found that their model helped to explain 80 anomalies, most of which were based on different firm characteristics. In this respect, their model outperformed the Fama and French three-factor and Carhart four-factor models. They inferred that many of these anomalies in stock returns were effectively explained by investment and profit factors. Another study by Stambaugh and Yuan (2017) proposed an alternative four-factor model containing market and size factors plus management and performance mispricing factors. To construct their two mispricing factors, they formed two clusters of a number of anomalies and then computed long/short factors from them. Their model was able to do a good job of explaining 80 different anomalies and exceeded the performance of the Fama and French five-factor model and Hou, Xue, and Zhang four-factor model. Hence, an effective way to construct a parsimonious set of factors is from the anomalies themselves.

Extending their previous work, Fama and French (2018) put forward a six-factor model that added momentum to their five-factor model. In this model they defined long/short factors in different ways to test a variety of size, value, profit, capital investment, and momentum factors. The winner model contained market and size factors plus small stock factors for size, value, capital investment, and momentum. In a related paper, Fama and French (2020) proposed the use of cross-section factors that are estimated from cross-sectional market prices of risk. That is, in the second step of the Fama and MacBeth (1973) procedure to test a model, the cross-sectional regression produces $\lambda_k$ estimates associated with the factor loadings for $k$ factors. These $\lambda_k$s are mimicking portfolio returns dubbed *cross-section factors* that were substituted into their five- or six-factor models in place of the original factors. Another innovation was to specify a conditional mathematical model with time-varying firm characteristics as the loadings on the cross-section factors in a mathematical conditional model. This mathematical model outperformed the regression models tested in their study. In effect, cross-section factors use machine learning instead of researcher judgment to design factors.

In another recent study using machine learning, Lettau and Pelger (2020) applied Principal Components Analysis (PCA) to search for correlation patterns in stock returns that represent so-called *latent factors*. They found that five latent factors were suggested by five-dimensional risk patterns in stock returns. The first factor was highly correlated with the CRSP market index, and other factors were related to value and momentum factors. Tests with stock portfolios associated with well-known asset pricing anomalies, including size, BM, investments, profitability, momentum, and others, showed that their five-factor model had small mispricing errors (or $\alpha_i$s) and therefore explained stock returns.

In sum, *theoretical methods* led to the creation of the CAPM, its companion models, and the APT. Over time, these models were supplanted by better fitting models based on *discretionary methods* that emphasized researcher judgment, including the three-, four-, five-, and six-factor models. Researchers constructed various long/short zero-investment portfolios as multifactors that were added to the CAPM market factor. More recently, *machine learning methods* have been proposed that produce factors based on artificial intelligence (AI). Cross-section and latent factors employ statistical and computer algorithms to form factors. In this man versus machine battle, who will win? Will some hybrid approach emerge in the future? As we will see in the next chapter, an unlikely outcome may be a return to theoretical methods with a new model dubbed the *ZCAPM*.

## Questions

1. What is momentum in asset returns? Can it be used to construct a long/short factor? How did Carhart (1997) modify the three-factor model to take into account momentum?
2. In Carhart's (1997) empirical tests, did momentum affect stock returns of mutual funds? What practical advice to investors in mutual funds did his research reveal?
3. Fama and French (2015) built upon their three-factor model to develop a five-factor model. What motivated them to add two more factors to their model? Write their five-factor model.
4. Fama and French (2015) tested their five-factor model in the sample period 1963–2013. What test asset portfolios did they use? Was the five-factor model supported?
5. Hou et al. (2015) developed a model that is very close to the Fama and French four-factor model. Write the equation for their model. What is the theoretical foundation for their model? What did they use as the test assets to empirically test their model? What did they find?
6. Stambaugh and Yuan (2017) developed a four-factor model. They added two new factors to the market and size factors. How did they construct these new factors? In empirical tests of over 80 anomalies, what did they find? They also created a three-factor model. How did this model perform?
7. Write the Fama and French (2018) six-factor model. They expanded this model to include different variations of these factors for a total of 48 factors. Which model worked the best?
8. More recently, Fama and French (2020) proposed a modified version of their five-factor model in which the multifactors are replaced by long/short mimicking portfolios estimated from a cross-sectional regression. What is the two-step process they implemented to do this?
9. Fama and French (2020) proposed two additional models that allow for time-varying risk parameters. Write the equations for these two conditional models. In empirical tests, which model was the best one? In these tests, how did they test one of the models that had no intercept (mispricing $\alpha$) term?
10. Normally, joint tests that the intercepts ($\alpha_i$s) equal zero are in-sample tests. What is a criticism of this testing approach?
11. Lettau and Pelger (2020) proposed the use of Principal Component Analysis (PCA) to identify latent asset pricing factors. How does PCA find factors in stock returns? How many latent factors did they find in empirical tests? Are PCA latent factors related to traditional factors used in asset pricing models?
12. Distinguish between theoretical methods, discretionary methods, and machine learning methods of developing asset pricing models. What are examples of each of these methods?

## Problems

1. Draw a diagram of returns on the Y-axis and time in months over the past year on the X-axis. Using this diagram, illustrate how momentum portfolios are formed.
2. Draw a diagram comparing the machine learning methods of Fama and French's (2020) cross-section factors and Lettau and Pilger's (2020) latent factors.

## References

Back, K., N. Kapadia, and B. Ostdiek. 2013. Slopes as factors: Characteristic pure plays. Working paper, Rice University.
Back, K., N. Kapadia, and B. Ostdiek. 2015. Testing factor models on characteristic and covariance pure plays. Working paper, Rice University.
Barillas, F., and J. Shanken. 2018. Comparing asset pricing models. *Journal of Finance* 73: 715–754.
Barroso, P., and P. Santa-Clara. 2015. Momentum has its moments. *Journal of Financial Economics* 116: 111–120.
Carhart, M.M. 1997. On persistence in mutual fund performance. *Journal of Finance* 52: 57–82.
Cochrane, J.H. 1991. Production-based asset pricing and the link between stock returns and economic fluctuations. *Journal of Finance* 46: 209–237.
Cochrane, J.H. 2011. Presidential address: Discount rates. *Journal of Finance* 56: 1047–1108.
Daniel, K., and T. Moskowitz. 2016. Momentum crashes. *Journal of Financial Economics* 122: 221–247.
Fama, E.F., and J.D. MacBeth. 1973. Risk, return, and equilibrium: Empirical tests. *Journal of Political Economy* 81: 607–636.
Fama, E.F., and K.R. French. 1992. The cross-section of expected stock returns. *Journal of Finance* 47: 427–465.
Fama, E.F., and K.R. French. 1993. The cross-section of expected returns. *Journal of Financial Economics* 33: 3–56.
Fama, E.F., and K.R. French. 1995. Size and book-to-market factors in earnings and returns. *Journal of Finance* 50: 131–156.
Fama, E.F., and K.R. French. 1996. The CAPM is wanted, dead or alive. *Journal of Finance* 51: 1947–1958.
Fama, E.F., and K.R. French. 2015. A five-factor asset pricing model. *Journal of Financial Economics* 116: 1–22.
Fama, E.F., and K.R. French. 2018. Choosing factors. *Journal of Financial Economics* 128 234–252.
Fama, E.F., and K.R. French. 2020. Comparing cross-section and time-series factor models. *Review of Financial Studies* 33: 1892–1926.
Ferson, W.E. 2019. *Empirical Asset Pricing: Models and Methods*. Cambridge, MA: The MIT Press.
Ferson, W.E., S.K. Nallareddy, and B. Xie. 2013. The "out-of-sample" performance of long-run risk models. *Journal of Financial Economics* 107: 537–556.
Gibbons, M.R., S.A. Ross, and J. Shanken. 1989. A test of the efficiency of a given portfolio. *Econometrica* 57: 1121–1152.
Gordon, M.J. 1962. *The Investment, Financing, and Valuation of the Corporation*. Homewood, IL: R.D. Irwin.

Hou, K., C. Xue, and L. Zhang. 2015. Digesting anomalies: An investment approach. *Review of Financial Studies* 28: 650–705.

Jegadeesh, N., and S. Titman. 1993. Returns to buying winners and selling losers: Implications for stock market efficiency. *Journal of Finance* 48: 65–91.

Kozak, S., S. Nagel, and S. Santosh. 2020. Shrinking the cross section. *Journal of Financial Economics* 135: 271–292.

Lettau, M., and M. Pelger. 2020. Factors that fit the time series and cross-section of stock returns. *Review of Financial Studies* 33: 2274–2325.

Merton, R.C. 1972. An analytical derivation of the efficient portfolio frontier. *Journal of Financial and Quantitative Finance* 7: 1851–1872.

Novy-Marx, R. 2013. The other side of value: The gross profitability premium. *Journal of Financial Economics* 108: 1–28.

Ross, S.A. 1976. The arbitrage theory of capital asset pricing. *Journal of Economic Theory* 13: 341–360.

Simin, T. 2008. The poor performance of asset pricing models. *Journal of Financial and Quantitative Analysis* 43: 335–380.

Stambaugh, R.F., and Y. Yuan. 2017. Mispricing factors. *Review of Financial Studies* 30: 1270–1315.

# 10 A Special Case of the Zero-Beta CAPM: The ZCAPM

A new CAPM dubbed the *ZCAPM* was recently proposed by Kolari, Liu, and Huang (KLH) (2021). In their book, the authors derived the ZCAPM as a special case of the more general zero-beta CAPM of Black (1972).[1] The theoretical ZCAPM is comprised of only two factors: mean excess market returns and the cross-sectional standard deviation of returns for all assets in the market more simply referred to as *return dispersion*. Sensitivity of asset returns to these two factors is measured by beta risk and so-called *zeta risk*, respectively. Their derivation of the ZCAPM relied heavily on the mean-variance investment parabola of Markowitz (1959), the CAPM equilibrium framework of Treynor (1961, 1962), Sharpe (1964), Lintner (1965), and Mossin (1966), and Black's zero-beta CAPM with two factors.

Relative to multifactor models, empirical tests using U.S. stock returns strongly supported the special case of the ZCAPM and, therefore, the more general zero-beta CAPM. Out-of-sample, cross-sectional Fama and MacBeth (1973) regression tests of the factor loadings (or beta risk and zeta risk coefficients) showed that zeta risk associated with return dispersion is more significantly priced than other factors in popular multifactor models. Based on the sample period 1965–2018, the authors compared the ZCAPM to the CAPM, Carhart (1997) four-factor model, Fama and French (1992, 1993, 1995, 1996, 2015, 2018), three-, five- and six-factor

[1] The material in the book is based on earlier academic studies of U.S. stock market returns by the authors in Liu et al. (2012, 2019) and Liu (2013) as well as real-world investment services in collaboration with the Teachers Retirement System of Texas (TRS). Additionally, recent papers by Kolari et al. (2022a, b) extend their previous work to a number of major industrialized countries as well as a longer U.S. sample period.

**Supplementary Information** The online version contains supplementary material available at https://doi.org/10.1007/978-3-031-16784-3_10.



J. W. Kolari and S. Pynnönen, *Investment Valuation and Asset Pricing*,
https://doi.org/10.1007/978-3-031-16784-3_10

models, Hou et al. (2014) four-factor model, and Stambaugh and Yuan (2017) four-factor model. Many different test asset portfolios (including individual stocks) were used as well as split sample tests with subperiods.

Surprisingly, the ZCAPM consistently outperformed multifactor models in terms of both higher $R^2$ values of goodness-of-fit and significance of the return dispersion factor. While multifactors are statistically significant in many cases, which confirms many published studies, they are not as significant as return dispersion in virtually all tests. Moreover, when using industry portfolios, which are exogenous to the factors in models, the ZCAPM dominated other models by large margins in many instances. Recall that discretionary methods incorporating multifactors in asset pricing models were initiated by Fama and French (1992, 1993) to boost the goodness-of-fit of the market model form of the CAPM and other companion CAPM specifications. The finding that goodness-of-fit can be improved by a CAPM-based asset pricing model is a remarkable turn of events.

In this chapter we review ZCAPM evidence in KLH's book in addition to findings related to many of the multifactor models covered in Chapters 8 and 9. Interestingly, KLH argue that the ZCAPM has some relation to discretionary methods relying on long/short multifactors. Each long/short portfolio in these models (e.g., the Fama and French three-factor model) is a rough measure of cross-sectional returncross-sectional return dispersion. For example, the size factor is small stocks' returns minus big stocks' returns. This factor comes from the cross-sectional distribution of all stock returns in the market. It represents one slice of the total return dispersion that describes the distribution of stock returns at a point in time. Other factors, such as value, profit, capital investment, momentum, etc., capture other slices within the total return dispersion. Together, multifactors incorporate most of the total return dispersion. However, each multifactor factor can change over time in terms of their location within the total return dispersion. Another interesting aspect of multifactors is that they sometimes can become negative (e.g., big stock returns are greater than small stock returns). The ZCAPM takes into account this kind of outcome as the empirical form of the ZCAPM allows for both positive and negative zeta risk associated with return dispersion.

Thus, as discussed by the authors, multifactor models are related to the ZCAPM and thereby the CAPM. Multifactor models are other forms of the ZCAPM that are more appropriately modeled using total return dispersion rather than different slices of return dispersion. Even new models using machine learning methods that utilize long/short portfolios as multifactors are related to the ZCAPM. It appears that the CAPM is not *dead* after all but is *alive and well*!

## 10.1 Theoretical ZCAPM

To derive the ZCAPM, KLH utilized Markowitz's mean-variance investment parabola. Figure 10.1 shows the parabola with expected portfolio returns $E(R_P)$ on the Y-axis and the time-series variance of returns $\sigma_P^2$ on the X-axis. For example, if we wanted to create the mean-variance parabola for one day in the market,

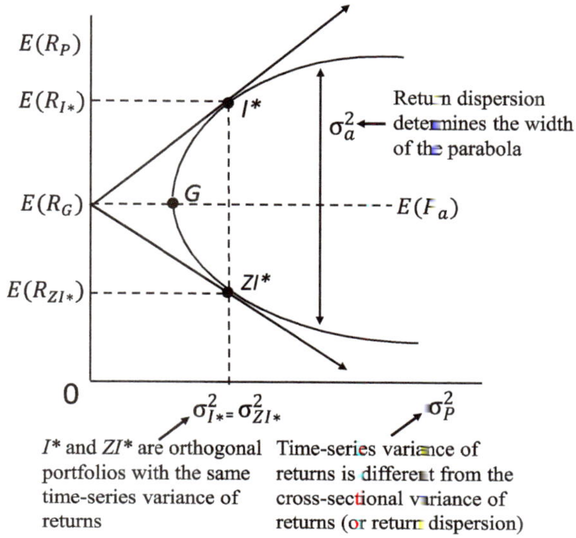


**Fig. 10.1** Locating orthogonal portfolios $I^*$ and $ZI^*$ on the mean-variance parabola (*Source* Kolari et al. 2021, p. 59)

we could obtain the time-series variance of returns (X-axis) by using returns for an asset computed every 10 minutes during the trading day. The mean 10-minute return and variance of returns for each asset are plotted in the graph as a point. $G$ is the minimum variance portfolio on the parabola with expected return $E(R_G)$. Portfolios to the right of $G$ on the upper half of the parabola lie on the efficient frontier (i.e., portfolios with the highest expected return unit total risk as measured by the variance of returns). Portfolios to the right of $G$ on the lower half of the parabola are inefficient minimum variance portfolios.

Before proceeding further, let's review Black's (1972) zero-beta CAPM. Dropping the time subscript $t$ due to a one-period model, the expected return for the $i$th asset is specified as follows:

$$E(R_i) = E(R_{ZI}) + \beta_{i,I}[E(R_I) - E(R_{ZI})], \tag{10.1}$$

where $E(R_I)$ is the expected return on an efficient portfolio on the upper boundary of the parabola, $E(R_{ZI})$ is the expected return on an orthogonal zero-beta portfolio on the lower boundary of the parabola, and $\beta_{i,I}$ is beta risk associated with excess return of efficient portfolio $I$. The expected return of the zero-beta portfolio replaces the riskless rate $R_f$ in the CAPM as the borrowing rate. Unlike the CAPM, that requires the use of the market portfolio $M$ on the efficient frontier, Black's zero-beta CAPM allows the use of any pair of efficient/inefficient minimum variance portfolios on the parabola that are orthogonal to one another. If $M$ could somehow be located, then $ZM$ would be the zero-beta portfolio.

Returning to Fig. 10.1, suppose that the parabola is a picture based on asset returns for one day in the market. In their book, KLH mathematically proved that the width or span of the parabola is largely determined by the cross-sectional standard deviation (or variance) of returns for all assets denoted $\sigma_{at}^2$ in a given period of time $t$ (e.g., one day).[2] This previously unknown result makes sense. The opportunity set of all the assets in the market is plotted within the parabola. The Y-axis shows the distribution of asset returns in the market. This distribution has a mean and variance of returns. The variance is obviously the width of the parabola, such that the mean market return must logically be approximately in the middle of the distribution. They denoted the mean market return at time $t$ as $E(R_{at})$. In another result not previously recognized, the mean market return is proposed to be approximately equal to the expected return on the minimum variance portfolio $E(R_{Gt})$, which splits the parabola into two halves on the axis of symmetry shown as the dashed line in Fig. 10.1. The simple logic is that the mean market return $E(R_{at})$ lies approximately in the middle of the distribution of returns on the $Y$-axis.

Most researchers prior to these findings believed that the mean market return (e.g., the value-weighted CRSP index or S &P 500 index) was located somewhere in the vicinity of the efficient frontier. However, according to KLH, the mean market return is far below the efficient frontier. As you will recall in previous chapters, researchers have tested the CAPM with U.S. stock returns using the value-weighted CRSP index as a proxy for the efficient market portfolio $M$. If this index lies somewhere along the axis of symmetry, it obviously is far below the true market portfolio $M$. This mean market return location helps to explain empirical tests of the CAPM that find a flatter relation between expected returns and beta risk estimates than predicted by the CAPM. This flatter relation would result in a higher intercept or $\alpha$ term than otherwise. Consistent with the Roll (1977) critique, an inefficient estimate of the market portfolio cannot be used to test the CAPM. If one accepts these new insights about the mean-variance parabola, then researchers have erroneously rejected the CAPM by using an inefficient market index $m$ as a proxy for $M$.

Using the geometry shown in Fig. 10.1, the authors located two orthogonal portfolios denoted $I^*$ and $ZI^*$ on the parabola. Symmetric rays extending from $E(R_G) \approx E(R_a)$ yield two tangent points to the minimum variance boundary of the parabola. Portfolio $I^*$ lies on the efficient frontier, and portfolio $ZI^*$ is on the inefficient, minimum variance boundary of the parabola. This orthogonal pair of portfolios is unique due to having the same time-series variance of returns and therefore are marked with $*$ superscripts as $\sigma_{I^*}^2 = \sigma_{ZI^*}^2$. Since the ZCAPM is a one-period model, as in Black's zero-beta CAPM, the time subscript $t$ is dropped. These two portfolios are important because their expected returns can be defined as follows:

$$E(R_{I^*}) \approx E(R_a) + \sigma_a \tag{10.2}$$

$$E(R_{ZI^*}) \approx E(R_a) - \sigma_a. \tag{10.3}$$

---

[2] Interested readers can refer to the random matrix theory and Markowitz's mean-variance portfolio proofs in their book.

That is, to reach these portfolios in Fig. 10.1, an investor needs to move along the axis of symmetry at $E(R_a)$ to the right of portfolio $G$ until they reach the point at which the time-series variance of portfolios $I^*$ and $ZI^*$ are equal to one another, or $\sigma_{I^*}^2 = \sigma_{ZI^*}^2$. From this point, moving up or down by the cross-sectional variance of returns (return dispersion) $\sigma_a^2$ can be used to locate portfolios $I^*$ and $ZI^*$, respectively.[3] Notice here that the geometry of the ZCAPM is much different from the CAPM. The CAPM locates market portfolio $M$ by means of a ray from the riskless rate $R_f$ to a tangent point with the efficient frontier of the parabola. The ZCAPM moves horizontally along the axis of symmetry and then vertically up or down to locate orthogonal portfolios on the efficient/inefficient boundaries of the parabola.

Next, they substitute the definitions of $E(R_{I^*})$ and $E(R_{ZI^*})$ in Eqs. (10.2) and (10.3), respectively, into zero-beta CAPM Eq. (10.1) as follows:

$$\begin{aligned}
E(R_i) =& E(R_{ZI^*}) + \beta_{i,I^*}[E(R_{I^*}) - E(R_{ZI^*})] \\
=& E(R_a) - \sigma_a + \beta_{i,I^*}\{[E(R_a) + \sigma_a] - [E(R_a) - \sigma_a]\} \\
=& E(R_a) + (2\beta_{i,I^*} - 1)\sigma_a \\
E(R_i) =& E(R_a) + Z_{i,a}^*\sigma_a,
\end{aligned} \tag{10.4}$$

where $Z_{i,a}^* = 2\beta_{i,I^*} - 1$. This relation is the theoretical ZCAPM in the absence of a riskless asset.

Assuming a riskless asset $f$ exists with rate $R_f$, they subsequently consider three assets *I*, *ZI*, and $f$. In this three-asset case, the expected return of the $i$th asset can be defined as:

$$E(R_i) = w_{I^*}E(R_{I^*}) + w_{ZI^*}E(R_{ZI^*}) + w_f R_f. \tag{10.5}$$

This equation can be re-written into the initial form of the theoretical ZCAPM:

$$E(R_i) = (w_{I^*} + w_{ZI^*})E(R_a) + (w_{I^*} - w_{ZI^*})\sigma_a + w_f R_f, \tag{10.6}$$

where $w_{I^*}$, $w_{ZI^*}$, and $w_f$ are asset weights that sum to one. It is assumed that investors can hold long and short positions in these assets. Rearranging terms, we get:

$$E(R_i) - R_f = (w_{I^*} + w_{ZI^*})[E(R_a) - R_f] + (w_{I^*} - w_{ZI^*})\sigma_a. \tag{10.7}$$

Finally, using Eq. (10.4), this equation can be re-written in the final form of the theoretical ZCAPM:

$$E(R_i) - R_f = \beta_{i,a}[E(R_a) - R_f] + Z_{i,a}^*\sigma_a, \tag{10.8}$$

[3] We have simplified the notation somewhat here. The authors use $f(\theta)\sigma_a^2$ instead of simply $\sigma_a^2$ in Eq. (10.2), where $f(\theta) > 0$ is a complex function of other terms.

where $\beta_{i,a} = w_{I^*} + w_{ZI^*}$ is the beta risk coefficient measuring the sensitivity of the *i*th asset's excess returns to average market excess returns of all assets, and $Z^*_{i,a} = w_{I^*} - w_{ZI^*}$ is the zeta risk coefficient measuring the sensitivity of an asset's excess returns to the market return dispersion of all assets.[4] Because both the average market return $E(R_a)$ and market return dispersion $\sigma_a$ are observable in the real world,[5] the problem of finding proxies in the real world is greatly reduced. Again, good proxies *m* for the expected return on the market portfolio *M* in the CAPM or zero-beta portfolio *ZM* in the zero-beta CAPM are difficult to construct and subject to controversy. Thus, the ZCAPM has the advantage of estimable proxies of its two factors.

It is important to recognize that beta risk in the ZCAPM is different from the CAPM. In the CAPM, beta risk is associated with the expected return on efficient market portfolio *M*, which is very difficult to identify or locate in the real world. However, in the ZCAPM, beta risk is related to the average return on the portfolio of all assets *a* in the market (not *M*) that is not efficient. Additionally, the zeta risk coefficient $Z^*_{i,a}$ can have a positive or negative sign to take into account both portfolios $I^*I^*$ and $ZI^*$ on the boundary of the parabola. As pointed out by Kolari et al. (2021, p. 75):

> This two-sided, opposite market volatility risk is a distinctive feature of the ZCAPM that arises by virtue of the mean-variance investment parabola with span determined by return dispersion.

Figure 10.2 provides an illustration of the ZCAPM. The beta risk of the *i*th asset is based on the relation between the *i*th asset's excess returns, or $R_i - R_f$ on the Y-axis, and average excess market returns, or $R_a - R_f$ on the X-axis. Zeta risk is determined by the relation between the asset's excess returns, or $R_i - R_f$, and market return dispersion, or $\sigma_a$. Here we see the two-sided, opposite effects of zeta risk on asset returns.

Figure 10.3 gives another more simplified view of two-sided return dispersion effects. Assume there are two time periods $t = 1$ and 2 in addition to two assets *B* and *C*. Return dispersion in the market increases from $\sigma_{a1} = 1\%$ at time 1 to 2% at time 2. Due to this increase in cross-sectional market volatility from time 1

[4] The following equilibrium conditions are implied by the ZCAPM:

1. assuming all funds are invested in either $I^*$ or $ZI^*$, then $\beta_{I^*,a} = \beta_{ZI^*,a} = 1$ and $Z^*_{I^*,a} = 1$ or $Z^*_{ZI^*,a} = -1$, respectively;
2. assuming no riskless asset, Eq. (10.8) reduces to Eq. (10.4) (i.e., $\beta_{i,a} \equiv w_{I^*} + w_{ZI^*} = 1$); and
3. assuming the restriction $w_f > 0$ (i.e., no borrowing at the riskless rate is allowed), then $\beta_{i,a} < 1$.

[5] They are observable in the sense that they can be estimated with standard mean and variance statistical measures of market characteristics.

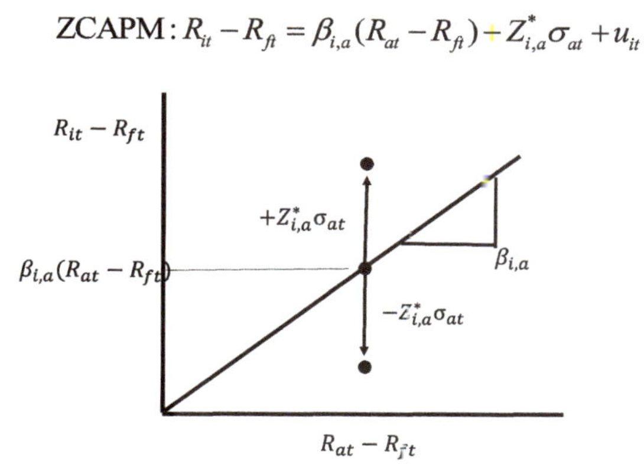


**Fig. 10.2** The ZCAPM with beta risk related to average excess market returns and zeta risk associated with positive and negative sensitivity to return dispersion (*Source* Kolari et al. 2021, p. 72)

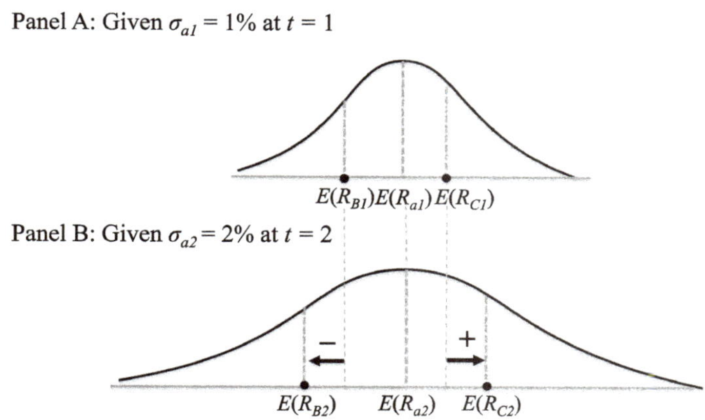


**Fig. 10.3** Two-sided, opposite effects of return dispersion on the expected returns of two assets (*Source* Kolari et al. 2021, p. 94)

to 2, asset C experiences increasing returns but the returns of asset B decrease at time 2. Of course, if return dispersion decreased over time, asset C would experience decreasing returns and asset B increasing returns. Thus, return dispersion has opposite effects on the returns of assets depending on where they are located in the distribution of returns.

In combination with beta risk, the dual systematic risk effects of return dispersion in the market give the mean-variance parabola its upper and lower boundaries. We can think of the upper (lower) boundary as having some amount of positive (negative) zeta risk—for example, $Z^*_{i,a} = 0.8$ $(-0.8)$. Along the upper (lower) boundary, assets will have increasing levels of beta risk. Hence, beta and zeta risk are important in defining the architecture of the mean-variance parabola.

As a visual example, Fig. 10.4 shows some results for 25 U.S. stock portfolios based on the ZCAPM in Kolari et al. (2021).[6] The top horizontal boundary (or frontier) contains the five stock portfolios with the highest average zeta risk. The frontier has an upward slope due to increasing levels of beta risk among these five portfolios. The bottom boundary contains five stock portfolios with the lowest zeta risk in addition to varying levels of beta risk from low to high. At each beta risk level, there is a vertical beta risk curve (i.e., represented by a dashed line) that intersects different zeta risk curves. Taken together, the intersecting latticework of beta-zeta risk portfolios in the graph takes on the general form of a mean-variance parabola. In effect, stock portfolios within the parabola have beta and zeta risk characteristics that jointly determine their expected returns. Rather than being randomly distributed within the parabola, portfolios are ordered by their systematic risks related to average market returns and market return dispersion. Hence, equilibrium asset prices are established within the parabola due to these two market forces.

## 10.2 Empirical ZCAPM

How can we model the positive and negative effects of return dispersion on real-world asset returns? Kolari, Liu, and Zhang proposed the following novel empirical ZCAPM:

$$R_{it} - R_{ft} = \alpha_i + \beta_i(R_{at} - R_{ft}) + Z_i D_{it}\sigma_{at} + u_{it}, \quad t = 1, \ldots, T \tag{10.9}$$

where $Z_i$ measures sensitivity to return dispersion $\sigma_{at}$, $D_{it}$ is a signal variable with values $+1$ and $-1$ representing positive and negative return dispersion effects on stock returns at time *t*, respectively, $u_{it} \sim$ iid N(0, $\sigma_i^2$), and other notation is as before. The dummy signal variable $D_{it}$ is not observable and therefore is considered to be an unknown or latent (hidden) variable. Unfortunately, due to the hidden variable $D_{it}$, commonly used ordinary least squares (OLS) regression cannot be used to estimate the empirical ZCAPM.

To take into account signal variable $D_{it}$, the well-known statistical method of expectation-maximization (EM) regression can be employed.[7] In EM, hidden variable $D_{it}$ is defined as an independent random variable with the following two-point

[6] The authors estimated the ZCAPM to compute beta and zeta risk coefficients for thousands of U.S stocks (see Sect. 10.2 for an overview of the empirical ZCAPM). In 1964 the ZCAPM was estimated for stocks which were then sorted into quintiles by their beta and zeta coefficients to form the 25 portfolios. Next, portfolios' returns were computed in the out-of-sample month of January 1965. This process was rolled forward one month at a time to generate monthly series of beta, zeta, and one-month-ahead returns for each portfolio from January 1965 to December 2018. For each portfolio, average returns and the standard deviations of these monthly returns were computed. All portfolios were long-only with no short positions.

[7] Originally invented by Dempster et al. (1977), EM regression is widely used in the sciences. See also studies by Jones and McLachlan (1990), McLachlan and Peel (2000), and McLachlan and

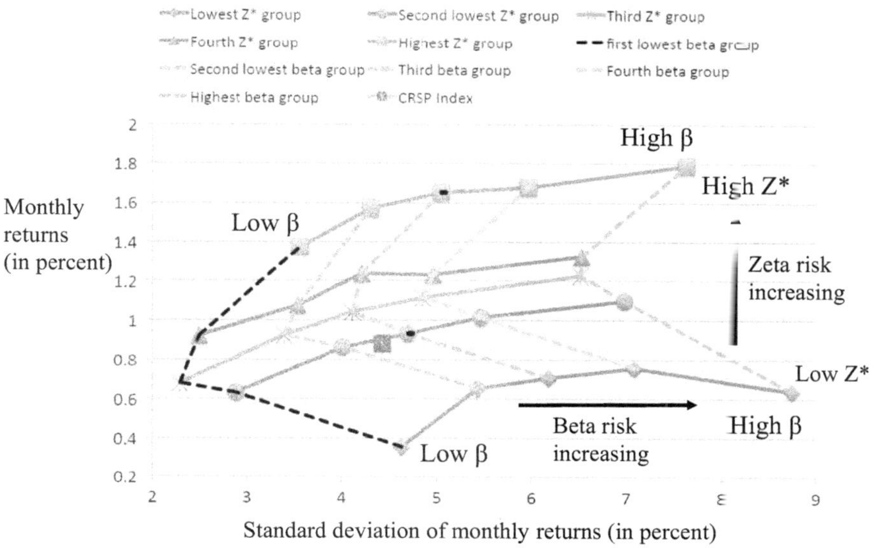


**Fig. 10.4** This graph shows the average beta risk, zeta risk, and one-month-ahead equal-weighted returns for 25 beta-zeta sorted portfolios. These long-only portfolios approximate the shape on an investment parabola. In each one-year estimation window, the empirical ZCAPM is estimated using daily returns to obtain the beta and zeta risk parameters. The analysis period is January 1965–December 2018 (*Source* Kolari et al. 2021, p. 272)

distribution:

$$D_{it} = \begin{cases} +1 \text{ with probability } p_i \\ -1 \text{ with probability } 1 - p_i, \end{cases} \quad (10.10)$$

where $p_i$ (or $1 - p_i$) is the probability of a positive (or negative) return dispersion effect, and $D_{it}$ is independent of $u_{it}$. No previous studies utilize EM regression in an asset pricing model.

Notice that, in the empirical ZCAPM relation (10.9), the interaction term $Z_{i,a}D_{i,t}$ has two possible values equal to $+Z_{i,a}$ or $-Z_{i,a}$ based on the sign of signal variable $D_{i,t}$. Since the mean of binary signal variable $D_{i,t}$ equals $2p_i - 1$, we can define $Z^*_{i,a} = Z_{i,a}(2p_i - 1)$, which results in the final form of the empirical ZCAPM:

$$R_{it} - R_{ft} = \beta_{i,a}(R_{at} - R_{ft}) + Z^*_{i,a}\sigma_{at} + u_{it}, \quad t = 1, \ldots T. \quad (10.11)$$

Krishnan (2008), among others. Wikipedia gives an excellent discussion of the EM algorithm with literature citations.

EM regression provides estimates of beta risk coefficient $\beta_{i,a}$ as well as zeta risk coefficient $Z^*_{i,a}$ that coincides with theoretical ZCAPM relation (10.8). The positive or negative sign of $Z^*_{i,a}$ is determined by the probability $p_i$ of signal variable $D_{it}$ in sample period $t = 1, \ldots, T$. If $p_i > 1/2$ (or $< 1/2$), $Z^*_{i,a}$ will have a positive (or negative) sign. In words, $Z^*_{i,a}$ gives the average increase or decrease of asset returns in response to a one-unit change in return dispersion $\sigma_{at}$.

Unlike other empirical asset pricing models, the empirical ZCAPM does not have an intercept ($\alpha$) term. The EM algorithm does not utilize an intercept to minimize squared error terms as in OLS regression. For this reason, KLH repeated cross-sectional tests discussed in the next section with and without intercepts in time-series multifactor models. They found that the cross-sectional tests of factor prices were unaffected for the most part by time-series regressions that set the intercept to zero. However, no Gibbons et al. (1989) (GRS) tests of the joint equality of $\alpha$s are possible for the empirical ZCAPM to compare to other models.

For interested readers, KLH have placed Matlab, R, and Python programs for EM estimation of the empirical ZCAPM on GitHub (https://github.com/zcapm). Their R programs estimate the ZCAPM faster than the Matlab and Python programs. Programs for running Fama–MacBeth cross-sectional regression tests are provided on the GitHub website also.

## 10.3 Empirical Evidence

Let's look at some of the empirical evidence on the ZCAPM in KLH's book. They employed daily U.S. stock returns from the period 1964 to 2018. The value-weighted CRSP index return was used to proxy $R_{at}$ on each day $t$. The value-weighted market return dispersion on each day $t$ was computed as follows:

$$\sigma_{at} = \sqrt{\frac{n}{n-1}\sum_{i=1}^{n} w_{it-1}(R_{it} - R_{at})^2}, \tag{10.12}$$

where $n$ is the total number of stocks, $w_{it-1}$ is the previous day's market value weight for the $i$th stock (i.e., market capitalization of the stock divided by the market capitalization of all $n$ stocks), $R_{it}$ is the return of the $i$th stock on day $t$, and $R_{at}$ is value-weighted average return of all available stocks in the CRSP database on day $t$. In their sample period, the average daily market return was 0.04% (i.e., 0.88% per month) compared to 0.99% for daily return dispersion. These descriptive statistics indicate that return dispersion is quite large compared to mean market daily returns. Also, because there was almost zero correlation between these two-asset pricing factors, the factors $R_{at}$ and $\sigma_{at}$ are orthogonal to one another for the most part and therefore contain different market information.

The authors conducted out-of-sample (or one-month-ahead), cross-sectional Fama and MacBeth (1973) tests for a number of different test asset portfolios. Empirical ZCAPM relation (10.11) was estimated using one year of daily returns.

The U.S. Treasury bill rate proxied the riskless rate. Following standard practices, Fama–MacBeth analyses were rolled forward one month at a time to generate a series of estimated market prices of beta and zeta risk loadings (denoted $\lambda_a$ and $\lambda_{RD}$, respectively). To comparatively evaluate the performance of the ZCAPM, they ran tests for the CAPM, Carhart (1997) four-factor model, and Fama and French (1992, 1993, 2015, 2018) three-, five-, and six-factor models. In forthcoming empirical evidence, we show results for not only the ZCAPM but these popular single and multifactor models covered in previous chapters. Also, results are compared to often-cited four-factor models by Hou et al. (2015) and Stambaugh and Yuan (2017).

### 10.3.1 Risk and Return Relations

To begin their analyses, KLH reported evidence on the relation between beta risk and zeta risk with respect to one-month-ahead stock returns. Using the 97 portfolios discussed above, the empirical ZCAPM in Eq. (10.11) was run using daily returns for one year to obtain $\beta_{i,a}$ and $Z^*_{i,a}$ estimates for each portfolio. The actual returns $R_{it+1}$ in the next one month were retained. The process was repeated by rolling forward one month to get new estimates of $\beta_{i,a}$ and $Z^*_{i,a}$ as well as the next one-month returns $R_{it+1}$ for portfolios. Repeating this process from 1964 to the end of 2018, they generated a series of 648 monthly values for $\beta_{i,a}$, $Z^*_{i,a}$, and $R_{it+1}$. Next, the average values of these values were computed for each portfolio.

For test asset portfolios, they used 25 size and BM sorted portfolios from Kenneth French's data website.[8] These portfolios are often used by Fama and French as well as other researchers in asset pricing model tests. Figures 10.5 and 10.6 graphically show the relation between average one-month-ahead excess returns (Y-axis) and average beta and zeta risk coefficients (X-axis), respectively. It is apparent from Fig. 10.5 that returns are not related to beta risk. Most of the portfolios have betas near one, which is the beta of the CRSP market risk. Moreover, a slightly inverse relation can be seen, which is opposite of CAPM theory. Concerning these results, as discussed earlier, beta risk is different in the ZCAPM than CAPM.

In stark contrast, Fig. 10.6 reveals a very strong relation between returns and zeta risk. Given zeta risks for the 25 portfolios, their future returns in the next month line up almost perfectly with the order of their previously estimated risks. This finding is extraordinary. Additionally, KLH sorted the 25 portfolios into beta risk quintiles and then zeta risk quintiles within each beta risk quintile. This sorting reveals that small stocks tended to have larger betas than big stocks. This pattern occurs in Fig. 10.5 also.

[8] See https://mba.tuck.dartmouth.edu/pages/faculty/ken.french/data_library.

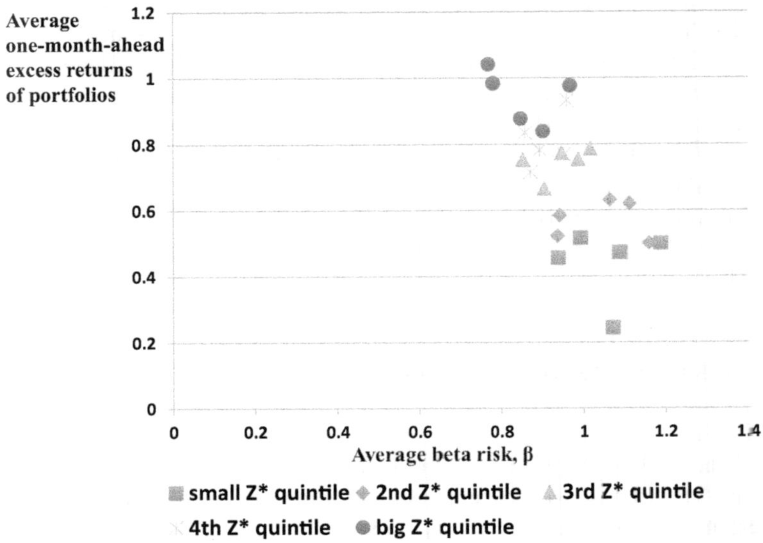


**Fig. 10.5** Out-of-sample cross-sectional ZCAPM relationship between average one-month-ahead realized excess returns in percent (Y-axis) and average beta risk $\beta_{i,a}$ in the previous 12-month estimation period (X-axis). Results are shown for 25 size-BM portfolios used in the Fama and French studies. Portfolios are sorted into zeta risk $Z^*_{i,a}$ quintiles and then beta risk $\beta_{i,a}$ quintiles within each $Z^*_{i,a}$ quintile. The analysis period is January 1965–December 2018 (*Source* Kolari et al. 2021, p. 141)

## 10.3.2 Predicted and Actual Return Relations

Are predicted returns using the ZCAPM related to future actual returns? Recall from Chap. 4 that Fama and MacBeth (1973) argued that *normative models*, which are intended to help investors make better decisions, are only valid to the extent that past information is related to future returns. To evaluate predicted versus actual returns, we estimated beta and zeta risk parameters using the empirical ZCAPM with one year of daily returns. In the next month on an out-of-sample basis, estimated beta and zeta coefficients were multiplied by average excess market returns $R_{at} - R_{ft}$ and market return dispersion $\sigma_{at}$ on each day $t$ to compute predicted (or fitted) excess returns for each portfolio. These daily predicted excess returns are used to compute a one-month predicted excess return in the next month. The realized (or actual) excess return in the next out-of-sample month is recorded also. This process is rolled forward month-by-month until December 2018 to get out-of-sample monthly series of predicted and realized excess returns for each portfolio. Lastly, averages of these excess returns from January 1965 to December 2018 are computed. In forthcoming Table 10.1, we utilize these average excess returns to assess the goodness-of-fit of different models. To do this, we regress average realized excess returns on average predicted excess returns for each model to estimate their $R^2$ value.

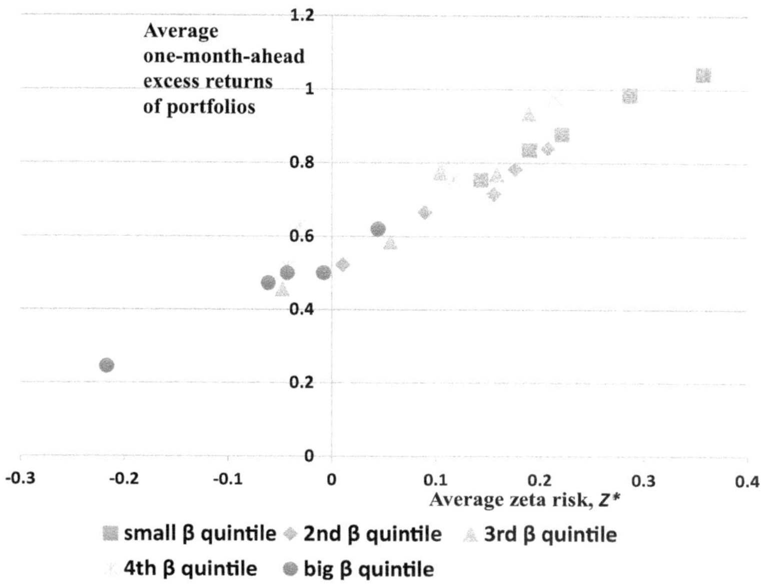


**Fig. 10.6** Out-of-sample cross-sectional ZCAPM relationship between average one-month-ahead realized excess returns in percent (Y-axis) and average zeta risk $Z^*_{i,a}$ in the previous 12-month estimation period (X-axis). Results are shown for 25 size-BM portfolios used in the Fama and French studies. Portfolios are sorted into beta risk $\beta_{i,a}$ quintiles and then zeta risk $Z^*_{i,a}$ quintiles within each $\beta_{i,a}$ quintile. The analysis period is January 1965–December 2018 (*Source* Kolari et al. 2021, p. 140)

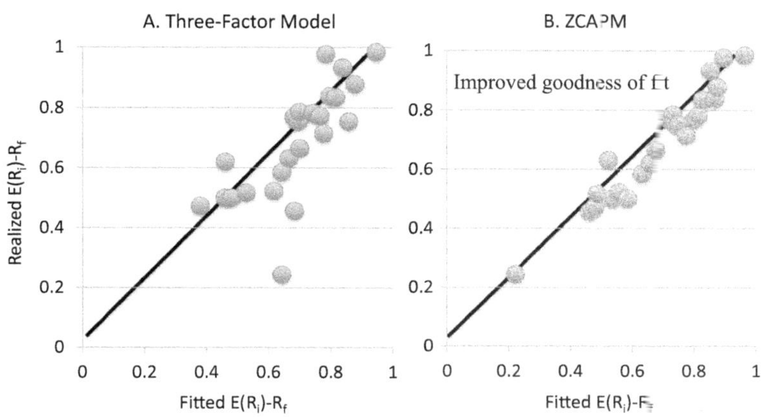


**Fig. 10.7** Out-of-sample cross-sectional relationship between average one-month-ahead realized excess returns in percent (Y-axis) and average one-month-ahead predicted (fitted) excess returns in percent (X-axis) for 25 size-BM sorted portfolios: Fama and French three-factor model in Panel A and empirical ZCAPM in Panel B. The analysis period is January 1965 to December 2018 (*Source* Kolari et al. 2021, p. 146)

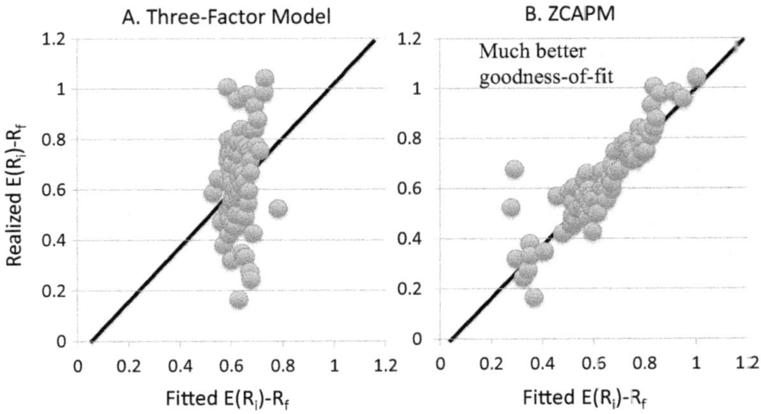


**Fig. 10.8** Out-of-sample cross-sectional relationship between average one-month-ahead realized excess returns in percent (Y-axis) and average one-month-ahead predicted (fitted) excess returns in percent (X-axis) for 25 size-BM sorted plus 47 industry portfolios: Fama and French Fama and French three-factor model in Panel A and empirical ZCAPM in Panel B. The analysis period is January 1965–December 2018 (*Source* Kolari et al. 2021, p. 147)

Using the 25 size and BM sorted portfolios, Fig. 10.7 shows the results for the Fama and French three-factor model versus the empirical ZCAPM. The three-factor model performs well in these tests. The (out-of-sample) predicted and realized excess returns in these out-of-sample analyses line up closely to the 45-degree line. By comparison, the ZCAPM performs even better. Notice that the three-factor model has one stray portfolio, which is the small-size portfolio with low BM (growth).[9] However, this stray portfolio is priced by the ZCAPM as it lies exactly on the 45-degree line.

Figure 10.8 repeats these experiments with the 25 size and BM portfolios plus 47 industry portfolios. Here we see that the three-factor model is not useful, but the ZCAPM does a fairly good job. Industries are exogenous to the three-factor model, unlike the endogenous size and BM portfolios (i.e., as discussed in Chapter 8, the size and value factors are related to the size and BM portfolios). In this regard, referring back to Fig. 10.6, the size and BM portfolios are exogenous to the ZCAPM. Even so, the ZCAPM outperforms the three-factor model. Together, these results suggest that the ZCAPM has better goodness-of-fit than the three-factor model. The tables have turned! Goodness-of-fit is higher in the CAPM model than the multifactor model.

[9] This portfolio is the smallest-size/lowest-BM (growth) stock portfolio with the lowest average realized excess return. It is well known that the three-factor model has difficulty explaining this small, growth portfolio (e.g., see Fama and French (1996)).

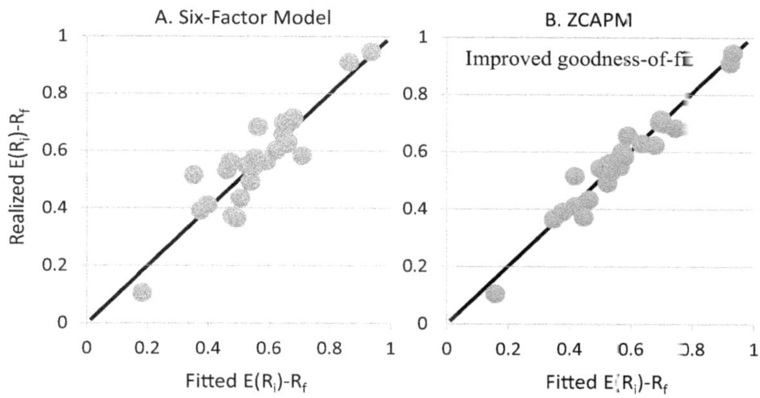


**Fig. 10.9** Out-of-sample cross-sectional relationship between average one-month-ahead realized excess returns in percent (Y-axis) and average one-month-ahead predicted (fitted) excess returns in percent (X-axis) for 25 profit-investment sorted portfolios: Fama and French six-factor model in Panel A and empirical ZCAPM in Panel B. The analysis period is January 1965 to December 2018 (*Source* Kolari et al. 2021, p. 150)

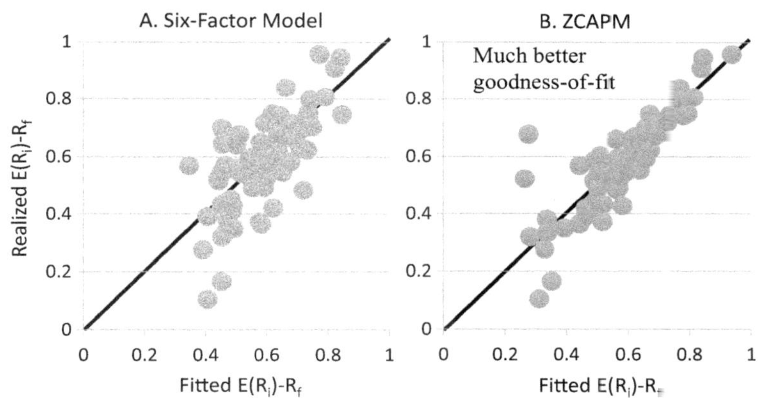


**Fig. 10.10** Out-of-sample cross-sectional relationship between average one-month-ahead realized excess returns in percent (Y-axis) and average one-month-ahead predicted (fitted) excess returns in percent (X-axis) for 25 profit-investment sorted plus 47 industry portfolios: Fama and French Fama and French six-factor model in Panel A and empirical ZCAPM in Panel B. The analysis period is January 1965–December 2018 (*Source* Kolari et al. 2021, p. 151)

Figures 10.9 and 10.10 repeat these analyses using the Fama and French six-factor model. Here the 25 size and BM portfolios are replaced with 25 profit-investment sorted portfolios from Kenneth French's data website. Clearly, the six-factor model performs quite well and does better than the three-factor model, but the ZCAPM still outperforms it. Also, the six-factor model has difficulty in fitting returns for industry portfolios. When test asset portfolios are used that are not related to long/short factors, the multifactor models are more likely to fall down.

### 10.3.3 Fama and MacBeth Cross-Sectional Tests

Out-of-sample Fama and MacBeth (1973) cross-sectional tests for the CAPM, ZCAPM, and a number of discretionary multifactor models are reported in Table 10.1. These selected results were taken from Kolari et al. (2021) and are representative of the many test results reported in their book. The ZCAPM is benchmarked against the CAPM and popular Carhart four-factor model as well as Fama and French three-, five- and six-factor models. In step one, the ZCAPM and other models are estimated with one year of daily returns beginning in 1964. In step two, one-month-ahead (out-of-sample) returns in January 1965 are regressed on previously estimated risk parameters in step one. The process is rolled forward one month at a time and repeated until the one-month-ahead return in December 2018. A monthly series of 648 estimated market prices of risk, denoted $\lambda_k$, for the $k$th factor and 648 one-month-ahead returns are generated for each test asset portfolio. Averages of $\lambda_k$s are shown in the table.

The first notable finding in Table 10.1 is the relatively high $R^2$ values of the ZCAPM compared to the other models. In Panels A and C, the ZCAPM achieves $R^2$ estimates of 94% and 96%, respectively. This goodness-of-fit is near perfect! Almost all variation in cross-sectional stock returns in these portfolios is explained by the ZCAPM. The near perfect fit of the ZCAPM is remarkable in light of fact that these tests utilize one-month-ahead (out-of-sample) returns. The CAPM has fairly good fit at 48% for the 25 size and BM sorted portfolios (Panel A) but is zero for 47 industry portfolios (Panel B). The highest multifactor model $R^2$ value of 80% is achieved by the six-factor model in the 25 size and BM portfolios (Panel A) but falls to 50% for 47 industry portfolios (Panel B) and only 35% for 97 combined portfolios (Panel D). In the latter two portfolio tests, the ZCAPM posted respectable 70% and 83% $R^2$ values. These results suggest that the ZCAPM outperforms the CAPM and multifactor models in general and by large margins with industry portfolios in particular.

Looking at the market prices of risk, or $\lambda_k$s, in Table 10.1, the market price of return dispersion ($\lambda_{RD}$) has the highest $t$-values of statistical significance ranging from 4.03 to 5.42 in the different panels. Size factor loadings ($\lambda_{SMB}$) never reach statistical significance at the 5% level. Loadings for other factors, including value ($\lambda_{HML}$), momentum ($\lambda_{MOM}$), profit ($\lambda_{RMW}$), and capital investment ($\lambda_{CMA}$), are intermittently significant in different models and test asset portfolios. And, market factor loadings are normally insignificant but are significant with a negative sign for the 25 size and BM portfolios in some models (opposite of CAPM theory).

Notice that none of the multifactor loadings achieves a $t$-statistic greater than 3. In extensive tests of over 300 multifactors, Harvey et al. (2016) and Chordia et al.

**Table 10.1** Out-of-sample Fama–MacBeth cross-sectional tests for ZCAPM regression factor loadings compared to other asset pricing models in the period January 1965–December 2018: 12-month rolling windows

| Model | $\hat{\alpha}$ | $\hat{\lambda}_m$ | $\hat{\lambda}_{RD}$ | $\hat{\lambda}_{SMB}$ | $\hat{\lambda}_{HML}$ | $\hat{\lambda}_{MOM}$ | $\hat{\lambda}_{RMW}$ | $\hat{\lambda}_{CMA}$ | $R^2$ |
|---|---|---|---|---|---|---|---|---|---|
| *Panel A: 25 size-BM sorted portfolios* | | | | | | | | | |
| CAPM | 0.98<br>(4.03) | −0.35<br>(−0.35) | | | | | | | 0.48 |
| ZCAPM | 0.78<br>(3.26) | −0.19<br>(−0.77) | 0.46<br>(4.22) | | | | | | 0.94 |
| Three-factor | 0.93<br>(4.98) | −0.41<br>(−1.96) | | 0.17<br>(1.27) | 0.31<br>(2.64) | | | | 0.63 |
| Four-factor | 1.12<br>(5.84) | −0.60<br>(−2.83) | | 0.16<br>(1.29) | 0.29<br>(2.57) | 0.08<br>(0.35) | | | 0.69 |
| Five-factor | 0.98<br>(4.94) | −0.45<br>(−2.06) | | 0.21<br>(1.73) | 0.28<br>(2.49) | | 0.13<br>(1.10) | 0.11<br>(0.84) | 0.75 |
| Six-factor | 1.07<br>(5.39) | −0.55<br>(−2.52) | | 0.22<br>(1.80) | 0.30<br>(2.69) | 0.16<br>(0.68) | 0.12<br>(1.03) | 0.06<br>(0.45) | 0.80 |
| *Panel B: 47 industry portfolios* | | | | | | | | | |
| CAPM | 0.57<br>(2.95) | 0.03<br>(0.15) | | | | | | | 0.00 |
| ZCAPM | 0.49<br>(2.71) | 0.11<br>(0.53) | 0.32<br>(4.07) | | | | | | 0.70 |
| Three-factor | 0.43<br>(2.21) | 0.11<br>(0.48) | | 0.02<br>(0.14) | 0.14<br>(1.17) | | | | 0.15 |
| Four-factor | 0.46<br>(2.31) | 0.08<br>(0.37) | | 0.04<br>(0.31) | 0.08<br>(0.73) | 0.43<br>(2.09) | | | 0.39 |
| Five-factor | 0.36<br>(1.78) | 0.19<br>(0.83) | | 0.07<br>(0.51) | 0.09<br>(0.76) | | 0.20<br>(2.03) | 0.24<br>(2.48) | 0.18 |
| Six-factor | 0.51<br>(2.53) | 0.04<br>(0.16) | | 0.04<br>(0.32) | 0.06<br>(0.52) | 0.39<br>(1.92) | 0.20<br>(2.05) | 0.17<br>(1.78) | 0.50<br>(1.78) |
| *Panel C: 25 beta-zeta sorted portfolios* | | | | | | | | | |
| CAPM | 0.49<br>(3.23) | −0.06<br>(−0.26) | | | | | | | 0.11 |
| ZCAPM | 0.29<br>(1.91) | 0.17<br>(0.83) | 0.35<br>(4.03) | | | | | | 0.96 |

(continued)

(2020) documented evidence that most multifactors are false discoveries.[10] For this reason, these authors recommended that asset pricing factors should surpass a $t$-statistic threshold of 3 to be considered significant in cross-sectional tests.

[10] We should mention that some researchers have found that many anomalous factors tend to disappear after their publication in finance journals (e.g., see McLean and Pontiff (2016), Linnainmaa and Roberts (2018), and others). Nonetheless, numerous anomalous factors persist over time.

**Table 10.1** (continued)

| Model | $\hat{\alpha}$ | $\hat{\lambda}_m$ | $\hat{\lambda}_{RD}$ | $\hat{\lambda}_{SMB}$ | $\hat{\lambda}_{HML}$ | $\hat{\lambda}_{MOM}$ | $\hat{\lambda}_{RMW}$ | $\hat{\lambda}_{CMA}$ | $R^2$ |
|---|---|---|---|---|---|---|---|---|---|
| Three-factor | 0.66<br>(3.34) | −0.05<br>(−0.24) | | −0.28<br>(−1.49) | 0.14<br>(1.00) | | | | 0.65 |
| Four-factor | 0.54<br>(3.50) | −0.03<br>(−0.15) | | −0.25<br>(−1.51) | 0.25<br>(1.76) | 0.28<br>(1.61) | | | 0.70 |
| Five-factor | 0.52<br>(3.06) | −0.03<br>(−0.13) | | −0.19<br>(−1.11) | 0.25<br>(1.56) | | 0.17<br>(1.18) | 0.09<br>(0.77) | 0.67 |
| Six-factor | 0.62<br>(3.86) | −0.11<br>(−0.54) | | −0.14<br>(−0.88) | 0.30<br>(1.90) | 0.26<br>(1.50) | 0.17<br>(1.30) | 0.02<br>(0.14) | 0.76 |
| *Panel D: 97 combined portfolios* | | | | | | | | | |
| CAPM | 0.64<br>(3.93) | −0.06<br>(−0.31) | | | | | | | 0.05 |
| ZCAPM | 0.48<br>(3.24) | 0.09<br>(0.47) | 0.38<br>(5.42) | | | | | | 0.83 |
| Three-factor | 0.52<br>(3.55) | 0.002<br>(0.01) | | 0.06<br>(0.49) | 0.18<br>(1.64) | | | | 0.06 |
| Four-factor | 0.53<br>(3.75) | −0.01<br>(−0.06) | | 0.09<br>(0.75) | 0.17<br>(1.64) | 0.43<br>(2.54) | | | 0.28 |
| Five-factor | 0.44<br>(2.97) | 0.09<br>(0.45) | | 0.12<br>(1.02) | 0.14<br>(1.35) | | 0.21<br>(1.99) | 0.21<br>(2.36) | 0.22 |
| Six-factor | 0.57<br>(4.02) | −0.04<br>(−0.24) | | 0.14<br>(1.20) | 0.17<br>(1.68) | 0.40<br>(2.40) | 0.19<br>(1.94) | 0.16<br>(1.84) | 0.35 |

This table reports selected results from Kolari et al. (2021). Out-of-sample (one-month-ahead) estimated prices of risk were estimated using the standard two-step Fama-MacBeth cross-sectional tests. Estimated prices of risk are denoted $\hat{\lambda}_k$ for the $k$th factor in monthly percent return terms ($t$-statistics in parentheses). Factors are denoted as $m$ (CRSP index, see footnote), *RD* (return dispersion), *SMB* (size), *HML* (value), *MOM* (momentum), *RMW* (profit), and *CMA* (capital investment). Value-weighted returns were used in the period January 1965–December 2018. Different sets of test asset portfolios were employed as shown in Panels A–D. The results shown below are based on Kolari et al. (2021, Table 7.1, p. 166)

[a]In the ZCAPM, the price of beta risk associated with CRSP index excess returns is denoted $\hat{\lambda}_a$ rather than $\hat{\lambda}_m$ in the other models

This hurdle is relatively high. Rarely are widely used factors able to exceed this threshold, especially in out-of-sample cross-sectional tests. Using this criterion, only zeta risk loadings in the ZCAPM pass recent standards for the validity of factors. Other models are subject to question in view of these findings.

Overall, the results in Table 10.1 show that the empirical ZCAPM outperforms the CAPM and popular multifactor models in standard Fama and MacBeth cross-sectional tests. KLH also conducted cross-sectional tests of the Hou et al. (2015) $q$-factor model with four factors (viz., market, equity capitalization, investment to assets ratio, and return on equity) as well as the Stambaugh and Yuan (2017) mispricing model with four factors (market, size, management, and performance).

None of the $t$-statistics for estimated $\lambda_k$s exceeded three. Moreover, the goodness-of-fit was less than the ZCAPM, especially for industry portfolios as in the tests of other models in Table 10.1. Hence, using similar test assets and sample periods, the ZCAPM outperformed these four-factor models in cross-sectional tests.

More recent work by Kolari et al. (2022b) extended the U.S. stock return analyses in KLH to a longer sample period of 1927 to 2020. The results corroborated those in KLH. Also, Kolari et al. (2022a) extended the analyses to Canada, Japan, Germany, and Japan. Again the results confirmed findings in KLH—namely, the ZCAPM outperformed multifactor models especially when using exogenous industry portfolios.

A natural question is: Why does the ZCAPM consistently outperform multifactor asset pricing models? As discussed in KLH and mentioned earlier, the long/short multifactors are themselves rough measures of return dispersion. They capture different slices of the total return dispersion as measured by $\sigma_{at}$. At times the market prices of multifactor loadings can turn negative (e.g., see the 25 beta-zeta portfolios in Panel C). These negative prices are difficult to explain in the context of the multifactor models. However, in line with the ZCAPM, they are picking up negative zeta risk. As more factors are added to multifactor models, they come closer to capturing total return dispersion. Of course, the multifactors can change over time and shift their position within the distribution of total returns. In general, all multifactors are subsumed or contained within total return dispersion.

Fama and French and others loosely link multifactor models to the hedge portfolio theories of Merton's (1973) intertemporal CAPM and Ross' (1976) arbitrage pricing theory (APT). Further linking theory to empirical models, KLH assert that multifactor models are closely linked to total return dispersion in the ZCAPM. Viewed as return dispersion measures, multifactors are therefore related to both KLH's ZCAPM and Black's (1972) zero-beta CAPM in addition to the CAPM of Treynor (1961, 1962), Sharpe (1964), Lintner (1965), and Mossin (1966). In a very real sense, all of these models are cousins of the CAPM! As already discussed, the main complaint against the CAPM by Fama and French and others was its poor empirical fit to stock returns. The ZCAPM overcomes this objection by dramatically improving the empirical fit of a CAPM-based model.

## 10.4 Summary

Kolari, Liu, and Huang (KLH) (2021) recently proposed a new CAPM dubbed the *ZCAPM*. The ZCAPM has two factors: mean excess market returns and the cross-sectional standard deviation of returns for all assets in the market or simply *return dispersion*. Return sensitivity to these two factors is measured by beta risk and zeta risk, respectively. The ZCAPM is grounded in the Markowitz (1959) mean-variance investment parabola, equilibrium conditions of the famous CAPM by Treynor (1961, 1962), Sharpe (1964), Lintner (1965), and Mossin (1966), and the zero-beta CAPM of Black (1972).

KLH mathematically derived the ZCAPM as a special case of Black's (1972) zero-beta CAPM. Two key insights proposed by KLH are: (1) the width or span of the mean-variance parabola at time $t$ is largely determined by market return dispersion; and (2) the mean market return is approximately in the middle of the parabola somewhere along its axis of symmetry. Using these insights, they identified two unique orthogonal portfolios on the parabola denoted $I^*I^*$ and $ZI^*$ that have the same time-series variance of returns. Upon substituting the formulas for the expected returns of these two portfolios into Black's equation for the zero-beta CAPM, they obtained a special case that represents the theoretical ZCAPM. Adding a riskless rate, they derived the final form of the theoretical ZCAPM.

KLH specified a novel empirical ZCAPM with a dummy signal variable (equal to $+1$ or $-1$) to capture either positive or negative return dispersion effects on asset returns. Since this signal variable is unobservable, they used expectation-maximization (EM) regression methods to estimate the probability that the signal variable is $+1$ or $-1$. Multiplying this probability times the zeta risk regression coefficient, they obtained an estimate of zeta risk (denoted $Z^*$) for a stock. Beta risk (denoted $\beta$) is the regression coefficient associated with mean excess market returns. The empirical ZCAPM is a parsimonious two-factor model that employs factors that can be readily estimated from available market data. There is no need to obtain a proxy for an efficient market portfolio $M$ as in the CAPM or a zero-beta portfolio $ZM$ as in the zero-beta CAPM.

Empirical tests of the ZCAPM yielded impressive results. Using cross-sectional analyses, KLH showed that a close relation exists between stock returns in the next month and previously estimated zeta risk coefficients. Also, using step-ahead or out-of-sample returns in the next month, predicted (fitted) excess returns from the ZCAPM were closer to realized (actual) excess returns in comparisons to the CAPM and Fama and French (1993, 2015, 2018) multifactor models.

More formal Fama and MacBeth (1973) cross-sectional tests using out-of-sample stock returns strongly supported the ZCAPM over the CAPM and multifactor models. Comparative tests of the Carhart (1997) four-factor model, Fama and French three-, five-, and six-factor models, Hou et al. (2015) four-factor $q$ model, and Stambaugh and Yuan (2017) four-factor model showed that:

(1) estimated $R^2$ values from the empirical ZCAPM were noticeably higher on a consistent basis in tests of different portfolios than those for the CAPM and multifactor models; and
(2) zeta risk loadings estimated from the ZCAPM normally had $t$-statistics greater than 3, but multifactors in other models did not exceed this recommended threshold.

A major difficulty of the CAPM as well as multifactor models is their poor pricing performance with respect to exogenous industry portfolios. By contrast, the ZCAPM did a good job of pricing industry portfolios.

Why does the ZCAPM outperform popular multifactor models? The main reason is that multifactor models depend on long/short portfolios as factors that are rough measures of return dispersion. A more complete and accurate measure of return dispersion is the cross-sectional standard deviation of returns in the market. From this perspective, all multifactor models are related to the ZCAPM and therefore the CAPM also. The main complaint of poor empirical fit among CAPM models is overcome by the ZCAPM. Indeed, the ZCAPM consistently outperforms the multifactor models in out-of-sample cross-sectional tests. Rather than the CAPM being empirically dead, it is reborn in the form of the empirical ZCAPM. The history of asset pricing has come full circle. The early theoretical models of the CAPM led to discretionary models with empirically justified multifactors. However, the ZCAPM subsumes multifactors within its total return dispersion factor. Can machine learning methods be developed to further enhance the empirical ZCAPM? Are there better proxies for mean market returns and the cross-sectional return dispersion? By improving these proxies, the empirical ZCAPM could be enhanced. It will be interesting to see what the future of asset pricing holds!

## Questions

1. Draw a picture of Markowitz's mean-variance investment parabola. Label the Y-axis as $E(R_P)$ for expected returns and X-axis as $\sigma_P^2$ for the variance of returns. Where is the minimum variance portfolio $G$? In your figure, show how Kolari, Liu, and Huang (KLH) (2021) located two orthogonal portfolios with equal time-series variance of returns: $I^*$ on the efficient frontier, and $ZI^*$ on the inefficient boundary of the parabola. According to KLH, what defines the width or span of the parabola? Show this in your diagram along with the mean market return.
2. In their picture of the mean-variance investment parabola, Kolari, Liu, and Huang (KLH) (2021) argued that commonly used general stock market indexes (e.g., the value-weighted CRSP index or S &P 500 index) are inefficient. Where do they locate these general indexes within the parabola? If this is true, what is the implication to tests of the CAPM using the market model?
3. Assuming a riskless asset exists, write the equation for the theoretical ZCAPM. What do beta risk and zeta risk measure in this model? Does the ZCAPM have an empirical advantage in terms of testing over other forms of the CAPM?
4. According to Kolari, Liu, and Huang (KLH) (2021), zeta risk (denoted by $Z_{i,a}^*$) in the ZCAPM can be positive or negative in sign. Illustrate this two-sided zeta risk in a diagram with the $i$th asset's excess returns denoted $R_i - R_f$ on the Y-axis and average excess market returns denoted $R_a - R_f$ on the X-axis. In your diagram, what is beta risk? Show how positive and negative zeta risk affect the excess returns of assets.
5. Show how two-sided return dispersion effects impact expected stock returns. Assume there are two time periods $t = 1$ and 2 in addition to two assets $B$ and $C$. Return dispersion in the market increases from $\sigma_{a1} = 1\%$ at time 1 to 2% at time 2. Due to this increase in cross-sectional market volatility from

time 1 to 2, show how expected asset returns of assets B and C are affected. What if return dispersion decreased over time?

6. Kolari, Liu, and Huang (KLH) (2021) argued that the mean-variance parabola is shaped by the dual systematic risk effects of beta risk and zeta risk. How is the architecture of the parabola affected by these systematic risks?
7. Kolari, Liu, and Zhang (KLH) (2021) conducted out-of-sample (or one-month-ahead), cross-sectional Fama and MacBeth (1973) tests of a number of different test asset portfolios. The final form of the empirical ZCAPM was estimated using one year of daily returns. The U.S. Treasury bill rate proxied the riskless rate. To begin their analyses, KLH reported evidence on the relation between beta risk and zeta risk with respect to one-month-ahead stock returns. Using 97 stock portfolios, the empirical ZCAPM was run using daily returns for one year to obtain $\beta_{i,a}$ and $Z^*_{i,a}$ estimates for each portfolio. The actual returns $R_{it+1}$ in the next one month were retained. The process was repeated by rolling forward one month to get new estimates of $\beta_{i,a}$ and $Z^*_{i,a}$ as well as the next one-month returns $R_{it+1}$ for portfolios. Repeating this process from 1964 to the end of 2018, they generated a series of 648 monthly values for $\beta_{i,a}$, $Z^*_{i,a}$, and $R_{it+1}$. Next, the average values of these values were computed for each portfolio. What did they find?
8. Following standard practices, Kolari, Liu, and Zhang (KLH) (2021) implemented Fama–MacBeth cross-sectional regression tests. The analyses were rolled forward one month at a time to generate a series of estimated market prices of beta and zeta risk loadings (denoted $\lambda_a$ and $\lambda_{RD}$, respectively). To comparatively evaluate the performance of the ZCAPM, they ran tests for the CAPM, Carhart (1997) four-factor model, and Fama and French (1992, 1993, 2015, 2018) three-, five-, and six-factor models. For the often used 25 size and BM sorted portfolios from Kenneth French's data website, they produced graphs comparing realized excess returns to fitted excess returns for the three-factor model of Fama and French (1992, 1993) versus the empirical ZCAPM. What did these graphs show? What about the results for 47 industry portfolios? What do these results mean?
9. Kolari, Liu, and Zhang (KLH) (2021) repeated the question above by comparing other multifactor models to the empirical ZCAPM. For the six-factor model of Fama and French (2018) compared to the empirical ZCAPM, using 25 profit-investment sorted portfolios, what did they find? For industry portfolios?
10. In empirical tests of the ZCAPM, is there an explanation for why multifactor models were dominated by the ZCAPM? Fama and French (1993, 1995, 2015, 2018) link that multifactor models to Merton's (1973) intertemporal CAPM and Ross' (1976) arbitrage pricing theory (APT). Can the ZCAPM be linked to these theoretical models?

## Problems

1. Given their new geometry of the parabola, how did Kolari, Liu, and Huang (KLH) (2021) define the expected returns for the special case of orthogonal portfolios $I^*$ and $ZI^*$ on the parabola? Describe this new geometry for locating these portfolios. How does this geometry differ from the CAPM and market portfolio $M$.
2. If we substitute the definitions of $E(R_{I*})$ and $E(R_{ZI*})$ into the zero-beta CAPM Eq. 10.1, we can derive a theoretical ZCAPM without a riskless rate. Show how to get the theoretical ZCAPM in this case.
3. Kolari, Liu, and Zhang (KLH) (2021) proposed a novel empirical ZCAPM to capture positive and negative sensitivity to return dispersion (i.e., zeta risk). Write their empirical model. What is $D_{it}$ in this model? Using the definition of $D_{it}$, write the final form of the empirical ZCAPM. Why must the expectation-maximization (EM) regression method must be used to estimate this final form?
4. How did Kolari, Liu, and Zhang (KLH) (2021) compute mean market returns as well as the return dispersion for U.S. stocks? Are equal-weighted or value-weighted return used in their computations of these factors?
5. Kolari, Liu, and Zhang (KLH) (2021) conducted out-of-sample Fama and MacBeth (1973) cross-sectional regression tests for the empirical ZCAPM and a number of other models, including the market model and multifactor models. What did these tests reveal about the goodness-of-fit? About the significance of estimated market prices of risk for different factors?

## References


Black, F. 1972. Capital market equilibrium with restricted borrowing. *Journal of Business* 45: 444–454.

Carhart, M.M. 1997. On persistence in mutual fund performance. *Journal of Finance* 52: 57–82.

Chordia, T., A. Goyal, and A. Saretto. 2020. Anomalies and false rejections. *Review of Financial Studies* 33: 2134–2179.

Dempster, A.P., N.M. Laird, and D.B. Rubin. 1977. Maximum likelihood from incomplete data via the EM algorithm. *Journal of the Royal Statistical Society* 39: 1–38.

Fama, E.F., and K.R. French. 1992. The cross-section of expected stock returns. *Journal of Finance* 47: 427–465.

Fama, F.F. and K.R. French 1995. Size and book-to-market factors in earnings and returns. *Journal of Finance* 50: 131–155.

Fama, E.F., and K.R. French. 1993. The cross-section of expected returns. *Journal of Financial Economics* 33: 3–56.

Fama, E.F., and K.R. French. 1996. The CAPM is wanted, dead or alive. *Journal of Finance* 51: 1947–1958.

Fama, E.F., and K.R. French. 2015. A five-factor asset pricing model. *Journal of Financial Economics* 116: 1–22.

Fama, E.F., and K.R. French. 2018. Choosing factors. *Journal of Financial Economics* 128: 234–252.

Fama, E.F., and J.D. MacBeth. 1973. Risk, return, and equilibrium: Empirical tests. *Journal of Political Economy* 81: 607–636.

Gibbons, M.R., S.A. Ross, and J. Shanken. 1989. A test of the efficiency of a given portfolio. *Econometrica* 57: 1121–1152.

Harvey, C.R., Y. Liu, and H. Zhu. 2016. and the cross-section of expected returns. *Review of Financial Studies* 29: 5–68.

Hou, K., C. Xue, and L. Zhang. 2015. Digesting anomalies: An investment approach. *Review of Financial Studies* 28: 650–705.

Jones, P.N., and G.J. McLachlan. 1990. Algorithm AS 254: Maximum likelihood estimation from grouped and truncated data with finite normal mixture models. *Applied Statistics* 39: 273–282.

Liu, W. 2013. *A New Asset Pricing Model Based on the Zero-Beta CAPM: Theory and Evidence.* Doctoral dissertation, Texas A &M University.

Liu, W., J.W. Kolari, and J.Z. Huang. 2012. A new asset pricing model based on the zero-beta CAPM. Best paper award in investments at the annual meetings of the Financial Management Association, Atlanta, GA, October.

Liu, W., J.W. Kolari, and J.Z. Huang. 2019. Creating superior investment portfolios. Working paper, Texas A &M University.

Kolari, J.W., W. Liu, and J.Z. Huang. 2021. *A New Model of Capital Asset Prices: Theory and Evidence*. Cham: Palgrave Macmillan.

Kolari, J.W., J.Z. Huang, H.A. Butt, and H. Liao. 2022a. International tests of the ZCAPM asset pricing model. *Journal of International Financial Markets, Institutions &Money* 79: 101607.

Kolari, J.W., W. Liu, J.Z. Huang, and H. Liao. 2022b. Further tests of the ZCAPM asset pricing model. *Journal of Risk and Financial Management* 15: 1–23.

Linnainmaa, J., and M. Roberts. 2018. The history of the cross-section of stock returns. *Review of Financial Studies* 31: 2606–2649.

Lintner, J. 1965. The valuation of risk assets and the selection of risky investments in stock portfolios and capital budgets. *Review of Economics and Statistics* 47: 13–37.

Markowitz, H.M. 1959. *Portfolio selection: Efficient Diversification of Investments*. New York, NY: Wiley.

McLachlan, G.J., and T. Krishnan. 2008. *The EM Algorithm and Extensions*, 2nd ed. New York, NY: Wiley.

McLachlan, G. J., and D. Peel. 2000. *Finite Mixture Models*. New York, NY: Wiley Interscience.

McLean, R.D., and J. Pontiff. 2016. Does academic publication destroy predictability? *Journal of Finance* 71: 5–32.

Merton, R.C. 1973. An intertemporal capital asset pricing model. *Econometrica* 41: 867–887.

Mossin, J. 1966. Equilibrium in a capital asset market. *Econometrica* 34: 768–783.

Roll, R. 1977. A critique of the asset pricing theory's tests, part I: On past and potential future testability of the theory. *Journal of Financial Economics* 4: 129–176.

Ross, S.A. 1976. The arbitrage theory of capital asset pricing. *Journal of Economic Theory* 13: 341–360.

Sharpe, W.F. 1964. Capital asset prices: A theory of market equilibrium under conditions of risk. *Journal of Finance* 19: 425–442.

Stambaugh, R.F., and Y. Yuan. 2017. Mispricing factors. *Review of Financial Studies* 30: 1270–1315.

Treynor, J.L. 1961. Market value, time, and risk. Unpublished manuscript.

Treynor, J.L. 1962. Toward a theory of market value of risky assets. Unpublished manuscript.

# Event Studies

# 11

One of the most common applications of asset pricing models is event studies.[1] As discussed in Chapter 2, consistent with the Random Walk Hypothesis (RWH), stock prices move randomly over time such that price changes are independent of one another over time. This price behavior supports the notion of efficient markets. To more rigorously test efficient markets, Fama et al. (1969) introduced the concept of an event study by examining the stock price reactions of companies to stock split announcements. They wanted to know the speed of adjustment of stock prices in response to news about stock splits by companies, which is an indicator of market efficiency. Importantly, the authors developed a new methodology to study the movement of stock prices over time. An event study of stock splits was proposed using the market model form of the CAPM to measure *abnormal returns* not explained by systematic market risk. Abnormal returns are firm-specific or idiosyncratic returns after taking into account systematic risk effects on returns. Empirical analyses of residual error terms used to measure abnormal returns showed that stock returns increase prior to stock splits and then level off thereafter. They interpreted these findings to mean that stock splits signal to investors that the firm will increase dividends in the future. Stock returns rise prior to splits due to investors recognizing the increasing profitability of the firm. The split itself signals that those expectations are confirmed by the firm. Interestingly, firms that later decreased (increased) dividends experienced lower (unchanged) stock returns after the split. These abnormal return patterns confirmed that splits are dividend signals from the

[1] See, for example, Dolley (1933), Myers and Baker (1948), Baker (1956, 1957, 1958), Ashley (1962), Ball and Brown (1968), and many others.

**Supplementary Information** The online version contains supplementary material available at https://doi.org/10.1007/978-3-031-16784-3_11.



J. W. Kolari and S. Pynnönen, *Investment Valuation and Asset Pricing*,
https://doi.org/10.1007/978-3-031-16784-3_11

prospective investors. Finally, stock prices reacted immediately on the day of split announcements in line with market efficiency.

Over time researchers have conducted event studies to investigate the stock market reaction to many different kinds of news announcements. For example, many studies have examined firm-specific events besides stock splits, including managerial decisions, earnings, and other accounting-related announcements.[2] Other studies look at economy-wide events, including regulatory changes and macroeconomic announcements.[3] Today, event studies not only provide evidence on the question of market efficiency but how investors perceive different kinds of information that will impact stock prices.

This chapter reviews the traditional event study methodology introduced by Fama, Fisher, Jensen, and Roll and developed by researchers over more than 50 years. In this regard, event studies can be categorized as short or long run. Typically, studies within a 1-year timeframe are considered to be short run. Those extending 1-to-5 years after events are long-run studies. As we will see, short- and long-run studies apply different statistical methods. Also, long-run studies have become very controversial as abnormal returns should not persist over many years in an efficient market.

## 11.1 Short-Run Event Studies

Brown and Warner (1980, 1985) and MacKinlay (1997)[4] have provided excellent discussions and references with respect to traditional, short-run event study analysis. In this section, we overview how asset pricing models are used to conduct short-run event studies.

### 11.1.1 Basic Steps in an Event Study

Event study analyses rely upon asset pricing models. We next go through the basic steps to conduct a short-run event study. We assume daily returns but weekly or monthly returns can be used too.

1. Define the *event* of interest—for example, an earnings announcement by a company. Often the event must be operationalized more precisely. For example, Campbell et al. (1997, Chapter 4) assigned each earnings announcement to one of the three categories: good news, no news, and bad news. If the actual earnings exceeded (fell below) expected or forecasted earnings by 2.5% or more,

[2] For example, see studies by Sunder (1973, 1975), Aharony and Swary (1980), Binder (1985), and others.

[3] For example, see studies by Schwert (1981a, b), Schipper and Thompson (1983), Brockett et al. (1999), Sharpe (2001), Knif et al. (2008), and others.

[4] See also Campbell et al. (1997) and Binder (1998).

the announcement was designated as good (bad) news. Other earnings closer to expected were considered no news.

2. Collect a *sample of firms* that had the event. Relevant companies are required to have sufficient data to estimate asset pricing model parameters.
3. Determine for each sample firm of the *event day*.
4. Based on the event day, define the *event window*. The event date is labeled as day 0 and other days around the event day comprise the event window. Event days with negative values occur before the event day, and positive values occur on post-event days. For example, days $-1, 0, +1$ mean one day before the event day, the event day, and the next day after the event day.

   The event window can be (for example) $\pm 5$ trading days around the event day, i.e., consisting of 11 trading days $-5, -4, -3, -2, -1, 0, 1, 2, 3, 4, 5$. The event window can be longer if desired; for example, Campbell et al. used an event window of $\pm 20$ trading days around the announcement or about one month before and one month after the event (41 trading days).
5. Define the *estimation window* prior to the event window. With daily data, the length of the estimation window may be (for example) 250 trading days, or about one year. Given the above 11-day event window from days $-5$ to $+5$, trading days from $-255$ to $-6$ would encompass the estimation window.
6. Using an asset pricing model, compute the *abnormal returns* for each firm on each event day in the event window. We discuss this calculation in detail below.
7. Make *inferences* about the behavior of the abnormal returns based on appropriate statistical tools, including descriptive statistics, graphics, and tests. Report the statistical findings and discuss their economic significance also (i.e., the magnitudes of abnormal returns from the perspective of investors).

### 11.1.2 Abnormal Returns

To evaluate the impact of an event on the stock returns of a company, we need to compute the *abnormal return* (*AR*). The *AR* is defined as the deviation of the actual return from the predicted return on each day in the event window:

$$AR_{it} = R_{it} - E(R_{it}|X_t), \tag{11.1}$$

where $R_{it}$ is the actual return at time *t*, and $E(R_{it}|X_t)$ is the predicted return. The latter return is the conditional expected return given information $X_t$ under normal conditions (i.e., without the event effect). Generally speaking, $E(R_{it}|X_t)$ is called the mean model that measures the normal performance of returns. Summing up the abnormal returns over the event window from $\tau_1$ to $\tau_2$ yields *cumulative abnormal returns* (*CAR*s):

$$CAR_i(\tau_1, \tau_2) = \sum_{s=\tau_1}^{\tau_2} AR_{it}. \tag{11.2}$$

There are several ways to specify and estimate the mean model. The simplest approach is to specify $E(R_{it}|X_t)$ equal to the unconditional expected return $\mu_i = E(R_{it})$, which can be estimated by the sample mean over the estimation window. A more common way to measure abnormal returns is to use an asset pricing model. Following Fama et al. (1969), let's take the simplest case of the market model written as $E(R_{it}|R_{mt}) = \alpha_i + \beta_i R_{mt}$, where $R_{mt}$ is the proxy market return.[5] Extending the market model approach, event studies have utilized a multifactor model written as $E(R_{it}|X_t) = \alpha_i + \beta_{i1} F_{1t} + \cdots + \beta_{ip} F_{pt}$ where the information set $X_t$ is based on multifactor $F_{jt}$ values (e.g., the Fama and French [1993, 2015] three- and five-factor models with $j = 1, \ldots, p$). Interestingly, Brown and Warner (1985) have found that statistical results in event studies are not critically dependent on the chosen asset pricing model. Hence, short-run event study results are not very sensitive to the asset pricing model employed.

Given the factor model, the regression parameters $\alpha_i$ and $\beta_{ij}$, $j = 1, \ldots, p$ are estimated by ordinary least squares (OLS) using the estimation window returns for each sample stock $i = 1, \ldots, n$. Estimates for the abnormal returns in the event window are *prediction errors*:

$$AR_{it} = R_{it} - (\hat{\alpha}_i + \hat{\beta}_{i1} F_{1t} + \cdots + \hat{\beta}_{ip} F_p), \tag{11.3}$$

where $t$ is the event time within the event window for $i = 1, \ldots, n$ different assets.

In short-run event studies, statistical tests of event effects can be broadly divided into two categories: parametric and nonparametric. Parametric tests rely on the assumption that returns follow some parametric probability distribution like the Gaussian normal distribution. Nonparametric tests relax this assumption and therefore tend to be more robust. Even so, this robustness does not come without some cost. For instance, if the underlying assumptions of the parametric return generating process hold, parametric tests tend to be more powerful, which means that they will detect the event effect with higher probability than nonparametric test if indeed there is a significant event (i.e., Type II error is reduced). Conversely, if the underlying assumptions are violated, parametric tests can be prone to false alarms in the sense that they detect significant event effects when there are none (i.e.,

---

[5] Here the conditioning information set $X_t = R_{mt}$, and the conditional expectation itself is simplified to the linear model $E(R_{it}|R_{mt}) = \alpha_i + \beta_i R_{mt}$, where the coefficients are assumed to be time independent.

Type I error is increased).[6] Because the vast majority of event studies utilize parametric testing, we focus on this approach here. For interested readers, Appendix A provides a short introduction to nonparametric approaches.

### 11.1.3 Parametric Testing

Statistical testing for an event effect involves testing whether the population mean of the abnormal returns deviates from zero after a news announcement. That is, we want to know whether the observed deviation of actual returns from predicted returns is due to natural random variation in stock returns or due to new information that causes stock prices to change. The null hypothesis is:

$$H_0 : \mu = 0, \tag{11.4}$$

where $\mu$ is the population mean of abnormal returns across all event firms. Similarly, denoting the population mean of cumulative abnormal returns as $CAR_i(\tau_1, \tau_2)$ over event days from $\tau_1$ to $\tau_2$ as $\mu(\tau_1, \tau_2)$, the null hypothesis of no cumulative event effect is:

$$H_0 : \mu(\tau_1, \tau_2) = 0. \tag{11.5}$$

#### Non-Standardized Return Tests

A generic form of the *t*-statistic for testing the null hypotheses in Eqs. (11.4) and (11.5) is the traditional *t*-ratio:

$$t = \frac{\bar{x}}{\text{s.e}(\bar{x})}, \tag{11.6}$$

where $\bar{x}$ is the sample mean of *AR*s (or *CAR*s) of sample event firms, and $\text{s.e}(\bar{x})$ is the standard error of the sample mean.

Assuming that the event windows of different firms are not overlapping in calendar time, the *t*-statistic in Eq. (11.6) for testing the null hypothesis (11.4) for *AR*s becomes:

$$t_{AR} = \frac{\overline{AR}_0}{\text{s.e}(\overline{AR}_0)}, \tag{11.7}$$

[6] In statistical testing, Type I error means falsely rejecting the null hypothesis when it is true (false alarm), and Type II error means accepting the null hypothesis when it is not true (missed alarm). The probability of Type I errors is set by the researcher. Typical values are 5% or 1%. The Type II error probability depends on the Type I error probability, sample size, distribution of the sample statistic, and the extent to which the true parameter value deviates from the null hypothesis value. Statistical *power* is measured by 1 − Type-II-probability, or the probability of detecting a false null hypothesis (correct alarm). It is important to use statistical tests that have maximum power in event studies.

where

$$\overline{AR}_0 = \frac{1}{n} \sum_{i=1}^{n} AR_{i0} \tag{11.8}$$

is the sample average of abnormal returns on event day $t = 0$, and s.e$(\overline{AR}_0)$ is the standard error of $\overline{AR}_0$. Similarly, for testing the null hypothesis (11.5) for *CAR*s, the $t$-ratio in Eq. (11.6) becomes:

$$t_{CAR} = \frac{\overline{CAR}_{\tau_1,\tau_2}}{\text{s.e}(\overline{CAR}_{\tau_1,\tau_2})}, \tag{11.9}$$

where

$$\overline{CAR}_{\tau_1,\tau_2} = \frac{1}{n} \sum_{i=1}^{n} CAR_i(\tau_1, \tau_2), \tag{11.10}$$

and s.e$(\overline{CAR}_{\tau_1,\tau_2})$ is the standard error.[7] If the event windows are completely nonoverlapping, the abnormal returns between firms can be considered independent. In this case, the central limit theorem (CLT) implies that the null distributions of both of these statistics are approximately standard normal, or $N(0, 1)$.

There is considerable literature on the development of robust $t$-statistics in event studies. These studies seek to provide more accurate tests of event effects that measure whether stock price changes are significant or not. For example, Harrington and Shrider (2007) noticed that news events can cause the variances of stock returns to increase. The authors recommended an adjustment to standard errors in the $t$-statistic to account for this issue. Another potential issue that can affect standard errors is returned autocorrelation (i.e., correlation of stock returns over time). Because the above $t$-ratios utilize returns in the event window and not the estimation window, they are robust to both event-induced variance and autocorrelation.[8]

---

[7] The respective standard errors in Eqs. (11.7) and (11.9) are defined as:

$$\text{s.e}(\overline{AR}_0) = \sqrt{\frac{1}{n(n-1)} \sum_{i=1}^{n} (AR_{i0} - \overline{AR}_0)^2} \tag{11.11}$$

and

$$\text{s.e}(\overline{CAR}_{\tau_1,\tau_2}) = \sqrt{\frac{1}{n(n-1)} \sum_{i=1}^{n} (CAR_i(\tau_1, \tau_2) - \overline{CAR}_{\tau_1,\tau_2})^2}. \tag{11.12}$$

[8] The standard error used in the *CAR* $t$-statistic (11.9) is an example of *clustering robust* standard errors (with respect to serial correlation), where the event windows over which individual *CARs* are aggregated from the clusters. See Cameron et al. (2011), Dutta et al. (2018), and Kolari et al. (2018) for further information.

### Standardized Return Tests

It was soon observed that material statistical power gains could be achieved by using standardized abnormal returns rather than original returns. The best known statistical tests are the Patell (1976) $z$-statistic and Boehmer et al. (1991) $t$-statistic referred to as the BMP-test. In general, these more sophisticated tests better measure the statistical significance of stock returns in response to news events. While somewhat complex, these tests can be fairly easily computed by means of statistical software programs.

Standardized abnormal returns are defined as:

$$SAR_{it} = \frac{AR_{it}}{s_{AR_{it}}}, \tag{11.13}$$

where

$$s_{AR_{it}} = s_i\sqrt{1 + d_{it}} \tag{11.14}$$

is the sample standard deviation of $AR_{it}$ in which $s_i$ is the OLS residual standard deviation of the estimation window residuals and $d_{it}$ is the prediction error correction to account for sampling errors in the OLS regression coefficient estimates. Standardized cumulative abnormal returns ($SCAR$s) over $\tau$ event days are defined in the same manner:

$$SCAR_i = \frac{CAR_i}{s_{CAR_i}}, \tag{11.15}$$

where

$$s_{CAR_i} = s_i\sqrt{\tau + d_{i\tau}} \tag{11.16}$$

in which $s_i$ is the same as in Eq. (11.14).[9]

[9] With the market model $R_{it} = \alpha_i + \beta R_{mt} + e_{it}$, $d_{it}$ in Eq. (11.14) becomes

$$d_{it} = \frac{1}{T} + \frac{(R_{mt} - \bar{R}_m)^2}{\sum_{s=1}^{T}(R_{ms} - \bar{R}_m)^2}$$

and $d_{i\tau}$ in Eq. (11.16)

$$d_{i\tau} = \tau^2\left(\frac{1}{T} + \frac{(\bar{R}_{m\tau} - \bar{R}_m)^2}{\sum_{s=1}^{T}(R_{ms} - \bar{R}_m)^2}\right),$$

where $T$ is the estimation window length, $\bar{R}_m$ is the average market return in the estimation window, and $\bar{R}_{m\tau}$ is the average market return in the window over which $CAR$ is computed. Because calendar times of the event are assumed not overlapping, estimation and event windows are unique for each stock $i$, such that we use the subscript $i$ in $d_{it}$ and $d_{i\tau}$.

For *SAR*s computed using the market model, Patell (1976) proposed the following test statistic:

$$z_{\text{patell}} = \frac{\sum_{i=1}^{n} SAR_{it}}{\sqrt{\sum_{i=1}^{n} \frac{T_i-2}{T_i-4}}}, \tag{11.17}$$

where $T_i$ is the length of the estimation window of the $i$th stock. By the CLT in large samples, we know that $z_{\text{patell}} \sim N(0, 1)$.

The Patell statistic does not account for possible event-induced variance To fix this problem, Boehmer et al. (1991) proposed to utilize the event time $t$ estimated standard error in the test statistic. As such, their test statistic is analogous to the $t$-ratios in Eqs. (11.7) and (11.9) with *AR*s and *CAR*s replaced by their standardized counterparts. Hence, for *SAR*s, we now have:

$$t_{\text{bmp}} = \frac{\overline{SAR}_t}{\text{s.e}(\overline{SAR}_t)}, \tag{11.18}$$

where $\text{s.e}(\overline{SAR}_t)$ is the standard error of $\overline{SAR}_t$ computed similarly to Eq. (11.11) using $SAR_{it}$s. Again, assuming independence, the CLT implies that the null distribution of the test statistic is approximately $N(0, 1)$. Due to its robustness to event-induced variance, the BMP statistic has become one of the most popular test statistics in event studies.[10]

If the events are clustered in calendar time, meaning that all or a large part of the event firms share the same event day in calendar time, the above statistics tend to overreject the null hypothesis when there is no event effect. This bias is due to the contemporaneous correlation of stock returns. The use of appropriate mean models to estimate abnormal returns was previously thought to alleviate this symptom. However, Kolari and Pynnönen (2010) demonstrated that even a low cross-sectional correlation causes incremental overrejection as the sample size grows. Consequently, they proposed the following adjustment to the BMP statistic (adjusted BMP) when all firms share the same event day in calendar time:

$$t_{\text{abmp}} = t_{\text{bmp}} \sqrt{\frac{1-\bar{r}}{1+(n-1)\bar{r}}}, \tag{11.19}$$

where $\bar{r}$ is an estimate of the average cross-sectional correlation of the abnormal returns. This test can be compted using either the estimation period or event period

In general, for a factor model with $p$ factors, the correction terms are $d_{it} = x_t'(X'X)^{-1}x_t$ and $d_{i\tau} = \tau^2 \bar{x}_\tau'(X'X)^{-1}\bar{x}_\tau$, where $x_t = (1, F_{1t}, \ldots, F_{pt})'$ includes *event time t* returns, $\bar{x}_\tau = (1, \bar{F}_{1\tau}, \ldots, \bar{F}_{p\tau})'$ includes factor averages over the *CAR*-window of length $\tau$, and $(X'X)^{-1}$ is the inverse of the $(p+1) \times (p+1)$ matrix of *estimation window* cross-products of the constant term and factor returns.

[10] See Campbell et al. (1997, Chapter 4) for an excellent discussion and further details.

or these combined periods. If the event days are partially clustered, meaning that groups of firms share some but not all event days in calendar time, Kolari et al. (2018) proposed the following adjustment:

$$t_{\text{abmp2}} = \frac{t_{\text{bmp}}}{\sqrt{1 + \delta(n-1)\bar{r}}}, \tag{11.20}$$

where $\delta$ is the fraction of overlapping calendar days in the computed abnormal return. If all event days are different in calendar time, $\delta = 0$ and $t_{\text{abmp2}}$ reduces to $t_{\text{bmp}}$. However, if all event days are the same, $\delta = 1$ and $t_{\text{abmp2}}$ reduces approximately to $t_{\text{abmp}}$.[11] Altogether, these test statistics provide robust statistical tools for researchers and professionals to conduct short-run event studies

### 11.1.4 Examples

**Example 1**: To demonstrate event study testing of abnormal returns, we employ daily stock returns for a sample of 50 seasoned equity offerings (SEOs) by U.S companies. We collect this sample of events in the period 1985– 2015. SEOs raise equity capital for firms to deploy in various capital expenditures (e.g., merger and acquisition bids, fixed plant expenses, etc.). They are highly visible events as new information about the future activities of a firm is revealed to investors. The event period (or event window) is $\pm 10$ days around the event day 0. The estimation period is 250 days prior to the event period, i.e., days from $-260$ to $-11$.

Table 11.1 reports results using the test statistics for event day 0 as well as the cumulative abnormal return windows $(-1, 1)$, $(-5, -1)$, $(+1, +5)$, and $(-10, +10)$. In this sample the event days are not clustered (i.e., SEOs for different firms happen on different days), so no cross-sectional correlation adjustments are needed. The event day return is $-2.54\%$, which is economically large and statistically significant in terms of the non-standardized $t_{CAR}$ test as well as standardized tests of the Patell and BMP. None of the other event windows shows significant abnormal returns. We infer that these results support market efficiency wherein market information is rapidly absorbed in stock prices and returns without delays or pre-event leakages. In general, investors viewed SEOs negatively as stock returns materially decreased on the event day.

**Example 2**: We next demonstrate event study testing for economy-wide announcements. Instead of focusing on individual firms, we investigate the impacts of announcements on industries. Using standard regression software, we consider selected announcements related to financial crises that occurred in 2008

[11] Approaches for taking into account cross-sectional correlation with clustering robust estimation methods as well as estimating the average cross-sectional correlation explicitly in the partial clustering case are discussed in Kolari et al. (2018).

**Table 11.1** Short-run event study results for 50 SEO events of U.S. firms from 1985 to 2015

| | Event window | | | | |
|---|---|---|---|---|---|
| | Event day | (−1, +1) | (−5, −1) | (+1, +5) | (−10, −10) |
| AR/CAR(%) | −2.54 | −2.31 | −1.21 | 0.27 | −3.84 |
| $t_{CAR}$ | −1.95 | −1.65 | −0.98 | 0.20 | −1.52 |
| *p*-value | 0.056 | 0.105 | 0.331 | 0.840 | 0.134 |
| $z_{\text{patell}}$ | −4.50 | −2.31 | −1.54 | 1.83 | −1.09 |
| *p*-value | 0.000 | 0.021 | 0.125 | 0.067 | 0.274 |
| $t_{\text{bmp}}$ | −2.20 | −1.40 | −1.41 | 1.33 | −1.12 |
| *p*-value | 0.033 | 0.196 | 0.165 | 0.190 | 0.269 |

and 2020.[12] Our investigation focuses on how news events impacted U.S. stock returns for different industry portfolios. We selected the following major news announcements in 2008 and 2020:

**2008 financial crisis news events**

- January 11: Bank of America agreed to buy failing savings bank Countrywide Financial for about $4 billion.
- March 16: The Federal Reserve agreed to guarantee $30 billion in assets held by securities firm Bear Stearns in connection with its government-sponsored sale to JP Morgan Chase.
- September 15: Lehman Brothers, a large securities firm, is not bailed out by the government and therefore files for bankruptcy. Bank of America agreed to purchase failing securities firm Merrill Lynch for $50 billion.
- October 3: Congress passed a bailout program for big banks (known as *TARP*). Wells Fargo agreed to buy failing Wachovia for about $14.8 billion.

**2020 COVID-19 pandemic news events**

- March 11: The World Health Organization (WHO) declared COVID-19 a global pandemic.
- March 26: The U.S. Congress passed the Coronavirus Aid, Relief, and Economic Security (CARES) Act. This legislation provided $2 trillion in aid to hospitals, small businesses, and state and local governments.

We downloaded daily stock returns from Kenneth French's online data library[13] for four industries: consumer discretionary, manufacturing, communications, and

[12] *USA Today* (September 8, 2013): https://eu.usatoday.com/story/money/business/2013/09/08/chronology-2008-financial-crisis-lehman/2779515/COVID-19.

AJMC: https://www.ajmc.com/view/a-timeline-of-covid19-developments-in-2020.

[13] https://mba.tuck.dartmouth.edu/pages/faculty/ken.french/data_library.html.

health. Days in the analyses are denoted as follows: $\tau_1$ = start estimation window, $\tau_2$ = end estimation window, $\tau_3$ = event day, and $\tau_4$ = end event window. As such, the event window consists of days $\tau_2 + 1, \ldots, \tau_4$ and the event day is a day within the event window, i.e., $\tau_2 < \tau_3 \leq \tau_4$.

To run the event study analyses, special event-study software is not needed. We can easily adapt standard regression/econometric software to do the analyses. We define a dummy variable for each day within the event window and add the dummies to the regression model. Here we use the Fama-French five-factor model as the mean model (normal return) for industry $p$ and enhance the model with the event window dummy variables as follows:

$$R^e_{pt} = \alpha_p + \beta_p R^e_m + s_p SMB_t + h_p HML_t + r_p RMW + c_p CMA_t + \delta_{\tau_2+1} D_{\tau_2+1} + \cdots + \delta_{\tau_4} D_{\tau_4} + \epsilon_{pt}, \tag{11.21}$$

where $R^e_p = R_p - R_f$ is the excess return for an industry portfolio over the riskless Treasury bill rate $R_f$, $R^e_m = R_m - R_f$ is the excess return for the market proxy, and $SMB$, $HML$, $RMW$, and $CMA$ are the well-known Fama-French zero-investment factor portfolios. Dummy variables $D_{\tau_2+j}$ equal 1 on event days $\tau_2 + j = t$ and 0 otherwise, which correspond to the days in the event window. Importantly, the respective coefficients $\delta_{\tau_2+j}$ measure event effects on each day within the event window.

Using standard regression programs available in SAS, Stata, R, or other statistical software packages, regression (11.21) can be estimated. The $\delta$-estimates equal the prediction errors of the regression model and therefore comprise the needed abnormal returns in Eq. (11.3) to measure the event effects. For instance, testing for the event day abnormal return reduces to testing whether the corresponding coefficient (or $\delta_{\tau_3}$) is zero. Testing cumulative abnormal returns, such as *CAR* (+1, +5), tests whether the sum of the respective coefficients is zero. Given $\tau_3$ denotes the event day, the null hypothesis is:

$$H_0 : \delta_{\tau_3+1} + \cdots + \delta_{\tau_3+5} = 0. \tag{11.22}$$

Using the above regression techniques, Table 11.2 reports the event study results. Again, the estimation window is 250 trading days before the event window of ±10 trading days around the event day. Panel A shows cumulative abnormal returns $CAR(-5, -1)$ for five days before the event day, Panel B tests abnormal returns on event day 0, and Panel C tests $CAR(+1, +5)$ for five days after the event day. The results show that event effects vary across industries. For instance, in Panel C for the October 3, 2008 announcement of Wells Fargo's purchase of Wachovia, there were negative $CAR(+1, +5)$s in the manufacturing and health industries but no effects on the communications industry. WHO's COVID-19 declaration on March 11, 2020 appears to have affected all industries but in different ways. The consumer and manufacturing industries had highly significant negative $CAR(+1, +5)$s, but the communications and health industries had significant positive $CAR(+1, +5)$s.

**Table 11.2** Abnormal returns for four industries using the Fama and French five-factor model: Selected news announcement dates during the 2008 financial crisis and 2020 COVID-19 crisis

| | Event date (Financial crisis) | | | | Event date (COVID-19) | |
|---|---|---|---|---|---|---|
| Industry | Jan 11, 2008 | Mar 16, 2008 | Sept 15, 2008 | Oct 3, 2008 | Mar 11, 2020 | Mar 26, 2020 |
| **Panel A:** *CAR* (−5, −1) | | | | | | |
| Consumer | 1.79<br>(0.002)*** | −0.36<br>(0.604) | 1.08<br>(0.219) | 1.28<br>(0.160) | 1.03<br>(0.124) | 0.40<br>(0.573) |
| Manufacturing | −1.15<br>(0.146) | 0.66<br>(0.426) | −1.20<br>(0.281) | −3.54<br>(0.003)*** | −2.56<br>(0.000)*** | 0.60<br>(0.433) |
| Communications | −2.97<br>(0.000)*** | 0.36<br>(0.639) | 1.48<br>(0.134) | 0.09<br>(0.929) | 0.01<br>(0.981) | −1.52<br>(0.010)*** |
| Health | 4.35<br>(0.000)*** | −0.77<br>(0.418) | 1.00<br>(0.395) | 1.90<br>(0.112) | 0.07<br>(0.942) | −5.02<br>(0.000)*** |
| **Panel B:** Event day 0 abnormal returns | | | | | | |
| Consumer | −0.99<br>(0.000)*** | −0.01<br>(0.979) | 0.97<br>(0.017)** | −0.63<br>(0.119) | −0.58<br>(0.040) | −0.36<br>(0.231) |
| Manufacturing | 0.01<br>(0.977) | 0.07<br>(0.843) | −1.23<br>(0.017)** | 1.02<br>(0.055)* | −1.31<br>(0.000)*** | 1.18<br>(0.000)*** |
| Communications | −0.47<br>(0.107) | 0.73<br>(0.036)** | 0.25<br>(0.582) | −0.31<br>(0.491) | 0.74<br>(0.001)*** | 0.02<br>(0.948) |
| Health | 1.34<br>(0.000)*** | 0.07<br>(0.868) | −0.16<br>(0.772) | −0.54<br>(0.305) | −0.14<br>(0.736) | 1.06<br>(0.012)** |
| **Panel C:** *CAR* (+1, +5) | | | | | | |
| Consumer | 1.33<br>(0.019)** | 2.03<br>(0.005)*** | −3.16<br>(0.001)*** | −0.81<br>(0.408) | −1.97<br>(0.004)*** | 0.16<br>(0.803) |
| Manufacturing | −1.30<br>(0.099)* | −3.62<br>(0.000)*** | 4.24<br>(0.000)*** | −6.47<br>(0.000)*** | −3.27<br>(0.000)*** | 1.39<br>(0.053)* |
| Communications | 1.05<br>(0.109) | −0.32<br>(0.680) | −2.28<br>(0.027)*** | 1.85<br>(0.090)* | 3.01<br>(0.000)*** | 0.02<br>(0.965) |
| Health | −1.17<br>(0.102) | 0.21<br>(0.830) | −1.59<br>(0.195) | −6.93<br>(0.000)*** | 3.32<br>(0.001)*** | 1.94<br>(0.037)** |

Abnormal returns are computed using the Fama and French five-factor model: $R_p^e = \alpha_p + \beta_p R_m^e + s_p SMB + h_p HML + r_p RMW + c_p CMA + \epsilon_p$, where $R_p^e = R_p - R_f$ is the excess return over the riskless Treasury bill rate for an industry portfolio, $R_m^e = R_m - R_f$ is the excess return for the market proxy, and $SMB$, $HML$, $RMW$, and $CMA$ are the zero-investment portfolio factors. The estimation window is 255 trading days before the beginning of the event window containing ±10 trading days around event day 0

*Note* $p$-values for the level of significance are shown in parentheses: * = 10*, ** = 5%, and *** = 1%

*Data source* https://mba.tuck.dartmouth.edu/pages/faculty/ken.french/data_library.html

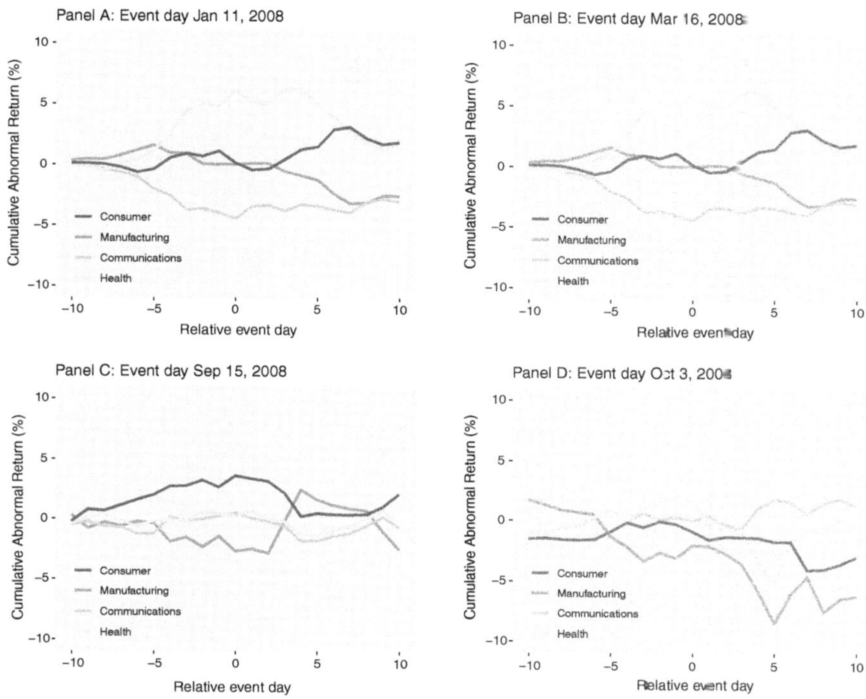


**Fig. 11.1** Cumulative abnormal returns for selected industries in response to 2008 financial crisis news events

Figures 11.1 and 11.2 graph the industry *CAR*s in the 21-day event windows for the news events. Notice in particular the larger negative effects of the financial crisis announcement on October 3, 2008 (Fig. 11.1, Panel D) and COVID-19 announcement on March 11, 2020 (Fig. 11.2, Panel A) with respect to the manufacturing sector compared to the other sectors. Interestingly, this industry seems to anticipate these events by a few days. Thus, investors were expecting these events to some extent, which is consistent with an efficient market.

## 11.2 Long-Run Event Studies

Both short- and long-run event studies are useful in terms of testing market efficiency. As we have seen, short-run studies focus on immediate effects and price adjustment in the days surrounding the event. By contrast, long-run event studies seek to capture potential persistence in event effects over time horizons from months to several years. Of course, persistent return effects over time are inconsistent with market efficiency. In an efficient market, investors should adjust returns

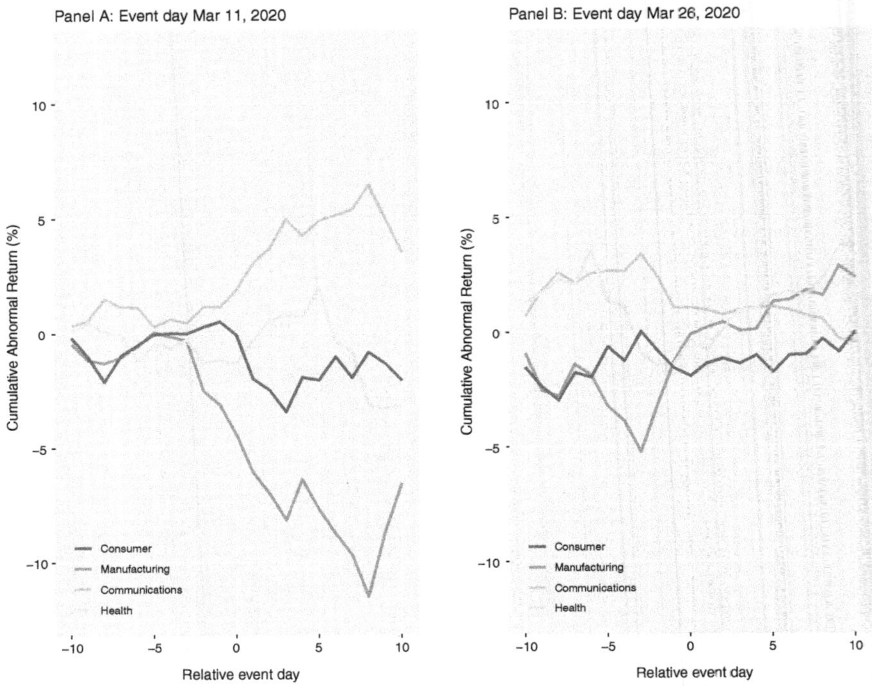


**Fig. 11.2** Cumulative abnormal returns for selected industries in response to 2020 COVID-19 crisis news events

to risks such that no abnormal returns (or differences between actual and predicted returns) exist in the long run.

While short-run event study methodology is well established, long-run event study methods continue to develop. Major long-run event study issues include proper normal expected return definitions and appropriate risk adjustment. It is reasonable to believe that a major firm event (e.g., a seasoned equity offer) will change firm fundamentals and therefore its risk profile. Also, in contrast to the short-run event studies, the test statistic specification in long-run studies is highly sensitive to the benchmark asset pricing model to measure predicted returns. The simple reason is that, within only a few days in short-run studies, a small bias in the predicted return is indiscernible from random noise. However, these small measurement biases can accumulate as the time horizon grows to several years, which can cause both statistically and economically large differences. Finally, risk shifts are likely due to major corporate events, which adds to potential measurement problems in estimating predicted returns. For these reasons, it is possible that an apparent long-run abnormal return is due simply to measurement problems.

Current long-run event studies utilize two different methods to assess post-event (risk-adjusted) abnormal return behavior: (1) buy-and-hold abnormal returns, (2) and calendar time abnormal returns. We next review these two test approaches.

### 11.2.1 Buy-and-Hold Abnormal Return Approach

Ikenberry et al. (1995), Barber and Lyon (1997), and Lyon et al. (1999) introduced the buy-and-hold abnormal return (*BHAR*) approach. This approach finances the investment in event firms by selling short similar non-event firms and holding the position to the end of the period (e.g., five years). A similar or matching non-event firm is called the *control firm*. Given the matching control firm, a $T$-month *BHAR* is defined as

$$BHAR_{iT} = \prod_{t=1}^{T}(1 + R_{it}) - \prod_{t=1}^{T}(1 + R_{it}^{c}), \tag{11.23}$$

where $R_{it}$ is the return on the event firm $i$ in post-event month $t$, and $R_{it}^{c}$ is the return on the matching non-event firm. Often the control firm is defined as a firm with similar size and book to market ratio characteristics as the event firm.

Under the null hypothesis of no event effect, the event firm and its match are expected to have similar expected returns, such the expected value of $BHAR_{iT}$ is zero. Given a sample of $n$ event firms, the $t$-ratio for testing the null hypothesis is

$$t_{BHAR} = \frac{\overline{BHAR}}{\text{s.e}(\overline{BHAR})}, \tag{11.24}$$

where $\overline{BHAR}$ is the sample mean, and $\text{s.e}(\overline{BHAR})$ is the standard error.[14]

Unfortunately, this test statistic has two Achilles' heels. One possible problem is the independence assumption, which requires that the event windows of all firms are completely non-overlapping in calendar time. In a long window extending (for example) 5 years, this assumption may well not hold. For this reason, because stock returns tend to be positively correlated, the standard error in $t$-ratio (11.24) becomes downward biased causing overrejection of the null hypothesis. A second problem is that *BHAR*s are prone to incomplete risk adjustment. Some adjustment for risk is accomplished by subtracting control firm returns from event firm returns. But the two firms can plausibly differ in terms of a number of important market risks. Recognizing this drawback, Fama (1998) has advocated for risk adjustment in computing abnormal returns, which favors the calendar time abnormal return (CTAR) approach to be discussed next. Despite its shortcomings, the *BHAR* approach has gained popularity due to its focus on investor experience. That is, *BHAR* is based on compounded returns earned by investors in a holding period.

---

[14] This standard error is computed as:

$$\text{s.e}(\overline{BHAR}) = \sqrt{\frac{1}{n(n-1)}\sum_{i=1}^{n}(BHAR_{iT} - \overline{BHAR})^2}. \tag{11.25}$$

Assuming the independence of $BHAR_{iT}$s, the asymptotic null distribution of $t_{BHAR}$ is standard normal.

### 11.2.2 Calendar Time Abnormal Return Approach

Introduced by Jaffe (1974), calendar timeabnormal returns (*CTAR*s) are risk-adjusted returns defined in terms of a calendar time portfolio. For example, for a 5-year investment horizon, the month $t$ return of an equal-weighted calendar time portfolio is the average of returns of those stocks that have had the event within the 5-year period. Applying the Fama-French three-factor model to adjust for market, size, and value risk factors, we have[15]:

$$R_{pt} - R_{ft} = \alpha_p + \beta_p(R_{mt} - R_{ft}) + s_p SMB_t + h_p HML_t + e_{pt}, \quad (11.26)$$

where $R_{pt}$ is the calendar time portfolio return, $R_{ft}$ is the riskless rate, $R_{mt}$ is the proxy market return, $SMB$ is the small minus big factor, $HML$ is the high minus low value factor, and $e_{pt}$ is the error term. Notably, the intercept $\alpha_p$ is the calendar time abnormal return (*CTAR*). In an efficient market in which all risks are impounded in asset prices, no abnormal return should persist in the long run. Hence, if $\alpha_p$ is nonzero, we can infer that an abnormal returns exist that is not explained by market risks.

It should be mentioned that a major controversy in finance exists with respect to long-run abnormal returns. As already mentioned, assuming efficient markets, all abnormal returns should be zero in the long run after proper risk adjustment. Hence, the presence of long-run abnormal returns suggests that market risks are not completely adjusted in computing predicted turns from an asset pricing model. On the other hand, assuming that inefficiency can exist in markets, behavioralists have argued that long-run abnormal returns reflect over- and underreactions by investors to market information due to psychological reasons. What do you think? What explains long-run abnormal returns?

It is important to note that Boehme and Sorescu (2002) adapted the *CTAR* approach to control firms in a manner similar to the *BHAR* approach. More specifically, they subtracted matched control firm returns from event firm returns on the left-hand-side of Eq. (11.26). By doing so, a nonzero $\alpha_p$ could be interpreted as an abnormal return, as opposed to mispricing error in the asset pricing model. Since mispricing error would be present in both event and control stock returns, they will cancel out in the event minus control stock return.

The null hypothesis of no (long-run) abnormal return reduces to testing whether $\alpha_p$ differs from zero:

$$H_0 : \alpha_p = 0. \quad (11.27)$$

The $t$-ratio is:

$$t_{\hat{\alpha}} = \frac{\hat{\alpha}_p}{\text{s.e}(\hat{\alpha}_p)}, \quad (11.28)$$

[15] We should note that, because the number of stocks in each month can vary from 1 to $n$ (the total number of stocks), weighted least squares are recommended in the regression estimation.

which tests for the significance of abnormal returns in the 5-year event period. A significant $\alpha_p$ estimate fails to accept (or rejects) the null hypothesis of no event effect.

Unfortunately, *BHAR* and *CTAR* often produce different inferences. As discussed above, *BHAR* emphasizes investor holding period returns, whereas *CTAR* is a risk-adjusted abnormal return measure based on market efficiency. Since long-run studies typically span many months, they can be used to investigate risk shifts of the sample firms in response to major news events. It is possible that both returns and risks change due to the impacts of events on firms. The following real-world example for testing abnormal returns illustrates these test approaches.

### 11.2.3 Example

Here we compare the *BHAR* and *CTAR* approaches to long-run event studies based on a sample of 200 seasoned equity offerings (SEOs) among U.S. firms from 1985 to 2015. Using a 5-year post-event period, the total sample period extends to the end of 2020. Comprehensive analyses of this event and other major corporate events are reported by Kolari et al. (2021). For *BHAR*, control firms are selected by matching size (market capitalization) and book-to-market (BM) ratio characteristics to event firms using CRSP and Compustat databases. Firm size is calculated at the end of December prior to the SEO announcement. The BM ratio is calculated at the end of the year prior to the event.

Table 11.3 reports the results for the event month as well as post-event months (i.e., 6-month as well as 1-, 2-, 3-, and 5-year periods). *BHAR* abnormal returns are the excess returns over respective holding periods, and *CTAR* abnormal returns are average returns per month. The signs of abnormal returns computed using these two methods are the same for the most part. One exception is 6 months, in which *BHAR*s are approximately 4% but *CTAR*s equal −0.31% monthly return or about −1.8% over six months. However, both of these abnormal returns are not statistically significant. A major difference in results occurs in the 1-year post-event period, wherein *BHAR*s equal an insignificant −4.77% but *CTAR*s equal a significant −0.81% per month or about −9.7% per year. Looking at other results, both approaches lead to the same inferences of significant 2-year abnormal returns and insignificant 3- and 5-year abnormal returns. In the post-event 5-year period, *BHAR*s and *CTAR*s suggest that SEO firms underperform their matches by an economically meaningful −22.1 percentage points and −0.28 percentage points per month or about −16.8% over 5 years, respectively. While economically large in magnitude, as observed by Kothari and Warner (2006), both approaches suffer from weak power that causes problems in detecting statistically significant events. In general, our results suggest that long-run abnormal returns occurred in response to SEOs by firms. Is the cause behavioral or is there a risk explanation for these negative abnormal returns? Alternatively, do managers sacrifice shareholder wealth to achieve their goals for the firm?

**Table 11.3** Long-run event study results for 200 SEO events of U.S. firms from 1985 to 2015

| | SEO | Post-event months/years | | | | |
|---|---|---|---|---|---|---|
| | Month | 6 months | 1 year | 2 years | 3 years | 5 years |
| *BHAR*(%) | −2.06 | 3.98 | −4.77 | −17.03** | −13.28 | −22.10 |
| *t*-value | −1.09 | 1.01 | −0.94 | −2.15 | −1.55 | −1.53 |
| *CTAR*(%) | −0.12 | −0.15 | −0.81** | −0.75** | −0.37 | −0.28 |
| *t*-value | −0.08 | −0.31 | −2.11 | −2.40 | −1.35 | −1.15 |
| Obs (*BHAR*) | 200 | 200 | 200 | 200 | 200 | 200 |
| Obs (*CTAR*) | 145 | 337 | 367 | 369 | 369 | 369 |
| N months | 200 | 1,199 | 2,393 | 4,584 | 6,334 | 8,767 |

Lastly, the number of observations used to compute *CTAR*s can be used to approximate the fraction of overlapping event months. From the SEO month column in Table 11.3, we see that 55 companies share the same event month.

## 11.3 Summary

This chapter reviewed basic steps for conducting short- and long-run event studies. Important steps include specification of the nature of the event, sample firms, event dates, event window, estimation window, and asset pricing model. Based on the empirical results, inferences are made regarding the statistical and economic significance of abnormal returns. Abnormal returns are the difference between actual and predicted returns. An asset pricing model is employed to estimate predicted returns. Short-run event studies typically focus on high frequency returns, such as daily returns. Parametric *t*-tests for the significance of abnormal returns use either non-standardized or standardized returns. Popular short-run tests of standardized abnormal returns have been developed by Patell (1976), Boehmer et al. (1991), and Kolari and Pynnönen (2010).

We demonstrated short-run event study tests using seasoned equity offerings (SEOs) announcements of firms within an 11-day event window. No significant abnormal returns were detected, which suggested efficient market reactions to SEO news announcements. We also investigated economy-wide announcements related to the 2008 financial crisis and 2020 COVID-19 pandemic. Among four different industries, we found that these news announcements had mixed positive and negative cumulative abnormal return (*CAR*) effects depending on the industry. Also, it appeared that investors anticipated some news announcements consistent with an efficient market. Graphical analyses of news events were shown to be helpful in visualizing the results of short-run event studies.

Long-run studies utilize lower frequency monthly data that can extend for years after events. We covered two different methods for assessing post-event abnormal returns: (1) the buy-and-hold abnormal return (*BHAR*) approach by Ikenberry et al. (1995), Barber and Lyon (1997), and Lyon et al. (1999), and the calendar time abnormal return (*CTAR*) approach by Jaffe (1974). While short-run methods are well established in the literature, long-run methods continue to develop. *BHAR*s capture long-run abnormal returns in a holding period from the perspective of an investor, whereas *CTAR*s are risk-adjusted measures based on the intercept ($\alpha$) term in an asset pricing model. We demonstrated these approaches by means of seasoned equity offering (SEO) announcements. The analyses showed that different results can be produced by these alternative test methods. In general, we found negative long-run abnormal returns after SEOS, which could be attributable to behavioral or risk explanations. Since long-run studies can span many months, they can be used to investigate risk shifts of the sample firms in connection with major news events also.

## Questions

1. Explain the concepts of event date, event time, event window, and estimation window.
2. Explain normal return, abnormal return, and cumulative abnormal return.
3. Discuss pros and cons of standardized event study tests with relation to non-standardized tests.
4. Suppose that you want to test the null hypothesis of no mean effect when event days are completely clustered. The sample size is $n = 100$ firms and the test statistic applied is BMP due to its good sample properties. You estimate the value of $t_{\text{bmp}} = 2.7$ with $p = 0.007$ in two-sided testing. As a result, you infer that the event effect is highly statistically significant. Since the average cross-sectional correlation of the abnormal returns is $\bar{r} = 0.02$, you argue that the small average cross-sectional correlation will not materially change the test results. Is this right?
5. In the text it was noted that the *BHAR* approach in long-run event studies is vulnerable to cross-sectional correlation. Is it vulnerable to autcorrelation or heteroskedasticity of the returns too?
6. Consider a long-run event study of SEO events with abnormal returns defined as the difference between the returns of the event firm and its matched control firm. What would you consider to be a major problem with this definition of the abnormal return?
7. Discuss some of the major pros and cons of nonparametric rank tests in event studies (see Appendix A).

## Problems

1. A key requirement for *efficient capital markets* is that prices fully and instantaneously reflect all available relevant information. Consider the event of an earnings announcement. Suppose that the current price of a stock is 100. Sketch

a stock price process for ±5 days around the event (using end of day prices) to reflect:

a. an efficient capital market when the announcement is
   *i.* a positive surprise with +5% price effect
   *ii.* a negative surprise with −5% price effect
   *iii.* neutral (i.e., according to analyst expectations) with no price effect
b. leakage of information before the event day when the surprise is
   *i.* positive (+5%)
   *ii.* negative (−5%)
c. a price process as in (a) when the full price adjustment takes place over a few days after the event.

2. The table below reports event day abnormal returns, standard deviations of the estimation window abnormal returns (i.e., OLS residuals of the market model), and rank number of the event day abnormal return for each stock relative to its estimation window abnormal returns in a sample of $n = 30$ stocks. The estimation window is $T_e = 200$ days so that $T = T_e + 1$ (i.e., estimation window returns + event return) is the total number of returns for each stock. The smallest return for each stock assumes rank number 1 and the largest 201. Using this ranking approach, the rank number 164 for the first stock indicates that the event day abnormal return of 1.21% is the 164th largest among the 201 returns from the combined estimation period and the event day. Test the null hypothesis of zero abnormal return using each of the following statistics:

a. $t_{AR}$
b. $z_{\text{patell}}$
c. $t_{\text{bmp}}$
d.* $z_{\text{sgn}}$
e.* $t_{\text{grank}}$.

**Optional*: In the optional problem (d), assume that the $d_{it} = 1/T_e$ in Eq. (A11.1). In optional problem (e), when computing Eq. (A11.4), you can use the theoretical standard error that in this case is:

$$s_{\bar{U}} = \sqrt{\frac{1}{nT}\sum_{i=1}^{T}(i/(T+1) - 1/2)^2},$$

where $T = T_e + 1 = 201$. Using this equation, the result is $s_{\bar{U}} = 0.0524$ (rounded to four decimal places).

| Stock | *AR* | Std dev | Rank |
|---|---|---|---|
| 1 | 1.21 | 1.04 | 165 |
| 2 | 0.27 | 1.01 | 134 |
| 3 | 1.01 | 1.13 | 162 |
| 4 | −0.81 | 1.03 | 47 |
| 5 | 0.32 | 0.84 | 116 |

| Stock | *AR* | Std dev | Rank |
|---|---|---|---|
| 6 | −0.87 | 0.98 | 60 |
| 7 | −0.41 | 1.20 | 82 |
| 8 | 1.13 | 0.94 | 159 |
| 9 | 1.16 | 1.17 | 161 |
| 10 | −0.20 | 0.98 | 84 |
| 11 | 0.89 | 1.17 | 153 |
| 12 | 0.97 | 1.08 | 150 |
| 13 | 1.68 | 1.14 | 180 |
| 14 | 1.13 | 0.99 | 171 |
| 15 | 1.79 | 1.05 | 186 |
| 16 | 0.42 | 1.18 | 111 |
| 17 | −1.64 | 1.10 | 19 |
| 18 | −0.71 | 0.96 | 56 |
| 19 | 0.91 | 1.20 | 154 |
| 20 | 0.29 | 1.15 | 124 |
| 21 | 2.10 | 1.18 | 187 |
| 22 | 0.22 | 1.06 | 114 |
| 23 | 0.19 | 1.03 | 116 |
| 24 | 1.32 | 1.06 | 172 |
| 25 | 2.29 | 0.92 | 199 |
| 26 | −3.05 | 0.95 | 1 |
| 27 | 0.77 | 0.85 | 161 |
| 28 | 0.86 | 0.97 | 162 |
| 29 | −1.38 | 0.97 | 14 |
| 30 | 1.32 | 0.99 | 175 |

## Appendix A: Nonparametric Testing

Section 11.1.3 discussed parametric tests wherein data are assumed to be generated from a particular process like the normal distribution. If this assumption holds, the implied test statistics are optimal for statistical testing. Even if the normality of returns does not hold, under fairly general assumptions, the Central Limit Theorem (CLT) guarantees incrementally accurate test results as the sample size grows. Nonparametric approaches are free from any assumption about the specific distribution of the returns. In this respect, the sign test and the ranks test are the two major categories of nonparametric tests.

The sign test assumes that the (cumulative) abnormal returns are cross-sectionally independent and, under the null hypothesis of no event effect, the positive and negative sign of the $CAR$ is equally likely. That is, $P(CAR \leq 0) = P(CAR > 0) = 1/2$. Defining dummy variables $D_i = 0$ when $CAR_i < 0$ and $D_i = 1$ when $CAR_i \geq 0$, and denoting $\bar{D} = \sum_{i=1}^{n} D_i/n$, then under the null hypothesis of no event effect $E(\bar{D}) = 1/2$ and $\text{var}(\bar{D}) = 1/(4n)$. Subsequently, we can define a test statistic

$$z_{\text{sgn}} = 2\sqrt{n}(\bar{D} - 1/2), \tag{A11.1}$$

which under the null hypothesis of no event effect is asymptotically $N(0, 1)$ distributed by the CLT.

The basic assumption of the sign test is that the return distribution is symmetric. For this reason, it is vulnerable to skewness of the distribution, in which case under the null distribution the probabilities of negative and positive signs deviate from one half.

Corrado (1989) developed a test based on ranks of returns. Kolari and Pynnönen (2011) refined the approach to cover both single day and cumulative abnormal returns. They defined estimation window standardized returns as $SAR_{it} = AR_{it}/s_i$, in which $AR_{it}$s are estimation window OLS residuals, and $s_i$ is the respective OLS standard error. For an event window, they defined standardized cumulative abnormal returns from event day $\tau_1$ to $\tau_2$ as

$$SCAR_i(\tau_1, \tau_2) = \frac{CAR_i(\tau_1, \tau_2)}{s_i(\tau_1, \tau_2)},$$

where $s_i(\tau_1, \tau_2)$ is the prediction error corrected OLS standard deviation of the cumulative abnormal return (see Kolari et al. 2018). Re-standardizing $SCAR_i(\tau_1, \tau_2)$ by their cross-sectional standard deviation helps to account for possible event-induced variance. The re-standardized $SCAR$s are defined as

$$SCAR_i^*(\tau_1, \tau_2) = \frac{SCAR_i(\tau_1, \tau_2)}{s(\tau_1, \tau_2)},$$

where

$$s(\tau_1, \tau_2) = \sqrt{\frac{1}{n-1}\sum_{i=1}^{n}(SCAR_i(\tau_1, \tau_2) - \overline{SCAR}_{\tau_1,\tau_2})^2}.$$

Using these together with the estimation window abnormal returns, Kolari and Pynnonen defined the following generalized standardized abnormal returns ($GSAR$s):

$$GSAR_{it} = \begin{cases} SAR_{it}, & \text{for the estimation window returns} \\ SCAR_i^*(\tau_1, \tau_2), & \text{for the cumulative event window return.} \end{cases} \tag{A11.2}$$

*GSAR*s are homogeneous in that, under the null hypothesis of no event (mean) effect, they have zero mean and unit variance. Using these results, rank transformations can be defined as

$$U_{it} = \text{rank}(GSAR_{it})/(T+1) - 1/2 \tag{A11.3}$$

for $i = 1, \ldots, n$, where $T$ indicates the number of estimation window returns plus the event window SCAR observation so that $T$ refers to the rank number associated with $SCAR_i^*(\tau_1, \tau_2)$. As such, these ranks capture both single day abnormal returns as well as cumulative abnormal returns. For testing the null hypothesis of no event effect, the authors derived the following rank test statistic:

$$t_{\text{grank}} = Z\left(\frac{T-2}{T-1-Z^2}\right)^{\frac{1}{2}}, \tag{A11.4}$$

where

$$Z = \frac{\bar{U}_T}{s_{\bar{U}}}$$

with

$$s_{\bar{U}} = \sqrt{\frac{1}{T}\sum_{t=1}^{T}\frac{n_t}{n}\bar{U}_t^2},$$

$$\bar{U}_t = \frac{1}{n_t}\sum_{i=1}^{n_t} U_{it},$$

and $n_t$ is the number of available cross-section returns at time $t = 1, \ldots, T$.

Under the assumption of cross-sectional independence, the asymptotic null distribution of $t_{\text{grank}}$ is Student's $t$-distribution with $T-2$ degrees of freedom. In addition to event-induced variance, $t_{\text{grank}}$ accounts for cross-sectional correlation of abnormal returns when the event days are clustered. Similar to Kolari et al. (2018), Pynnonen (2022) developed an adjustment for $t_{\text{grank}}$ to account for cross-sectional dependence in cases where the event windows are partially clustered.

The major attractiveness of nonparametric tests is their robustness to nonnormality. Also, rank tests are invariant to the usage of simple returns or log-returns as log-transformation preserves the order of observations Many researchers conduct both nonparametric and parametric tests to check the robustness of the results.

## References

Aharony, J., and I. Swary. 1980. Quarterly dividend and earnings announcements and stockholders' returns: An empirical analysis. *Journal of Finance* 35: 1–12.

Ashley, J.W. 1962. Stock prices and changes in earnings and dividends. *Journal of Political Economy* 70: 82–85.
Baker, C.A. 1956. Effective stock splits. *Harvard Business Review* 34: 101–106.
Baker, C.A. 1957. Stock splits in a bull market. *Harvard Business Review* 35: 72–79.
Baker, C.A. 1958. Evaluation of stock dividends. *Harvard Business Review* 36: 99–114.
Ball, R., and P. Brown. 1968. An empirical analysis of accounting income numbers. *Journal of Accounting Research* 6: 159–178.
Barber, B.M., and J.D. Lyon. 1997. Detecting long-run abnormal stock returns: The empirical power and specification of test statistics. *Journal of Financial Economics* 43: 341–372.
Binder, J.J. 1985. On the use of the multivariate regression model in the event studies. *Journal of Accounting Research* 23: 370–383.
Binder, J.J. 1998. The event study methodology since 1969. *Review of Quantitative Finance and Accounting* 11: 111–137.
Boehme, R.D., and S.M. Sorescu. 2002. The long-run performance following dividend initiations and resumption: Underreaction or product chance? *Journal of Finance* 57: 871–900.
Boehmer, E., J. Musumeci, and A.B. Poulsen. 1991. Event study methodology under conditions of event induced variance. *Journal of Financial Economics* 30: 253–272.
Brockett, P.L., H.-M. Chen, and J.R. Graven. 1999. A new stochastically flexible event methodology with application to Proposition 103. *Insurance: Mathematics and Economics* 25: 197–217.
Brown, S.J., and J.B. Warner. 1980. Measuring security price performance. *Journal of Financial Economics* 8: 205–258.
Brown, S.J., and J.B. Warner. 1985. Using daily stock returns: The case of event studies. *Journal of Financial Economics* 14: 3–31.
Cameron, A.C., J.B. Gelbach, and D.L. Miller. 2011. Robust inference with multiway clustering. *Journal of Business and Economic Statistics* 29: 238–249.
Campbell, J.Y., A.W. Lo, and A.C. MacKinlay. 1997. *The Econometrics of Financial Markets*. Princeton, NJ: Princeton University Press.
Corrado, C. J. 1989. A Nonparametric test for abnormal security-price performance in event studies. *Journal of Financial Economics* 23: 385–395.
Dolley, J.C. 1933. Characteristics and procedure of common stock split-ups. *Harvard Business Review* 11: 316–326.
Dutta, A., J. Knif, J.W. Kolari, and S. Pynnonen. 2018. A robust and powerful test of abnormal stock returns in long-horizon event studies. *Journal of Empirical Finance* 47: 1–24.
Fama, E.F. 1998. Market efficiency, long-term returns, and behavioral finance. *Journal of Financial Economics* 49: 283–306.
Fama, E.F., and K.R. French. 1993. Common risk factors in the returns on stocks and bonds. *Journal of Financial Economics* 33: 3–56.
Fama, E.F., and K.R. French. 2015. A five-factor asset pricing model. *Journal of Financial Economics* 116: 1–22.
Fama, E.F., L. Fisher, M.C. Jensen, and R. Roll. 1969. The adjustment of stock prices to new information. *International Economic Review* 10: 1–21.
Harrington, S.E., and D.G. Shrider. 2007. All events induce variance: Analyzing abnormal returns when effect vary across firms. *Journal of Financial and Quantitative Analysis* 42: 229–256.
Ikenberry, D., J. Lakonishok, and T. Vermaelen. 1995. Market underreaction to open market share repurchases. *Journal of Financial Economics* 39: 181–208.
Jaffe, J.F. 1974. The effect of regulatory changes on insider trading. *Bell Journal of Economics and Management Science* 5: 93–121.
Knif, J., J.W. Kolari, and S. Pynnonen. 2008. Stock market reaction to good and bad inflation news. *Journal of Financial Research* 31: 141–166.
Kolari, J.W., and S. Pynnönen. 2010. Event study testing with cross-sectional correlation of abnormal returns. *Review of Financial Studies* 23: 3996–4025.
Kolari, J.W., and S. Pynnönen. 2011. Nonparametric rank tests for event studies. *Journal of Empirical Finance* 18: 953–971.

Kolari, J.W., B. Pape, and S. Pynnonen. 2018. Event study testing with cross-sectional correlation due to partially overlapping event windows. Mays Business School Research Paper No. 3167271. Available at SSRN: https://ssrn.com/abstract=3167271 or https://doi.org/10.2139/ssrn.3167271.

Kolari, J.W., S. Pynnonen, and A.M. Tuncez. 2021. Further evidence on long-run abnormal returns after corporate events. *Quarterly Review of Economics and Finance* 81: 421–439.

Kothari, S.P., and J.B. Warner. 2006. Econometrics of event studies. In *Handbook of corporate finance: Empirical corporate finance*, Vol. 1, ed. B.E. Eckbo, Chapter 1, 1–36. Amsterdam: North Holland.

Lyon, J.D., B.M. Barber, and C.-L. Tsai. 1999. Improved methods for tests of long-horizon abnormal stock returns. *Journal of Finance* 54: 165–201.

MacKinlay, C.A. 1997. Event studies in economics and finance. *Journal of Economic Literature* 35: 13–39.

Myers, J.H., and A.J. Bakay. 1948. Influence of stock split-ups on market price. *Harvard Business Review* 26: 251–265.

Patell, J. 1976. Corporate forecasts of earnings per share and stock price behavior: Empirical tests. *Journal of Accounting Research* 14: 246–276.

Pynnonen, S. 2022. Non-parametric statistic for testing cumulative abnormal stock returns. *Journal of Risk and Financial Management* 15: 149. https://doi.org/10.3390/jrfm15040149.

Schwert, G.W. 1981a. Using financial data to measure the effect of regulation. *Journal of Law and Economics* 24: 121–157.

Schwert, G.W. 1981b. The adjustment of stock prices to information about inflation. *Journal of Finance* 36: 15–29.

Schipper, K., and R. Thompson. 1983. The impact of merger-related regulations on the shareholders of the acquiring firms. *Journal of Accounting Research* 21: 184–121.

Sharpe, S.A. 2001. Reexamining stock valuation and inflation: The impact of analysts' earnings forecast. *Review of Economics and Statistics* 84: 632–648.

Sunder, S. 1973. Relationship between accounting changes and stock prices: Problem of measurement and some empirical evidence. *Journal of Accounting and Research* 1[illegible]: 1–45.

Sunder, S. 1975. Stock prices and related accounting changes in inventory valuation. *Accounting Review* 50: 305–315.

# Index





J. W. Kolari and S. Pynnönen, *Investment Valuation and Asset Pricing*,
https://doi.org/10.1007/978-3-031-16784-3

**N**



**O**



**P**

Ingram Content Group UK Ltd.
Milton Keynes UK
UKHW022323160523
421879UK00004B/331

9 783031 167836